MORE SOY COOKING

MORE SOY COOKING

Healthful Renditions of Classic Traditional Meals

Marie Oser

John Wiley & Sons, Inc.

New York • Chichester • Weinheim • Brisbane • Singapore • Toronto

CONTENTS

Contents

ℬ

viii

FOREWORD

The World Can Be Your Teacher

The truth about good nutrition is hidden from people who fail to use their own powers of observation. Pick up a globe of the earth. Look at different countries and think about what the people eat and how they live in order to discover the best diet to remain trim and healthy for your lifetime. You'll note that billions of Asians live on rice and vegetables, and nearly all of them radiate excellent health without an extra ounce of body fat. If you studied their medical records you would discover that coronary artery disease (heart attacks); breast, colon, and prostate cancer; multiple sclerosis; diabetes; and inflammatory arthritis are rare. The proof that this is not genetic (or racial) immunity to obesity and sickness is from your observation of the Asians who have moved to your hometown in the good old USA. As these immigrants and their descendents eat less rice, vegetables, and soy products and more meat, poultry, dairy products, and refined foods, they gain weight and succumb to our common afflictions.

My eyes were first opened to the cause and potential cure of disease in 1971 when I was a senior medical student. I was frustrated with my medical education because all I was being taught was descriptive details of chronic disease, their genetic connection, and/or the possibility of a mysterious virus as the cause. Never was a cause given that would provide me the opportunity to help my patients prevent or, better yet, cure their health problems. This changed when Dennis Burkitt, a famous British surgeon, gave a noontime conference at Blodgett Hospital in Grand Rapids, Michigan. He had trained in England, then moved to Africa, where he set up practice. He observed and reported the complete absence of obesity, heart disease, hemorrhoids, varicose veins, and hiatus hernia among the rural Africans and related this to their diet, which was high in plant fiber. African Americans today suffer from these problems in epidemic proportions. I recently learned the first case of rheumatoid arthritis was described in Africa in 1957 and the first case of Lupus was reported in 1960. Yet U.S.–born blacks have the highest rates of both of these life-threatening diseases.

Introduction

More Soy Cooking speaks to the role that the plant-based diet, with an emphasis on soyfoods, can play in nutrition and in disease prevention and management. Every day there seems to be a new study linking diet and disease. While we all know that food choice is the most obvious lifestyle factor under our control, many interested consumers don't quite know how to begin making changes. Some feel that it would be a burdensome undertaking to change lifelong habits or that they would miss the comfort of favorite foods. They have tried "low-fat" and "healthy" alternatives concocted with chemically altered ingredients. It's easy to become discouraged because this artificial approach invariably leads to products that don't taste good and tend to leave an aftertaste, often trading one problem for another.

More Soy Cooking continues in the vein of *Soy of Cooking*, introducing the goodness of soy into every course of every meal. However, here we take the concept a step further. In *More Soy Cooking*, the contrast between traditionally prepared dishes and those created with plant-based alternatives is highlighted by including a comparative analysis with each recipe. The analyses of these enticing dishes are dubbed "Enlightened" and compared with recipes using conventional ingredients that are labeled "Traditional." The enlightened recipes make use of traditional as well as new and innovative alternative ingredients and introduce the health-conscious consumer to widely available and easy-to-use products that do a stellar job of replacing their high-fat, cholesterol-laden counterparts. Problematic ingredients normally found in traditional Western cuisine are replaced by those that add wholesome goodness. Adding while subtract-

1

ing—what a concept! The techniques are simple and recommended substitutes are high quality, easy to use, and widely available.

More Soy Cooking contains information and concepts that can revitalize the menu for those who want to make the transition to healthy food choices. And who doesn't? Americans are in deplorable shape and sliding backward. Why? Because many physicians feel that most people won't take the steps necessary to make a significant difference. Consequently, their dietary recommendations have been generally weak and ineffective. There is a new breed of physician on the scene, however. Medical professionals like Doctors Ornish, Barnard, and McDougall speak to the *heart* of the problem. They offer programs that exclude virtually all animal products from the diet, with remarkable results. A plant-based approach is one that is truly low-fat, health-supporting fare. *More Soy Cooking* speaks from the heart, using applied science to create appealing, richly delectable, and satisfying food choices. New and lighter alternatives, along with my distinctive techniques and applications, present mainstream consumers with many palatable options.

If you are looking for healthy and delicious food, this is the place. Low in fat, high in fiber, rich in phytochemicals, and 100 percent cholesterol- and dairy-free—this is my mantra. Not only will you treasure these dishes, you will find that they are meals indistinguishable in appearance, flavor, and texture from the traditional dishes you know. *More Soy Cooking* will help you build your plant-based repertoire, delectably. À votre santé!

The Need for a Plant-Based Diet

The plant-based diet is just that: a diet regimen that contains foods derived from plants. This low-fat vegetarian, or vegan, diet includes four food groups: grains, legumes, vegetables, and fruit. Flesh foods like meat, fish, eggs, and dairy products lose their food group status in this more enlightened approach to health and wellness through optimal nutrition. Extensive modern research has shown that traditional dietary recommendations regarding the need for animal products have been in error. Irrefutable scientific evidence indicates that these very foods are implicated in the epidemic of heart disease, many forms of cancer, osteoporosis, and obesity.

Western diets are notoriously high in fat. The American Cancer Society, the National Cancer Institute, and the Surgeon General of the United States have all come to the conclusion that this rich diet is a major contributor to breast and other forms of cancer. However, not all fats are created equal. Fat can be saturated, polyunsaturated, or monounsaturated. These terms indicate the type of chemical structure associated with each. Saturated fats are found in meat and dairy products and are so dense that they are solid at room temperature. There are a few vegetable fats that are predominately saturated, and these include coconut oil, palm oil, and cocoa butter.

Unsaturated fats are found in vegetable oils and are fluid at room temperature. Vegetable oils are predominantly polyunsaturated and very low in saturated fat. I use only olive oil and olive oil cooking spray in my kitchen. Olive oil is monounsaturated fat and is considered the most desirable. Olive oil in moderate amounts not only tastes good but is heart-healthy and has been

3

The Protein Question

Many people still believe it isn't safe to eliminate meat and dairy products from the diet. Tell a meat eater you are vegan (total vegetarian) and invariably the first response is, "How do you get enough protein?" There is a dietary revolution in the air. Many well-known professionals link diets high in protein with bone mineral loss, or osteoporosis.

According to Dr. William Harris, author of the compellingly persuasive *The Scientific Basis of Vegetarianism,* the reply should be, "How much do you think you need?" Dr. Harris indicates that the recommended daily allowance (RDA) for protein intake is set too high and insures that over 97 percent of the population meeting the RDAs will exceed its nutrient and calorie requirements. Adults need little more than 0.5 grams of protein per kilogram of body weight. The U.S. RDA is calculated at 0.8 grams per kilogram of weight per day, and includes a safety margin to cover even those with very high protein needs. In order to calculate your own protein requirements, just divide your ideal weight by 2.2 to find your ideal weight in kilograms. Then multiply that number by 0.8. The result will be your daily protein requirement. An adult male whose ideal weight is 154 pounds needs only 56 grams of protein a day. The average American consumes about 103 grams of protein, 70 grams of which comes from animal sources. Even pregnant women need only about 75 grams of protein a day. Mark Messina, in *The Simple Soybean and Your Health,* says, "Most of us are getting more protein than the amount needed by a world class bodybuilder."

According to Dr. Neal Barnard, president of Physicians Committee for Responsible Medicine and author of *Food for Life,* "Americans consume more than twice the amount of protein they need. A high protein intake is detrimental to bone strength and overworks the kidneys." Indeed the high-protein foods that make up the core of the American diet are the very ones that contribute an extraordinary amount of cholesterol and fat to the diet as well.

The idea of protein complementing, a popular theory in the 1970s requiring carefully planned food combinations at every meal in order to assure adequate protein, has been discarded by the American Dietetic Association. They have acknowledged that plant-based diets that include all four food groups— grains, legumes, vegetables, and fruit—contain more than an adequate amount of high-quality protein, and that there is no need to combine "complementary" proteins at the same meal. "Dietary Guidelines for Americans," released by the U.S. Department of Agriculture in 1996, endorsed vegetarian diets as safe, and acknowledged that the failure to include vegetarian diets in the past was a serious oversight.

Vegetarian diets provide more than adequate sources of protein. Soy protein, for example, is considered essentially equal in quality to that found in meat, milk, or eggs. Protein derived from soybeans is recognized by the U.S. government as a protein alternative equivalent to meat. Dr. John McDougall, medical director of the McDougall Program at St. Helena's Hospital and Health Center in Deer Park, California, has said, "All the protein needed to grow large muscles is present in vegetable foods. Vegetables provide two to four times the protein anyone would need during any activity." He points out that potatoes provide 11 percent protein; corn 12 percent; oranges 8 percent; cauliflower 4 percent; while legumes such as beans, peas, and lentils provide 28 percent protein—the same as beef. He states further that these plant sources provide complete proteins, containing all of the essential amino acids. Nathan Pritikin, the widely acclaimed nutrition expert, said, "Vegetarians always ask about getting enough protein, but I don't know any nutrition expert who could plan a diet of natural foods resulting in protein deficiency, so long as you're not deficient in calories. You need only 5 or 6 percent of total calories in protein . . . and it is practically impossible to get below 9 percent in ordinary diets."

PLANT SOURCES OF PROTEIN

Almonds, blanched	1 ounce	5.8 g
Barley, cooked	1 cup	19.8 g
Broccoli, raw	1 spear	4.5 g
Brown rice, cooked	1 cup	5 g
Garbanzo beans	4 ounces	10 g
Gimme Lean	2 ounces	9 g
Jumbo vegetarian hot dog	each	17 g
Kidney beans	4 ounces	10.4 g
Lentils	4 ounces	10.2 g
Lightlife Veggie Burger	each	13 g
Lima beans	4 ounces	7.7 g
Millet, cooked	1 cup	8.4 g
Miso	½ cup	6.3 g

(continued)

PLANT SOURCES OF PROTEIN *(continued)*

Mung beans	4 ounces	8 g
Navy beans	4 ounces	9.9 g
Oatmeal, cooked	1 cup	6 g
Peanuts, dry-roasted	½ cup	17.3 g
Pinto beans	4 ounces	9.3 g
Pumpkin seeds, roasted	1 ounce	9.4 g
Ready Ground Tofu	3 ounces	7 g
Rye flour, dark	1 cup	18 g
Sesame seeds, toasted	1 ounce	4.8 g
Soybeans, boiled*	4 ounces	18.9 g
Soy flour	1 cup	29.4 g
Soynuts	½ cup	34 g
Spinach, raw	10-ounce pkg	5.8 g
Split peas	4 ounces	9.5 g
Sprouted soybeans	½ cup	4.6 g
Sunflower seeds, roasted	1 ounce	5.5 g
Textured Vegetable Protein, cooked	3.5 ounces	17.3 g
Tofu, firm	½ cup	19.9 g
Wheat flour, whole-grain	1 cup	16.4 g
Wheat germ, toasted	1 cup	32.9 g
White rice, cooked	1 cup	5.5 g

*Calcium values given for all legumes (dried beans) are for cooked (boiled) beans.

The Dairy Myth

Those of us who were around in the 1950s remember the milkman. Several times a week, milk, cheese, ice cream, and all manner of dairy products were delivered to the door well before breakfast. This was lauded as a wonderful modern convenience. However, since milk is a leading contributor of saturated fat in the American diet, actually beginning to clog arteries in childhood, consumers got much more than they bargained for.

The National Dairy Council claims to be an unbiased source of nutrition education and is one of the leading suppliers of educational materials to the school system. I remember that when my children went to public elementary school, I was actually required to write a note excusing them from drinking milk, despite the growing body of evidence that dairy foods are not essential for human health. In fact, Mark Messina, in *The Vegetarian Way* (coauthored with his wife, Virginia Messina, a registered dietitian), states, "Vegetarians who avoid dairy products may seem to be choosing a diet that is unusual by Western standards, but are actually choosing a typical diet by world standards. . . . The belief that milk is essential is clearly incorrect." So, where is one to get calcium, if not from dairy products? To listen to the Dairy Council, the only reliable source is dairy products. But, according to Dr. Robert Heaney, a professor at Creighton University School of Medicine's Osteoporosis Research Center, "The sheer quantity of calcium in dairy products makes them attractive, but they have no monopoly on calcium. There's no reason in the world why you couldn't get an adequate intake from vegetable sources."

Countries with the greatest calcium and protein intake typically also have the highest rates of osteoporosis and hip fracture. The United States, Sweden, Finland, and Great Britain have the highest rates of osteoporosis and hip fracture in the world. Among the populations with the lowest rates are those of Hong Kong, Singapore, and Ghana. The average American gets 807 milligrams (mg) of calcium a day from drinking milk, while in Ghana the average is 8 mg. Why does the Food and Nutrition Board of the American Academy of Sciences recommend a daily allowance of 800 mg? The World Health Organization recommends 400 to 500 mg daily. Apparently, the U.S. RDA is established higher to compensate for the typical high-protein American diet. Charles Attwood, a leading pediatrician, says, "It seems that milk, with its excessive protein, may be part of the calcium problem instead of the solution."

PLANT SOURCES OF CALCIUM

Almonds	1 ounce	70 mg
Apple	1 medium	10 mg
Artichokes, cooked	½ cup	54 mg
Asparagus, cooked	4 spears	22 mg
Baked beans, vegetarian	1 cup	128 mg

(continued)

PLANT SOURCES OF CALCIUM *(continued)*

Banana	1 medium	7 mg
Blackstrap molasses	2 tablespoons	274 mg
Bok choy, cooked	1 cup	158 mg
Brazil nuts	1 ounce	50 mg
Broccoli, cooked	1 cup	94 mg
Brown rice, cooked	1 cup	23 mg
Brussels sprouts, cooked	8 sprouts	56 mg
Butternut squash, cooked	1 cup	84 mg
Carrots, cooked	2 medium	38 mg
Cauliflower, cooked	1 cup	34 mg
Celery, cooked	1 cup	54 mg
Collard greens, cooked	1 cup	357 mg
Corn tortilla	one	42 mg
Couscous, cooked	1 cup	15 mg
Cranberry beans	1 cup	88 mg
Figs, dried	10	269 mg
Fortified soymilk	1 cup	200–500 mg
Garbanzo beans, canned	1 cup	78 mg
Great Northern beans	1 cup	121 mg
Green peas, cooked	1 cup	44 mg
Kale, cooked	1 cup	94 mg
Kidney beans	1 cup	50 mg
Lentils	1 cup	37 mg
Lima beans	1 cup	52 mg
Navy beans	1 cup	128 mg
Oatmeal, cooked	1 cup	20 mg
Onions, cooked	1 cup	58 mg
Orange juice	1 cup	300 mg
Orange, navel	1 medium	56 mg
Peanuts	1 ounce	26 mg
Pear, Bartlett	1 medium	19 mg
Pinto beans	1 cup	82 mg

Pita bread	one	31 mg
Raisins, golden	1 cup	76 mg
Raspberries	1 cup	35 mg
Rye bread	1 slice	20 mg
Soybeans, boiled*	1 cup	175 mg
Sweet potato, boiled	1 cup	70 mg
Tahini	2 Tb	128 mg
Tempeh	1 cup	154 mg
Textured Vegetable Protein, cooked	3½ ounces	106.7 mg
Tofu (calcium sulfate)	½ cup	120–392 mg
Turnip greens, cooked	1 cup	249 mg
Turtle beans	1 cup	103 mg
Wax beans, canned	1 cup	174 mg
White beans	1 cup	161 mg
White potato, baked	1 cup	20 mg
Whole wheat bread	1 slice	20 mg
Whole wheat flour	1 cup	49 mg

* Calcium values given for all legumes (dried beans) are for cooked (boiled) beans.

The International Connection

More Soy Cooking often takes the international route to healthy gourmet cookery. Many enticing dishes inspired by cuisines of foreign cultures introduce a broad selection of interesting grains, legumes, vegetables, and fruit. In international cooking, the spice and variety of colorful foods, rich in exotic flavors and aromas, offer attractive options to the health-conscious cook. This is especially true in the Asian and Mediterranean models, long regarded as a healthier approach to eating. A number of dishes based on other ethnic cuisines are also included, all designed with an eye to style and authenticity.

A considerable body of scientific data suggests a positive relationship between vegetarian diets and risk reduction for several chronic degenerative diseases and conditions. Many prominent and authoritative health profession-als have presented information regarding the role that diet plays in the preven-tion and treatment of disease.

T. Colin Campbell is in the forefront of medical and nutrition profession-als who advocate the vegetarian lifestyle for optimal health. He was the princi-pal researcher in the China-Oxford-Cornell Diet and Health Project, which studied the lifestyle patterns and health of 7,500 rural Chinese adults and their families. This study provided much of the scientific basis for the health bene-fits of a vegetarian diet. Campbell and his colleagues analyzed mortality data for 50 diseases, including 7 different cancers, from 65 counties and 130 villages in rural mainland China. The results of this study are some of the most widely respected data in the field of nutrition. Comparison of diets in rural China with average American diets shows that Chinese diets are much lower in total fat (6 to 24 percent of calories, except for certain nomadic groups in northern China), much higher in dietary fiber (10 to 77 grams per day), about 30 per-cent higher in total calorie intake, and substantially lower in foods of animal origin. Interestingly, obesity is far less prevalent in China than in the United States, even though the Chinese consume more total calories.

In China, an average of 11 percent of dietary protein is obtained from ani-mal sources, while the average American diet is comprised of about 60 to 80 percent animal-based foods. Breast cancer, large bowel cancer, and osteoporo-sis were far less common among the Chinese than in America. Dr. Campbell, regarding diet and its role in nutrition and disease prevention, says, "Quite simply, the more you substitute plant foods for animal foods, the healthier you are likely to be. I now consider veganism to be the ideal diet. A vegan diet (entirely plant-based), particularly one that is low in fat, will substantially reduce disease risks."

What's Eating North America?

Countries where low-fat, plant-based diets are common have very low cancer rates, while populations with meat-based diets tend to have high cancer rates. Numerous studies indicate that in many other areas of the world, such as Asia and the Mediterranean countries, rates of cancer and heart disease are far lower than in North America. In Japan, for example, breast cancer rates have been very low. At first, it was thought that this was an indication of a genetic link to these diseases. However, when Asian women who came to this country began developing breast cancer at the same rate as Americans, the scientific commu-

nity took notice. Because high-fat food increases the activity of the sex hormones estrogen and testosterone in the blood, it is thought to be a major factor for the increased risk of breast, uterine, ovarian, and prostate cancer where
the consumption of such foods is common. It became increasingly obvious that
there must be a connection. It appears that when people from other countries
adopt the American lifestyle, they begin to develop the very same diseases at the
same rates as the rest of us, and the finger has been pointed at our high-fat diet,
heavy with animal products and loaded with cholesterol.

Dr. John McDougall was among the first to recognize the importance of a
low-fat vegetarian diet. While living and working on the Big Island of Hawaii,
he had the opportunity to observe the effect of nutrition and health on people
of several different backgrounds and races. Often, three or four generations of
the same family would all live on the island. Characteristically, the first generation had been born in Japan, China, or the Philippines and had lived there the
first 15 to 25 years of their lives. The first generation stayed true to the eating
habits acquired in their native land. They enjoyed a diet made up largely of rice,
vegetables, a little fish, and very little meat. As Dr. McDougall tells it, because
they were raised in countries where cows were rare, they never acquired a taste
for cow's milk, cheese, or beef. However, as successive generations became
acclimated and assimilated, they were introduced to a different kind of eating—a very rich diet centered around meat, dairy products, and refined foods.
What was the essence of their parents' and grandparents' native diet, rice and
vegetables, became unimportant side dishes for the children.

To Dr. McDougall, the differences between the generations were distinct.
Large numbers of the older generation were in excellent health. He indicates
that they were trim, hardworking, and felt few aches and pains. In addition,
they had normal blood pressure and low levels of cholesterol, sugar, and uric
acid. Those who had grown up with the American lifestyle did not share their
older relatives' enviable health. They were developing gout, diabetes, colon cancer, high blood pressure, and heart disease. They were fat, felt bad, and looked
sick. The only difference between the generations was the radical change in
diet; the impact of this change in diet was indisputable.

There is much to learn from ancient cultures whose cuisines lend themselves
so easily to the health-supporting, plant-based approach. Knowledge is power,
and *More Soy Cooking* takes the plant-centered international diet to another
level, demonstrating how easy it is to achieve better health through sensible
nutrition. You'll be introduced to myriad easy-to-use and widely available
ingredients. See "Soyfoods and More: A Glossary" on page 22, where you will

find a wide assortment of delicious, wholesome alternatives. "Kitchen Tools, Techniques, and Tofu 101" on page 42 and the Resource Guide on page 285 provide further information.

Soy: Food of the Future

Replacing animal protein in the diet with soyfoods will help lower blood cholesterol levels and reduce the risk of heart disease.

Soyfoods have been the subject of scientific research for many years, and numerous studies suggest that including soyfoods in a low-fat diet may prevent many forms of cancer, heart disease, and osteoporosis. Soyfoods are high in protein but very low in saturated fat and completely free of cholesterol. One serving of cooked soybeans (½ cup) provides 14 grams of high-quality protein but only about 1 gram of saturated fat and no cholesterol.

Almost 30 years ago, researchers showed that protein from soyfoods could lower blood cholesterol. Since then, more than 40 studies involving human subjects have also shown this. A 10 percent decrease in cholesterol reduces the chance of having a heart attack by 20 to 30 percent, and soy protein decreases blood cholesterol levels by about 10 to 15 percent in people with elevated cholesterol. Even in people who have already reduced their blood cholesterol by eating a low-fat diet, consuming soy produces a further decrease in cholesterol.

Led by Dr. Neal Barnard of Physicians Committee for Responsible Medicine in Washington, D.C., researchers at Georgetown University studied the effects of a low-fat, vegetarian diet on premenstrual syndrome (PMS). PMS includes feelings of moodiness, tension, or irritability, as well as physical symptoms, such as water retention. Like menstrual pain, PMS appears to be influenced by nutrition. Published in the *Journal of Obstetrics & Gynecology* (February 1999), the study reviewed individual reports that low-fat, vegetarian diets can cause dramatic reductions in menstrual pain and that vegetarians also have fewer ovulatory disturbances. There are several reasons why this diet affects hormones. First of all, reducing the amount of fat in the food you eat reduces the amount of estrogen in your blood. This appears to be true for all fats—vegetable oils as well as animal fats. Some researchers have found that excess estrogen plays a role in PMS symptoms and that shifting the balance of the diet away from fatty foods and toward high-fiber plant foods is helpful. Certain foods that are common in vegetarian diets have special effects. Soy products, for example, contain phytoestrogens, which are very weak plant estrogens that reduce the natural estrogens' ability to attach to cells. The result is less estrogen stimulation of cells.

All legumes have a low glycemic index, and the glycemic index of soybeans is the lowest of any legume. The glycemic index is a measure of how much blood sugar rises when a particular food is consumed. Foods with a low glycemic index produce a smaller rise in glucose, therefore, consuming soyfoods can be helpful in controlling diabetes.

Also at Georgetown University, researchers prepared a pilot study that compared a high-fiber, low-fat, and entirely plant-based diet with the more commonly used American Diabetes Association (ADA) diet. The vegan (plant-based) meals were made from vegetables, grains, beans, and fruits, with no refined ingredients. These meals averaged just 10 percent fat and 80 percent complex carbohydrate. They also averaged 60 to 70 grams of fiber per day and contained no cholesterol. The comparison (ADA) diet contained somewhat more plant-based ingredients than the average American diet, but still relied on the conventional chicken- and fish-centered meals. The ADA diet was 30 percent fat and 50 percent carbohydrate. It provided about 30 grams of fiber and 200 milligrams of cholesterol per day.

The research subjects in both groups did a great job overall in adhering to their prescribed diets. However, the vegan group clearly had the edge in many of the results. Fasting blood sugars decreased 59 percent more in the vegan group than in the ADA group. And, while the vegans needed less medication to control their blood sugars, the ADA group needed just as much medicine as before. The vegans were taking less medicine, but were in better control. And while the ADA group lost an impressive 8 pounds each, on average, the vegans lost nearly 16 pounds each. Cholesterol levels also dropped more substantially in the vegan group compared to the ADA group. As reported by Dr. Andrew Nicholson of Physicians Committee for Responsible Medicine, the researchers at Georgetown were very encouraged by the strong results and planned to expand the study.

Replacing animal products with soyfoods is also good for the planet. Consumption of the traditional American diet diverts a disproportionate share of our resources, wasting enormous amounts of water and polluting the rest. The land needed to feed one person eating a meat-based diet can feed 20 vegetarians.

At this time, less than one tenth of the soybean crop grown around the globe is produced for food. The majority of the yield is crushed to produce soybean oil and soybean meal. The meal that is left after the oil is extracted is used for animal feed.

As compared to fats and carbohydrates, proteins are the most expensive ingredients used in processed foods. When the relative costs of animal and plant proteins are compared, based on 70 grams of protein per day, the number of days of protein requirements provided by one acre of land are as follows:

- Beef: 77 days
- Milk: 236 days
- Wheat flour: 527 days
- Soybeans: 2,224 days

Clearly, soybeans and wheat are far more efficient in providing protein compared to beef and dairy cattle. This is only a sample of the many compelling statistics that support plant-centered diet choices. As consumers take advantage of the diverse selection of soy products that displace flesh foods with all their attendant problems, they make healthy choices for themselves *and* for the planet.

Soybeans are indeed the food of the future—high in antioxidants, rich in phytochemicals and dietary fiber, and having a low glycemic index. Add to this soyfoods' ability to displace unhealthy animal products and you have the optimal low-fat/high-fiber diet—one that is plant based.

Functional Foods

"Let food be thy medicine and medicine be thy food."
—HIPPOCRATES, 500 B.C.

What are these "functional foods" we've been hearing so much about? Currently, one of the hottest areas in food science is in discovering ways to target specific health-enhancing properties of a particular food. The resulting knowledge about nontraditional components in common foods, such as fruits and vegetables, has led to some of them being called "functional foods." According to Clare Hasler, director of the University of Illinois Functional Foods for Health Program, "The definition of functional foods is still evolving but refers to foods that, by virtue of physiologically active components, provide benefits beyond basic nutrition and may prevent disease or promote health. These benefits are best realized from a wide variety of foods rather than supplements."

Scientific research in recent years has suggested that these subnutrient components provide potent disease-preventing benefits. Dr. Stephen de Felice, director of New York's Foundation for Innovation in Medicine, is credited with the first use of the term *nutraceutical,* which describes specific chemical compounds found in foods that may prevent disease.

Researchers are investigating the phytochemical components of traditional foods that may be responsible for many health benefits. *Phytochemical,* literally translated, means plant chemical and emphasizes the plant source of most of these protective, disease-preventing compounds. While these phytochemicals may one day be classified as essential nutrients, foods "fortified" with phyto-chemicals are already turning up on grocery shelves.

According to the Position Paper of the American Dietetic Association, phy-tochemicals and functional food components have been associated with the prevention or treatment of at least four of the leading causes of death in this country—cancer, diabetes, cardiovascular disease, and hypertension—and with the prevention or treatment of other medical ailments, including neural tube defects, osteoporosis, abnormal bowel function, and arthritis.

The most prominent of these phyto-superstars include garlic, soyfoods, tomato products, grapes, carrots, sweet potatoes, oats, flaxseed oil, broccoli and other cruciferous vegetables, citrus fruits, cranberries, green tea, and wine. As researchers investigate the specifics of how these functional foods work to prevent certain diseases, they are focusing on the particular functions of these phytonutrients—how they relate to one another synergistically and ultimately benefit human health.

In an article in a recent issue of *The Journal of Food Technology,* "Functional Foods: Their Role in Disease Prevention and Health Promotion," Clare Hasler, the summary author, noted that "overwhelming evidence from epidemiologi-cal, in vivo [in living animals], in vitro [in laboratory tests], and clinical trial data indicates that a plant-based diet can reduce the risk of chronic disease, par-ticularly cancer." Newly recognized plant chemicals have been credited with this reduced risk. For example, lycopene, the primary phytochemical found in tomatoes, has been associated in human clinical trials with reducing the risk of prostate and other cancers. Limonoids in citrus fruits, glucosinolates in crucif-erous vegetables, and catechins in green tea also appear to be protective against a variety of human cancers. Isoflavones in soy and lignans in flaxseed oil, which act as weak estrogens, may have a role in reducing the risk of breast cancer.

Nutritionally high-powered foods aren't new to anyone familiar with the natural foods industry. Health food stores have been selling nutrition-rich foods such as whole grains, lecithin, brewer's yeast, and soy products for over half a century. Nutritionists, food scientists, food marketers, and others are exploring how today's traditional foods, along with some exciting new food concepts, can offer consumers a healthier future. As consumers become more knowledgeable about nutrition and how diet is related to health, they will be able to make informed choices in selecting from a vast assortment of foods to come up with the right formula for good food and good health.

BENEFITS OF PHYTOCHEMICALS

Plants	Extracts	Health Benefits
Broccoli, kale, radish	Sulforaphane	Deters tumors
Cabbage	Isothiocyanate	Deters lung and other tumors
Cauliflower	Several	Deters breast tumors
Citrus plants	Quercetin	Relieves allergies, deters heart problems
Garlic, onion	Allicin	Deters lung and other tumors, breaks blood clots, reduces blood pressure, helps lower cholesterol and normalize irregular heartbeats
Ginger	Gingerol	Antioxidant; relieves arthritis, deters ulcers, helps heal skin sores
Green tea	EGCG	Antioxidant; deters tumors; reduces cholesterol; helps deter heart problems, strokes, infection
Ginkgo biloba	Flavones	Improves circulation; ameliorates headaches, depression, ringing in ears, impotence
Hawthorn plant	Flavonoids	Lowers cholesterol, deters allergies
Paprika	Canthaxanthin	Antioxidant
Rosemary plant	Rosmarinic acid	Deters tumors, helps ameliorate heart problems
Spirulina	Several	Detoxifies blood; stimulates production of the body's most powerful antioxidant, superoxide dismutase

Plants	Extracts	Health Benefits
Tomato	Lycopenes	Deters tumors and prostate disease
Tumeric	Curcumin	Relieves arthritis
Various plants	Coumaric acid	Deters tumors
Most plants	Chlorophyll	Detoxifies blood, deters tumors, helps heal bedsores

Soy-Centered Cuisine

There's no denying the deluge of health-related stories in recent years, as the media and even corporate wellness programs seek to satisfy consumers' increasing appetite for information on how to live better and longer. At the same time that medical concerns are stimulating the demand for soyfoods, the vegetarian market is on the rise. Industry analysts estimate the number of vegetarians in the United States to total 15 million, a figure that has more than doubled during the past decade.

Replacing animal foods with plant foods can be the most important health choice that you can make. And with soyfoods in the mix, plant-based diets can deliver variety, texture, and flavor along with many healthful benefits.

Soybeans contain all three of the acronutrients required for good nutrition—complete protein, carbohydrates, and fats—as well as vitamins and minerals, including calcium, folic acid, and iron. Soybeans are the only vegetable that contains complete protein, providing all eight amino acids in the amounts needed for human health. The amino acid pattern of soy is virtually identical to that of meat, milk, and eggs.

In this book we make full use of the tried-and-true soyfood of record, tofu, when enlightening our menu. While there are numerous new and traditional soyfoods available, tofu is the best known and least understood of all. Tofu is ideal for stir-frys and other medleys, most cooks would agree. However, there are several different types and textures, each with their own application. For instance, silken tofu in aseptic packaging is the best choice for dips, dressings, soups, casseroles, quiches, puddings, and icings. Silken tofu is also an excellent replacement for eggs in baked goods, acting as a binding agent. The Chinese firm style of tofu would be most useful in recipes that require the tofu to hold its shape through a lot of handling. There are many new and traditional types of tofu now available, and it is important that you choose the right style of tofu for a particular dish. "Kitchen Tools, Techniques, and Tofu 101" on page 42 gives a more detailed description of the forms, suitable applications, and methods that transform the texture of tofu and increase the absorption of flavorful marinades. Once you try the remarkable recipes in this collection, this versatile ingredient is likely to become a regular player in your culinary repertoire.

However, *More Soy Cooking* is not just about tofu! Far from it! In "Soyfoods and More" later in this chapter, traditional soyfoods from tofu to tempeh are detailed along with myriad new and lighter soyfoods. Many new products offer options that deliver a full count of flavor, texture, and "mouthfeel" without adding excess fat and cholesterol. Meat alternatives made from soy and/or wheat gluten (sometimes called seitan or wheat meat) are excellent sources of protein, iron, and B vitamins. Perhaps you've never considered using miso for anything other than soup. There are many varieties available that can add depth of flavor to other dishes and invite endless experimentation.

The more popular soyfoods such as tofu, some meat analogs, soy sauce, and soy flour can be found in most supermarkets, but you will find the greatest variety of soyfoods in health food stores. Asian groceries carry those soyfoods used in Asian cuisine, such as water-packed tofu, miso, tamari, and so on, and a number of products can be obtained through mail-order catalogs. If you have questions about soyfoods or any of the wholesome ingredients used in this collection, contact any of the information resources listed in the Resource Guide (page 285).

Textured soy protein, often called TSP or TVP (which stands for Textured Vegetable Protein and is a trademark of the Archer Daniels Midland Company), is made from defatted soy flour that is compressed and processed into granules or chunks. Use this versatile product in many applications, from tacos and lasagna to fajitas and "chicken" cacciatore! Produced in several styles, this dehydrated product has a remarkable shelf life. When it is rehydrated with boiling broth, it has a texture similar to ground, chunk, or strip beef or chicken. Once you become familiar with the assortment of widely available soyfood ingredients, you will be able to use them repeatedly, effortlessly creating delightful meals.

Looking to re-create a favorite dish healthfully? How about Sweet Italian

"Sausage" with Peppers (page 147)? Savory chunks of spiced veggie sausage are cooked in the traditional Italian style, with lots of bell peppers in a rich tomato sauce. Very authentic! Or Tuscan White Bean Soup (page 102)? Luscious Great Northern white beans and chunks of vegetarian Canadian bacon marry in this creamy, dairy-free rendition of a classic northern Italian soup. Perhaps it's Chinese Unchicken Salad (page 110) that will turn your head. You will love the easy techniques and healthful ingredients that come together to re-create this perennial classic. You will savor the enlightened puddings. My interpretation of dairy-free Creamy Rice Pudding (page 253) is so creamy and rich in flavor that you just won't believe it! There is even a Chocolate Rice Pudding (page 249) for you chocoholics out there—so delicious! These delectable vegan dishes are reproduced through the versatility of this magic bean in all of its guises! *More Soy Cooking* demonstrates how to replicate so many of your favorite dishes that you will use it often. Take advantage of the wide array of choices from appetizers to desserts, and you will be able to enjoy delicious gourmet-style meals and entertain healthfully to rave reviews. It's so easy when you know how.

Soyfoods and More: A Glossary

A marvel in taste and functionality, soy in all of its forms has many applications in food production and preparation. Because of recent research indicating that soyfoods may play an important role in reducing the risk of heart disease and many forms of cancer, there has been an unprecedented demand for soy-enhanced products from consumers in this era of increasing awareness of food-related health issues.

Heart disease, the leading cause of death in the United States, kills more than a hundred people each hour in this country. However, there is a wide variation in heart disease rates throughout the world, and the wide variation in lifestyle, especially diet, is thought to be the main reason. Because a number of clinical trials have shown that consumption of soy protein (compared to other proteins such as those from milk or meat) can lower total and LDL cholesterol levels, the U.S. Food and Drug Administration (FDA), on October 26, 1999, authorized the use of health claims about the role of soy protein in reducing the risk of coronary heart disease (CHD) on labels of foods containing soy protein. This rule is based on the FDA's conclusion that foods containing soy protein included in a diet low in saturated fat and cholesterol may reduce the risk of CHD by lowering blood cholesterol levels.

Foods with the goodness of soy can be as diverse as soymilk, tofu, meat analogs (substitutes) such as TVP, or other authentic re-creations fashioned from soy and wheat gluten, as well as enriched pasta and baked goods. Because soybean derivatives occur in, or can be added to, a wide variety of foods and beverages, it is possible to add soy products to the diet as many as four times a day (three meals and a snack).

The FDA recommends that consumers incorporate four servings of at least 6.25 grams of soy protein into their daily diet, with a total of at least 25 grams of soy protein each day. In order to claim the healthy effects of soy, a product must meet the following criteria (per serving):

- 6.25 grams soy protein or more
- Low fat (less than 3 grams)
- Low saturated fat (less than 1 gram)
- Low cholesterol (less than 20 milligrams)

Foods made with the whole soybean may also qualify for the health claim if they contain no fat in addition to that present in the whole soybean. These would include soy foods such as tofu, soymilk, soy-based burgers, tempeh, and soynuts.

Just how easy is it to consume 25 grams of soy protein in a day? The Indiana Soybean Board gives these examples of common soyfood servings and their average soy protein content:

3 ounces water-packed tofu: 8.5 grams
3 ounces silken firm tofu: 6 grams
8 ounces plain soymilk: 8 grams
8 ounces vanilla soymilk: 6 grams
¼ cup (1 ounce) soynuts: 12 grams
2 tablespoons soynut butter: 8 grams
2 ounces (½ cup) soy ground crumbles: 9 grams
1 soy burger: 10 grams
2 soy breakfast links: 6.5 grams
1 soy breakfast pattie: 6.5 grams
½ cup (4 ounces) tempeh: 16 grams
½ cup cooked or canned soybeans: 13 grams
½ cup green soybeans: 7 grams
½ cup black soybeans: 9 grams
¼ cup dry textured vegetable protein: 12 grams
1 soy protein bar: 14 grams

You can use this list to help you create your own daily combinations. However, these are just averages, and even though many of these products will not necessarily be featuring the health claim on their labels (because they may not fit the fat or protein criteria), they will still help you reach 25 grams of soy protein daily.

The Soyfood Alternatives

A Basic Guide to Substituting with Traditional Soy Products

Soymilk

- Substitute for cow's milk one-to-one in any recipe, with excellent results
- Blend with frozen fruit and a wholesome sweetener for a delicious dairy-free smoothie

Silken Tofu

- Blend into shakes, fruit smoothies, and puddings
- Substitute for sour cream in dips and dressings
- Replace eggs in baking: ¼ cup = 1 egg

Soy Flour

- Replace up to ¼ of the flour in quickbreads and pancakes
- Replace up to ⅛ of the flour in yeast bread recipes
- Use to thicken sauces and gravies
- Replace eggs in baking: 1 tablespoon soy flour + 1 tablespoon water = 1 egg

Soyfoods Central

The following is a summary of the variety of soyfoods that play important roles in the creation of the many delightful recipes in this collection. Use this book as your guide, and it won't be long before you count these versatile soyfoods among the essentials on your shopping list. Clever use of ingredients like creamy lite silken tofu, hearty tempeh, and the many ingenious soy-based meat analogs will allow you to re-create your favorite dishes with a much healthier bottom line.

Baked tofu   A delicious form of precooked, ready-to-eat tofu that can be sliced and added to salads and sandwiches right from the package. Baked tofu is available in several styles, including Savory Baked Tofu, Five Spice Baked Tofu, Hickory Smoked Tofu, and Teriyaki Baked Tofu. These versatile products have a flavor reminiscent of smoked meats or roast duck and function well as quick high-protein additions to stir-fry and baked dishes. They are available at health food stores nationwide in brands such as The Soy Deli or Tree of Life, among others.

Boca Burger Basics   This ready-to-use ground beef alternative, available in 12-ounce packages, is found in the freezer section of health food stores and supermarkets nationwide and can be used instead of ground meat in recipes.

Bragg Liquid Aminos   A mineral-rich liquid seasoning made from soybeans with 420 mg of soy protein per ½ teaspoon and many essential and nonessential amino acids. This tasty flavoring is not fermented, but can be used in the same way as soy sauce. It is available in health food stores nationwide from Live Food Products.

Dressings made with soy   There are some terrific salad dressings on the market that are made using tofu, miso, or shoyu. My favorites are sold under the brand names Nasoya and Simply Delicious. They are available in health food stores nationwide.

Firm nigari tofu   This very firmly pressed tofu with a dense texture is lower in fat than traditional water-packed tofu (3 grams per 4 ounces). Vacuum packed, this tofu will keep unopened in the refrigerator for up to two months. Once opened, it should be used in a few days. Made from organic soybeans and sold under The Soy Deli brand name, this tofu has a subtle sweetness and handles well because of its firm texture. It is available in health food stores and some supermarkets.

Gimme Lean   This wholesome meat alternative, made by Lightlife, is available in sausage and ground beef style and sold in the freezer section of health food stores, some supermarkets, and specialty stores nationwide. This easy-to-use product is exceedingly authentic in flavor, texture, and appearance and holds together very well when making patties, "meatballs," or loaves.

Ground beef alternatives   There are several soy products, such as Boca Burger Basics, Yves Ground Round, and Ready Ground Tofu, that are fat-free and ready to use. Some manufacturers offer preseasoned varieties like Italian or Savory. These analogs can be in any "loose meat"–type application. They are available at health food stores and many supermarkets nationwide.

Lean Links Italian   A low-fat vegetarian sausage link product from Lightlife Foods, Inc., that duplicates the appearance, taste, and texture of Italian sausage. Available at health food stores and some supermarkets and specialty stores nationwide.

Lite silken tofu A very low-fat tofu (1 gram of fat per 3 ounces), lite silken tofu is rich-tasting and has a smooth, creamy texture and a custardlike consistency. It is widely available in aseptic packages in supermarkets and health food stores nationwide as Mori Nu Silken Tofu Lite. Because of its aseptic packaging, this is the only tofu that can be eaten right from the box. Because it does not have to be precooked, it is a time-saving ingredient when making dips, spreads, and dressings. Its creamy versatility makes it an excellent substitute for eggs and dairy products in baked goods and cream sauces. Toddlers can enjoy a healthy snack of this creamy, custardlike product, cubed out of hand, or mashed with applesauce.

Miso This savory fermented soybean paste has a consistency somewhat like peanut butter. A mainstay of Japanese cuisine for centuries, miso may be aged for several years. A living natural food rich in enzymes and beneficial bacteria, miso should be stored in the refrigerator, where it will keep for several months. Easily digested and highly nutritious, miso adds depth of flavor to soups, sauces, marinades, dips, salad dressings, and main dishes. It is available in Japanese markets and health food stores from Cold Mountain, Westbrae, and other manufacturers.

Barley miso and country barley miso These are reddish brown in color, with a chunky texture and rich flavor. This is the flavor of miso that is strongly preferred by the American macrobiotic community.

Hatcho miso Dark cocoa brown in color, hatcho miso is richly flavored with slight overtones of chocolate. Unlike other miso, which is fermented with grain, hatcho is made with soybeans only.

Mellow white miso Pale beige in color with a subtle, sweet fragrance, this miso has a rich, creamy texture. Highly versatile, it makes a wonderful addition to sauces, fillings, dips, and dressings. **Mellow barley miso** is similar in color, but not as creamy.

Nayonaise This is the brand name for the tofu-based mayonnaise used in place of traditionally prepared mayonnaise. Made by Nasoya, this tasty, wholesome alternative contains no eggs, and therefore no cholesterol, and is also much lower in fat than traditional mayonnaise.

Soybeans What it's all about! This delicious legume is available in a number of forms, each with its own special characteristics.

Dried soybeans These must be presoaked before being cooked for several hours. Once cooked, they are a delicious ingredient ready to be used in many recipes. Dried soybeans are sold in bulk in many health food stores. They are also available in 1-pound packages from Arrowhead Mills.

Green vegetable soybeans in the pod (edamamé) These are available frozen at health food and specialty food stores, Asian markets, and many supermarkets. These green, or immature, soybeans—harvested at about 80 percent maturity—are quite flavorful and have none of the stronger "beany" taste associated with mature beans. Use them as a nutritious snack or a delicious addition to an appetizer buffet.

Soynuts Soynuts are roasted crunchy snacks similar to peanuts and are available in health food stores as well as many supermarkets and grocery stores. See page 77 for an easy way to make homemade soynuts, which are invariably fresher and tastier than the store-bought variety.

Sweet beans Shelled green soybeans are sold frozen in 1-pound packages in health food stores and some supermarkets; they are a hearty addition to vegetable stir-fry or medley dishes.

Soyco Parmesan cheese alternative This vegan grated Parmesan cheese is the best-tasting dairy-free cheese product on the market. Soyco is a division of Soymage/Galaxy Foods, whose Soymage product line is low fat or fat free, cholesterol free, lactose free, all natural, and 100 percent dairy free.

Soy flour This finely ground flour made from soybeans is very high in protein (35 percent—twice that of wheat flour) and low in carbohydrates. It is generally mixed with other flours, especially in baking, as it contains no gluten. Soy flour may also be used to bind sauces and replace eggs in baked goods. Soy flour is available in packages from Bob's Red Mill and Arrowhead Mills in health food stores and some supermarkets nationwide.

Soy grits Sometimes called soya granules, soy grits are whole soybeans that have been lightly toasted and cracked into small pieces. Added to recipes uncooked, they are great for boosting nutrition while adding texture and consistency to baked goods. Bob's Red Mill Soy Grits and Fearn Soya Granules are available in health food stores nationwide.

Soymage cream cheese This vegan cream cheese is used in recipes to add the unique texture associated with cream cheese.

Soymage sour cream You can use this vegan sour cream in any recipe calling for sour cream.

Soymilk   A nondairy beverage made by extracting the liquid from cooked soybeans, soymilk is a dairy-free and cholesterol-free alternative that is low in fat and sodium. Substitute for cow's milk in any recipe one-to-one. Soymilk is widely available in heath food stores and supermarkets nationwide.

Soymilk, 1% fat   Aseptically packaged, 1% fat soymilk is available from Pacific Foods, Westbrae Natural Foods, and several other manufacturers, as well as in supermarkets and health food stores across the country. I use the vitamin- and calcium-enriched 1% fat varieties of soymilk in cooking and baking.

Soymilk, Silk Vanilla, and Chocolate Silk   These delicious soymilks made by White Wave are smooth and creamy dairy-free beverages that are widely available in the refrigerated case alongside dairy milk at health food stores and supermarkets. Silk Soymilk was the subject of a blind taste test conducted by John Stossel on a segment of the *20-20* television show. The majority of the participants preferred the taste of Silk Soymilk over cow's milk.

Soyrizo Vegetarian Chorizo   This is a plant-based version of the highly seasoned pork sausage widely used in Mexican and Spanish cooking. Remove the casing and crumble before browning in a small amount of olive oil.

Soy sauce   Soy sauce is a generic term for the dark salty sauce made by fermenting boiled soybeans and roasted wheat or barley.

Shoyu   Shoyu is a naturally brewed, high-quality soy sauce. Processed in the traditional Japanese way, it is aged two to three years without coloring, additives, or preservatives. Shoyu is true soy sauce and is available in Asian markets and health food stores nationwide.

Tamari   A wheat-free natural soy sauce, tamari has a mellow flavor, slightly stronger than shoyu. Tamari is available in health food stores, Asian markets, and some supermarkets nationwide. Imported tamari is far superior to the domestically produced variety and is well worth the higher price, as its darker, richer flavor will go farther. Tree of Life tamari is organic and is available nationwide in health food stores.

Tempeh   Fermented from whole soybeans, tempeh is an easily digestible, live-cultured food. It has a chewy texture and a distinctive nutty flavor, contains more protein than tofu, and is the best-known source of vitamin B_{12} for strict vegetarians. Because tempeh is made from the whole bean, it is richer in flavor and nutrients than tofu. Tempeh can be found in the refrigerated or freezer section of health food stores in both prepared forms like tempeh burgers or as the cultured soyfood ingredient used in the many recipes in this collection. Tempeh is available across the country from Turtle Island Foods, White Wave, Pacific Tempeh, Lightlife, and Soy Power, among others.

Tempeh, Lightlife, and Soy Power, among others.

Textured Vegetable Protein (TVP)   TVP is made from defatted soy flour. Once rehydrated, it is a very credible meat substitute. Available in a variety of styles, including ground, chunk, and strip beef or chicken, TVP is used in the *unflavored* variety only in *More Soy Cooking*. Because of its very low fat content, unprepared TVP has an extended shelf life. A wide selection of this extremely economical, high- protein food source is available through The Mail Order Catalog (see Resources Guide, page 285).

Tofu   Soybean curd is made by coagulating soymilk with *nigari* (seaweed) or calcium chloride, in much the same way cheese is made from milk. Tofu is high in protein, very low in saturated fats, and its and cholesterol free, and its blandness and ability to absorb flavors make it a very versatile ingredient.

Yves Veggie Canadian Bacon   Yves veggie bacon is a wholesome alternative, very close to Canadian bacon or ham in appearance, aroma, and flavor. It is made with soy protein and wheat gluten and can be enjoyed right out of the package in sandwiches or salads. It is a delicious ingredient in stir-fry and baked dishes, adding protein and carbohydrates and very little fat.

Yves Veggie Ground Round   Available in original and Italian styles, this very authentic ground beef alternative is found in the refrigerated section of health food stores and some supermarkets nationwide.

Yves Veggie Pepperoni   This very popular presliced meat analog with an authentic appearance and taste is available in health food stores and some supermarkets nationwide.

Beyond Soyfoods

The recipes in *More Soy Cooking* include many plant-based ingredients that, while not soy-based, will also serve to replace unhealthy traditional products and to add beneficial nutrients, subnutrients, vitamins, and minerals to your diet. Combining these wholesome foods with soyfoods will contribute heartily to a well-balanced, plant-based regimen.

Active dry yeast   Used to leaven dough, this type of yeast is sold in packages containing 2½ teaspoons and also in 4-ounce jars in supermarkets and health food stores. Quick-rising yeast takes a third to half the time required for regular yeast. Store dry yeast in a cool, dry place.

Applesauce   In all recipes that call for applesauce as a fat replacer, you should use unsweetened applesauce. It is widely available in supermarkets and health food stores.

Arrowroot   Like tapioca, flour, or cornstarch, this powder can be used as a thickener.

Artichoke hearts   Canned quartered artichoke hearts are available from several manufacturers. Or buy whole ones and quarter them.

Arugula   Sometimes called rocket, arugula is a green leafy vegetable with a peppery, somewhat bitter flavor.

Assorted greens   When a recipe calls for assorted greens, you can use a variety of greens with a mixture of colors, tastes, and textures. Choose a mix from salad greens such as: arugula, radicchio, sorrel, oak- and red-leaf lettuces, mizuno, red and white cabbage, and dandelion greens.

Avocado   Rich-tasting, pear-shaped fruit with either smooth or textured skin and light green flesh. Hass, with thick, dark green, bumpy skin and buttery flesh, is considered to be the superior variety. Select avocados that yield to gentle pressure and store in the refrigerator for several days. To ripen an avocado, keep it at warm room temperature or in a closed brown paper bag.

Baby cut carrots   These are mature carrots that have been peeled and "baby cut" into small carrot shapes, not the delicate baby carrots used by chefs for garnish and eye appeal. Baby cut carrots are widely available in supermarkets and health food stores in 1- and 2-pound packages.

Baking powder   Nonaluminum, double-acting baking powder is available nationwide at health food stores and many supermarkets. Rumford, Featherweight, and Cellu brands are all nonaluminum.

Balsamic vinegar   Slightly sweet and fragrant with a distinctive depth of flavor, genuine balsamic vinegar is aged for a minimum of six years and produced in the Modena region of Italy.

Basmati rice   An aromatic long-grain rice, with a faintly nutlike flavor and aroma. This high-quality rice is considered by many cooks to be the world's finest. *More Soy Cooking* recipes calling for basmati rice use white basmati rice. Also available are brown basmati rice varieties, which take longer to cook. Check package for cooking instructions.

Beans

Borlotti beans   An Italian variety of medium-sized beans that are kidney shaped with pink or beige skins speckled in burgundy, these delicious beans add rich flavor. They are available dried or precooked in cans or jars. If borlotti beans are not available, pink kidney beans or pinto beans may be substituted.

Chile beans with chipotle peppers   These Sante Fe–style seasoned pinto beans flavored with smoky chipotle peppers are available from S&W Foods at supermarkets nationwide.

Garbanzo beans (sometimes called chickpeas or ceci beans)   These legumes are buff colored, irregularly shaped round beans with a firm texture and a mild nutlike flavor. The main ingredient in hummus, they are used extensively in Mediterranean, Indian, and Middle Eastern cuisine.

Great Northern beans   These are kidney-shaped white beans, either small or large, with a creamy texture and mild flavor. They are available dried or pre-cooked in cans. If unavailable, substitute white (navy) beans.

Pinquitos   These seasoned small, tender, pink beans are used in South-western or Mexican dishes. Available in supermarkets from S&W Foods.

Capers   Capers are flower buds pickled in vinegar brine. The pungent flavor of capers adds a piquant quality to sauces and vegetable medleys. Available in jars in supermarkets.

Cereal, multigrain   Multigrain Hot Cereal, made by Country Choice, is a mixture of rolled rye, barley, oats, and wheat designed to be made into a hot cereal that is similar to rolled oats. This hearty organic product can be used in baked goods like rolled oats.

Chiles, green   Available whole or chopped, canned green chiles are sold in supermarkets and specialty stores in the Mexican foods section.

Chipotle chiles in adobo sauce   Smoky chipotle chiles are whole chiles packed in a spicy adobo sauce. Available in small cans in supermarkets nation-wide.

Cornstarch   A fine-textured, powdery flour ground from the white heart of the corn kernel, cornstarch is used as a neutral-flavored thickening agent in sauces, fillings, and to give baked goods a delicate texture. It is also known as corn flour.

Couscous   Found in Middle Eastern cuisine, these tiny grains of pasta are made from milled wheat. Sold in this country presteamed, couscous need only be added to boiling water or broth, stirred, removed from heat, and set aside for 5 minutes to absorb the liquid. Available in plain, whole wheat, and a number of flavored varieties.

Curry powder   Curry powder is a spice blend used to flavor East Indian–style dishes. It generally includes ground dried chili, cumin, coriander, fenugreek, turmeric, and cloves. Blends labeled Madras are often hotter than other commercial products.

Diced canned tomatoes   Diced and peeled tomatoes are available from S&W Foods in plain and flavored styles.

Dijon mustard   Named for the city in France where it originated, this distinctive mustard is made from brown or black mustard seeds and has a pale yellow color and smooth consistency.

Dressings   A wide variety of dairy- and egg-free salad dressings from Follow Your Heart are available in the refrigerated case of health food stores. Delicious low-fat and cholesterol-free choices include Lemon Herb, Thousand Island, Creamy Garlic, and Honey Mustard (not vegan because of the honey).

Dried fruit   Delicious as snacks, dried fruits also add special flavor to cooked dishes and baked goods.

Currants   The type of currants used in cooking and baking are the small, dark, seedless, raisinlike dried Zante grapes. If these are unavailable you may substitute raisins.

Date pieces   Chopped dates, rolled in oat flour rather than sugar, are available in health food stores and specialty stores.

Dried apricots   Available as pitted whole or halved dried fruits, dried apricots have an intense flavor and moist, chewy texture. They can be eaten out of hand or used as an ingredient in sweet and savory dishes and in baking.

Dried blueberries   These are whole blueberries that have been kiln-dried to preserve their deep blue-black color and distinctive flavor. In shape and texture, they resemble raisins.

Dried cranberries   Resembling raisins in shape and texture, dried cranberries are lightly sugared and are available year-round. They can be eaten out of hand or used as an ingredient in baking and in sauces and chutneys.

Dried peaches   Sweet and slightly tangy, dried peaches are available halved or quartered. They are eaten out of hand or used as an ingredient in sweet and savory dishes and in baking.

Dried pineapple chunks   These are available in specialty stores and some supermarkets.

Dried minced garlic   This is widely available in the spice aisle at supermarkets and health food stores. Look for roasted dried minced garlic at specialty stores.

Eggless mayonnaise   There are several alternatives available to replace traditional mayonnaise, which is obscenely high in fat, calories, and cholesterol. Vegenaise by Follow Your Heart is superb and Original Gourmayo by Vegi-Deli is also quite good. Nasoya makes a tofu-based mayonnaise that is lower in fat and calories than the rest and is a very good alternative.

Egg replacer powder   EnerG Egg Replacer is a powdered product made from tapioca starch and leavenings. A most effective ingredient in baked goods, it is sold in health food stores and is also available through the EnerG catalog (see Resource Guide, page 285). Recipes in this collection that call for egg replacer were created using this product.

Evaporated cane juice   This is an unbleached, minimally processed alternative sweetener, which is light in color and finely granulated. It can be substituted on a one-for-one basis for refined white sugar. Available from Wholesome Sweeteners and Florida Crystals.

Flour   The finely ground and sifted meal of any edible grain.

   Kamut flour   Ground from a highly nutritious ancient wheat, kamut flour contains a unique type of gluten that is easier for the body to utilize than that in common wheat. Available in health food stores nationwide, and also from Arrowhead Mills and Bob's Red Mill. (See Resource Guide, page 285.)

   Oat flour   Oat flour may be purchased at health food or specialty stores, however, it takes only a few seconds to produce your own fresh oat flour. Simply measure and place the same amount of rolled oats as called for in the recipe in a food processor or blender and process into flour.

   Semolina flour   Semolina flour is coarsely ground from durum wheat. Pasta made with semolina flour is higher in protein and has a firm texture that holds up well. Gnocchi and better-quality pastas are made with semolina flour.

   Semolina flour mix   This is a blend of semolina flour and kamut flour made by Arrowhead Mills that produces a tasty and very manageable pasta dough. Available in health food stores and some supermarkets.

   Spelt flour   High in protein, containing all eight of the essential amino acids, and rich in B vitamins, spelt is related to wheat and like kamut is considered to be more easily tolerated by wheat-sensitive people. Available in health food stores nationwide and also from Arrowhead Mills and Bob's Red Mill.

Whole wheat flour   A whole-grain flour that contains the wheat germ, whole wheat flour has the highest nutritional, fiber, and fat content.

Whole wheat pastry flour   The best whole-grain flour to use in cakes and quickbreads, this finely milled flour is made from soft wheat. It has a low gluten content and is not used in yeast breads. Whole wheat pastry flour is available in health food stores nationwide and from Bob's Red Mill, Arrowhead Mills, and others.

Yellow cornmeal   Only whole-grain yellow cornmeal is used in these recipes.

Fruitsource   A wholesome sweetener, Fruitsource is made from grapes and grains. Available at natural food stores in both liquid and granulated forms. However, only liquid Fruitsource is used in *More Soy Cooking* recipes. Because it contains pectins, Fruitsource also functions as a fat replacer in baked goods.

Ginger brandy   This flavored brandy adds a unique flavor to dried fruits, baked goods, and savory dishes. If it is unavailable, any other type of brandy can be substituted.

Gingerroot   A knobby root with an aromatic, spicy flavor, ginger-root is found in supermarkets and specialty stores across the country. Fresh gingerroot is peeled and grated before it is added to the recipes in this collection.

Gomasio   Sometimes called sesame salt, gomasio contains toasted sesame seeds and sea salt. It is available in health food stores.

Gourmayo   This is a new line of vegan mayonnaise available in original and flavored styles: Chipotle, Herb & Garlic, and Pesto, among others. It is very tasty and there are lots of applications for the flavored varieties. Available from Vegi-Deli in health food stores nationwide.

Granny Smith apple   A very tart, green-skinned apple, mostly imported from New Zealand and Australia, but now also produced in California and Arizona. This juicy, crisp, all-purpose apple is excellent for cooking or eating out of hand.

Granulated garlic   Textured into grains, like sugar or salt, garlic in this form is far superior to garlic powder in flavor and aroma. Available at health food stores and some supermarkets.

Hip Whip   All natural, sugar- and dairy-free whipped topping, similar to Cool Whip. Available at health food stores nationwide from Now & Zen. Chocolate Mousse Hip Whip is also available.

Japanese eggplant   This small, relatively straight-sided, and narrow variety of eggplant has solid purple or variegated skin. It has tender and slightly sweet flesh.

Jasmine rice   A distinctly fragrant rice similar to basmati rice, for which it may be substituted, Jasmine rice is at the center of Thai cuisine.

Kale   A member of the cabbage family, kale has deep green frilly leaves sometimes tinged with purple. High in calcium, folic acid, and iron, kale also provides ample amounts of vitamin C and vitamin A.

Ketchup   Traditional ketchup is loaded with refined sugar. Fruit juice–sweetened ketchup is available from Muir Glen and Westbrae in health food stores nationwide.

Lasagna noodles   For my baked lasagna, I use Barilla lasagna noodles, which do not have to be precooked before baking. Imported from Italy, they are available at supermarkets nationwide.

Lighter Bake   Prune puree and applesauce join together to make a fat replacer for baked goods. This terrific product by Sunsweet is available in supermarkets nationwide.

Lite Coconut Milk   This product is much lower in fat and calories than regular coconut milk. Available from Thai Kitchen in supermarkets and health food stores.

Oat bran   This fiber-rich bran derived from oats adds a distinctive hearty flavor to baked goods. Available at health food and specialty stores.

Pearl barley   A hardy grain that is used primarily in soups and stews, pearl barley has been steamed and polished and the bran has been removed.

Mashed potato flakes   Barbara's Mashed Potatoes is a wholesome product made from whole, unpeeled Idaho potatoes. Distributed by Barbara's Bakery, it is available in health food stores.

Mirin   Lower in alcohol than Japanese sake, mirin is a sweet rice wine used in cooking.

Mushrooms   Very low in calories, fat- and cholesterol-free mushrooms give a meaty texture to many vegan dishes.

Baby portobellos   Sometimes called stuffing portobellos, these are a smaller variety of portobello mushrooms. They provide a reasonable cavity to hold a savory filling or can be sliced and added to many dishes. If they are not available, simply stuff the larger portobello and then divide into portions or use the largest cremini mushrooms.

Button mushrooms   These are mild-flavored cultivated white mushrooms in their smallest form. Select firm, plump mushrooms that are not bruised or slimy. Store in the refrigerator unwashed and lightly wrapped.

Cremini mushrooms   Similar in size and shape to common cultivated white mushrooms, cremini mushrooms are sometimes called Italian or brown mushrooms. They have a more assertive flavor and a rich brown skin concealing creamy tan flesh.

Shitake mushrooms   Available both fresh and dried, these distinctive mushrooms are used in stir-frys, soups, and salads.

Wild mushrooms   Some wild mushrooms are poisonous, so it is very important to be able to distinguish between those that are edible and those that are not. Morrel, chanterelle, oyster, shitake, enoki, Chinese black, wood ear, and porcini (sometimes called cepe) are examples of edible wild mushrooms.

Mushroom broth   Pacific brand organic mushroom broth is distributed in aseptic packaging. This very convenient product adds the rich flavor of mushrooms and contains no MSG.

Nutritional yeast   Available in health food stores, these delicious flakes are very high in protein and B vitamins. Not to be confused with brewer's yeast, which has a characteristically bitter taste, nutritional yeast adds a rich, cheese-like flavor and creaminess.

Vegetarian Support Formula   Made by Red Star, this is the only nutritional yeast containing vitamin B_{12}. Available at many health food stores and through The Mail Order Catalog (see Resource Guide, page 285).

Nuts   A number of my recipes, particularly those for baked goods, use nuts for added crunch and flavor. Nuts are a good source of protein (almonds have 30 grams per cup), but are also high in fat. I have found that ⅓ cup of nuts can add just the right crunch and impart plenty of flavor. These recipes are so very low in fat that you can afford a bit of "nutty indulgence."

Olive oil cooking spray A cooking oil product used to grease baking and cooking pans, it is widely available in supermarkets and health food stores nationwide.

Onions These pungent underground bulbs are essential to cuisines the world over.

Green onions Sometimes called spring onions, or scallions, green onions are perfect for stir-fry, salads, and soups. In order to retain its bright green color, the green section should be added during the last few minutes of cooking.

Leeks Leeks can be cooked as a vegetable or added to soups, stews, or vegetable medleys. Though related to garlic and onions, leeks have a more subtle flavor and milder fragrance than either. Leeks have a thick, white cylindrical stalk and look very much like enormous scallions. Fresh leeks have crisp, brightly colored leaves, and the smaller leeks are more tender. Leeks should be washed carefully (see "Techniques," page 47).

Red onions Mild and sweet, red onions perform equally well raw in salads, sandwiches, and antipasti or cooked in fajitas, medleys, focaccia, or pizza.

Shallots More like garlic than onions, shallots are composed of a head with multiple cloves covered with a papery skin. Used extensively in French cuisine, this mild member of the onion family combines the flavor of onions and garlic. Be careful not to brown shallots, as this will give them a bitter taste

Spanish and Bermuda onions These are sweeter than yellow or white onions, but not as sweet or as fragile as the Vidalia variety.

Sweet onions So sweet that some people eat them out of hand, the sweetest onions are grown in Vidalia, Georgia; Walla Walla, Washington; parts of Texas; and on the Hawaiian island of Maui.

White onions These can be as big as yellow onions in size, but their flavor is a good deal milder.

Yellow onions These all-purpose onions are the most pungent. Use in frying, main dishes, stews, and soups.

Orange blossom water The distilled essence of orange blossoms used to perfume sweets in eastern Mediterranean cuisine. It is used sparingly and fills the house with the fragrance of orange blossom.

Orzo A light and delicious rice-shaped pasta that is perfect in soups or as an innovative ingredient for the creative cook. Widely available in supermarkets.

Phyllo (or filo) pastry   These paper-thin leaves of dough are available in the freezer section of most supermarkets.

Polenta   Precooked San Gennaro polenta is a fat-free and gluten-free ready-to-use product sold shrink-wrapped in a cellophane sleeve. Available in a variety of flavors at health food stores and some supermarkets and specialty stores.

Polenta pasta   Made by the Gabriele Macaroni Company, this wheat-free and gluten-free corn-based pasta is available in a variety of cuts and flavors. It has a light and delicate texture and is available in health food stores nationwide.

Prune puree   Pureed prunes are a very effective fat replacer in baked goods. Prepared prune puree—sometimes called prune butter, prune filling, or lekvar—is available in supermarkets across the country and can be found with the kosher foods or in the baking aisle, under the brand names Solo Lekvar, Baker, and Sokol. See "Techniques" (page 47) for a simple recipe for homemade prune puree.

Quinoa   Although new to North Americans, quinoa has been cultivated in the South American Andes since 3000 B.C. High in protein, calcium, and iron, quinoa was called the "Mother Grain" by the ancient Incas. Like soybeans, quinoa is exceptionally high in lysine, an amino acid not overly abundant in the vegetable kingdom. This versatile grain is used like rice and is a relatively good source of phosphorus, calcium, iron, vitamin E, and several of the B vitamins. In addition to all this, quinoa tastes terrific!

Rice butter spread   This cholesterol-free alternative spread that is lower in fat than butter is available from Soyco in health food stores. Great on toast and for adding a buttery flavor when cooking or baking. Contains a small amount of casein, a dairy derivative.

Roasted sweet corn   Dried, roasted corn kernels are sold in 3-ounce packages by Melissa's in the produce section of supermarkets and health food stores nationwide.

Rose water   The distilled essence of rose petals, used to perfume sweets in eastern Mediterranean cuisine. Like orange blossom water, it is used sparingly and fills the house with fragrance. According to folklore, the soothing flavor is supposed to put you in a happy mood.

Saffron   The most expensive spice in the world, the yellow-orange stigmas of the crocus plant must be handpicked and then dried. This pungent, aromatic spice is an exotic flavoring that also adds a lovely hue to Mediterranean dishes. Fortunately, a little goes a long way.

Sea salt   Salt derived from evaporated seawater, which retains some natural trace minerals and contains no additives.

Seitan   Also called wheat gluten, this meat alternative is available packed in broth or shrink-wrapped in the refrigerated case at health food stores nation-wide. Brands include White Wave, Meat of Wheat, and Vegi-Deli, among others. When listed as such in this collection, the product recommended is one that is sold in the refrigerated section of health food stores packed in broth. Be aware that a 1-pound package of this type of wheat gluten will yield 8 ounces of seitan and 8 ounces of broth.

Stewed tomatoes   Flavored stewed tomatoes are used in a number of savory dishes in this collection. From S&W Foods, Mexican- and Italian-style stewed tomatoes add spice and flavor conveniently and are widely available in super-markets.

Sucanat Organic Sugar   This brand of evaporated cane juice is a slightly refined product that can be substituted one-for-one for refined granulated white sugar in any recipe. Available in health food stores and some specialty markets.

Organic Sucanat (Sugar Cane Natural)   This is similar to pourable brown sugar. Made from unrefined cane juice, this alternative sweetener is a whole food and therefore retains all of the vitamins and minerals found in nature. From Wholesome Sweeteners, it imparts many of the same characteristics as brown sugar and is found in health food stores nationwide.

Sun-dried tomatoes   These are ripe tomato halves that have been oven-dried, giving them a uniquely intense flavor. I use *only* the dry ones (which are reconstituted in boiling water) and never those packed in oil. Store unused dry-packed tomatoes airtight at room temperature for up to one year. Organic sun-dried tomatoes are available from Sonoma Foods.

Sunspire Chocolate Chips   These real chocolate chips are wholesome and dairy-free. There are several varieties, but my favorites are the Organic Dark Chocolate Chips, sweetened with evaporated cane juice. These chips are knock-your-socks-off delicious! They are sold in health food stores nationwide.

Tofu Hero (formerly Tofu Helper)   I developed these spice packs for Mori-Nu to turn a box of silken tofu into a meal in minutes. They are available in four varieties at health food stores and supermarkets nationwide from Mori-naga Nutritional Foods, Inc. You need add only boiling water or mayonnaise (depending on the variety) to mashed or cubed tofu. Note: This product has been incorporated into a number of *More Soy Cooking* recipes as a flavoring ingredient. In some instances, the directions will differ from those indicated on the package. Use the dry mix only, without added water, unless otherwise indicated in the recipe instructions.

Tropical Source Chocolate Chips   Delicious, dairy-free chocolate chips in a variety of flavors—such as espresso, peanut butter, and semisweet, among others—are made by Cloud Nine and are available at health food stores and some specialty markets.

Unsweetened pie cherries   The type of pitted cherries used in pie fillings, without additional ingredients, these can be found with the cans of prepared pie filling in the supermarket.

Vanilla extract   Pure vanilla extract is the ingredient of choice. Pure vanilla extract is a brown liquid that is clear and richly fragrant. In order to meet FDA standards it must contain 13.35 ounces of vanilla beans per gallon during extraction and 35 percent alcohol. In contrast, imitation vanilla is composed of artificial flavors, most of which are chemically treated by-products of the paper industry. Pure vanilla extract is about twice as expensive as imitation vanilla; however, the flavor, intensity, and quality will allow you to use about half as much.

Vegenaise   This is a very authentic mayonnaise alternative and a favorite in my kitchen. This eggless mayonnaise is available in original, expeller pressed, and grapeseed oil varieties in health food stores nationwide from Follow Your Heart.

Vegetarian broth   Chicken- or beef-flavor broth powder is used to reconstitute unflavored TVP products in many of the *More Soy Cooking* recipes. You will also find this product used in soup, stew, sauce, and gravy recipes. Available in some health food stores and through The Mail Order Catalog (see Resource Guide, page 285).

Vegetarian Worcestershire sauce   A condiment with all of the zest and flavor of the original, but without anchovies or any artificial ingredients. Available at health food stores from The Wizard or Robbies.

Vegi-Deli Chicken and Turkey Strips   These very authentic, plant-based poultry alternatives are especially good when marinated. They are made from wheat gluten and are low in fat and, of course, cholesterol-free. Available shrink-wrapped at health food stores nationwide.

Vegi-Deli pepperoni   Meatless pepperoni with the rich and satisfying taste of pepperoni—without the guilt—is made from wheat gluten and is low in fat and cholesterol-free. Available in three flavors: Original, Zesty Italian, and Hot 'N Spicy at health food stores nationwide.

Vital wheat gluten   Vital wheat gluten occurs naturally in all wheat flours, and helps improve the rise and texture of bread. It is highly recommended that you add vital wheat gluten to the flour in recipes for whole-grain breads. Please note: Vital wheat gluten is not the same as gluten flour, which is a combination of flour and vital wheat gluten.

Whole wheat tortillas   When buying tortillas, make sure to read labels carefully. Most tortillas will contain hydrogenated fat. Whole wheat tortillas are available at health food stores and supermarkets. If whole wheat is not available, tortillas made with unbleached flour are fine, as long as the ingredients do not list partially hydrogenated oil of any kind.

WonderSlim Cocoa (Wondercocoa)   This is real cocoa and it is fat-free, an advantage over already low-fat regular cocoa. The best news is that it is also caffeine-free and that the caffeine is extracted using a natural process. This cocoa is available in health food stores and some supermarkets nationwide.

Kitchen Tools, Techniques, and Tofu 101

$\wp$

Maintaining a healthy lifestyle is not at all complicated. It requires only the desire to improve the very quality of life that you enjoy. Perhaps you would like more energy, or to lose some weight. You have read about the link that is being drawn between diet and health and would like to pursue a more wholesome regimen. Applying the principles and procedures employed in the healthy kitchen involves making choices when purchasing ingredients and taking advantage of some helpful techniques. Wholesome food preparation is about techniques that inspire creativity, and as you become more familiar with these ingredients, tools, and techniques, you will develop your own style of creating delicious healthy meals.

Tools

Every cook develops his or her own style, one that evolves from a consideration of objectives, motivation, and necessity. Often the rigors and time constraints of everyday life or an impending crisis in the kitchen will force us to discover new uses for old favorites that would otherwise be overlooked. You can find all manner of kitchenware for every conceivable application, but just about any kitchen utensil has more than one use. For example, to grate gingerroot there are special Japanese ceramic ginger graters, but I find that a small, handheld stainless steel grater is all I need. And while there are special citrus zesters available, the same small grater is quite effective, though you should be careful not to grate through to the bitter white pith beneath the skin.

I love kitchen gadgets, but I certainly have my share of clever inventions that looked cool and turned out to be not so great. I have found some terrific kitchen tools that have become favorites in my culinary routine.

In my kitchen, there is a wide array of spatulas, knives, whisks, measuring cups and spoons, and mixing bowls. There are whisks of every size and shape for different uses—from larger whisks for mixing and aerating sauces to very small whisks that are perfect for creaming miso or blending cornstarch or egg replacer powder with liquids. Spatulas, both hard plastic or soft rubber-tipped, are essential for effectively scraping bowls and pans. A soft mushroom brush, while not essential, is an effective way to clean mushooms without causing them to become waterlogged; the stiff vegetable brush I use to scrub potatoes is indispensable.

There are many sizes and shapes of bakeware—springform, Bundt, and tube, oblong, square, and round—each shape and size a crucial factor in gauging the results. Pay close attention to the type of pan called for in baking.

I tend to use a tight circle of cooking appliances, baking pans, measures, and such in the kitchen. These are the tried-and-true kitchen utensils that work so well with the techniques that I have developed over the years. Here are the tools that assist me in producing my culinary repertoire.

Food processor   The hardest-working appliance in my kitchen, this versatile tool streamlines the preparation of so many tasks, whether fundamental or sophisticated. It is my blender and mixer for everything from pie, yeast, and pasta doughs to puddings, sauces, dressings, and dips. I will sometimes use the food processor for slicing or shredding large quantities, such as shredding carrots for a carrot cake or salad. In general, though, I prefer to chop, mince, and dice by hand.

Electric frying pan   This is another workhorse in my culinary routine, and the only chore it never performs in my healthy kitchen is cooking fried or deep-fried foods. (The high volume of fat used and absorbed into the food and ultimately into the body would be considered deadly in my approach to healthy living.) I use a large pan for increased surface heat, and the electric frying pan seems to provide an even distribution of heat that cooks down juices more efficiently.

Microwave oven   Fast and convenient, the microwave oven is useful for warming liquids, boiling water and broth, thawing frozen foods, and reheating leftovers, sauces, and gravies. Vegetables cooked in the microwave will retain their color better than those cooked conventionally. Microwaving is fine for a quick baked potato, but a conventional oven produces finer-textured and tastier flesh and crisp skin.

Micro-steamer   This nifty vegetable steamer from Tupperware produces tender, brightly hued steamed vegetables in record time without water.

Tortilla warmer   A very useful clay baking dish that is designed to warm tortillas and keep them hot and moist, this handy item can be found at department stores and gourmet shops.

Pressure cooker   Pressure cookers are tightly sealed and energy efficient. Using a pressure cooker can reduce cooking times by as much as two thirds. Modern models are usually made from stainless steel with reinforced bottoms, which allow for more even heat distribution, and are equipped with built-in safety release valves. I particularly like the texture and flavor of brown rice cooked under pressure.

Stovetop- and Oven-safe cookware (Corningware)   This product line is so versatile. I like the ability to begin a recipe on the stove, continue the cooking process in the oven, and serve and store the dish all in the same pan. In cooking with Corningware, it is important to note that while cooking on the stovetop, the contents should be stirred regularly and the temperature should not be set too high for an extended period. This will prevent the food from sticking.

Saucepans, sauté pans, frying pans   Size, weight, and shape are all important when choosing saucepans. Stainless steel is nonreactive and noncorrosive and is the best choice for durability and wear. Aluminum disk– or copper-bottomed saucepans provide the best distribution of heat.

Expandable steamer basket   This perforated, stainless steel basket converts any covered saucepan into a steamer. Generally available in two sizes: 8½ inches and 10½ inches.

Glass bakeware (Pyrex)   Heat-tempered baking pans, pie plates, and casserole dishes can go from the refrigerator to the oven to the table and back into the refrigerator. I particularly like the 2-quart covered casserole for side dishes, baked puddings, and gratins. Because batter cooks more quickly in glass than in metal baking pans, reduce the recommended oven temperature by 25° when using glass cake pans.

Jelly roll pan   A wide, shallow, rectangular pan that measures 17 by 12 inches is most often used to make thin, aerated cakes that are filled and rolled. This pan's generous size exposes most of the batter to oven heat; a large pan of brownies or cookie bars will be done in 30 minutes or less.

Measuring tools   Accurate measuring is all-important in producing delectable results.

Dry measuring cups   Available in metal or plastic, nested measuring cups for dry ingredients should be filled to the rim. Spoon ingredient into the cup and level off with a spatula. Never "tap down" when filling.

Liquid measuring cups   Heat-tempered, spouted glass measuring cups in various sizes are marked with both American and metric units. They allow accurate reading of levels and also are excellent vessels for creaming miso or nutritional yeast with liquids. They can also be used for stirring down silken tofu to measure volume. Plastic liquid measuring cups are also available.

Measuring spoons   Sets of six elongated spoons from ⅛ teaspoon to 1 tablespoon are the most useful.

(Measuring tip: measure oil before anything sticky, like molasses or Fruitsource; if oil is not called for in the recipe, spray the spoon or cup lightly with cooking oil spray. The oil will make the sticky liquid slide out of the spoon or cup more easily.)

Knives   There are knives designed for every purpose; however, in the vegetarian kitchen a few quality knives can handle most tasks.

The petite or chef's knife   A wide-bladed, 10-inch knife with a gently curved triangular blade is best used for crushing and mincing fresh garlic cloves and chopping fresh herbs and vegetables.

Bread knife   Usually 8 to 10 inches long with a blunt-tipped ridged blade, the bread knife can slice through both hard crust and soft interior.

Grapefruit knife   This knife conforms to the general size and shape of citrus fruit and has a serrated, curved blade 3½ to 4 inches long. Grapefruit knives can also be used to separate melon from rind, hull tomatoes, and core onions.

Paring knife   The small paring knife, with about a 4-inch blade, is used to pare fruits and vegetables, peel gingerroot, remove stems and eyes from vegetables, pit plums, nectarines, and peaches—and, for the artistic among us, to create radish roses, celery curls, and pickle fans. It can also be used to slice and dice small foods or to quarter apples and potatoes.

Cake knife   In addition to slicing through cakes and tortes, serrated cake knives are also used to slice and serve pies.

Spoons and spatulas Every kitchen needs a few sizes of the slotted spatula for flipping foods like pancakes and burgers. Large mix-and-stir spoons can also double as serving spoons. Slotted or perforated spoons are used to stir foods like pasta and a ladle is best for dishing out soups and stews.

Spreader spatula With a rounded, flexible metal blade a few inches wide, the flat-surfaced spatula spreader is most useful for spreading frosting, but can be used to cut sandwiches, muffins, and rolls.

Potato masher Designed to reduce cooked potatoes into a fluffy mass, this utensil is used in my kitchen most often to mash tofu into curdlike pieces when making eggless egg salad, a tofu scrambler, or ricotta cheese–type fillings.

Kitchen shears With strong, sharp blades forged in either chrome-plated carbon steel or stainless steel, general-purpose kitchen shears are designed to be hardy. The best shears are fitted with a pivot screw that allows the parts to be disassembled for cleaning and for adjustment of pressure. Quality kitchen shears can handle a number of tasks, from trimming fibrous artichoke leaves to slicing pizza.

Vegetable peeler The best vegetable peelers have ergonomically designed handles and make quick work of separating vegetables like potatoes from their skins, without cutting too deeply into the flesh of the vegetable.

Wire mesh strainer Coarse, stainless steel mesh strainers range from 5 to 14 inches in diameter. A 9½-inch mesh strainer is useful for rinsing grains like basmati or quinoa, or for rinsing and sorting beans. Look for a strainer with a flat-bottomed bowl-like construction, which allows hands-free draining of liquids from foods.

Salad spinner I highly recommend spinning salad greens as dry as possible so they can hold dressing well and to prevent them from wilting. I like the three-piece plastic ensemble that consists of a solid outer bowl, and inner slotted basket, and a hand crank. The spinners with a cord-pull for spinning seem to break more readily.

Lemon reamer A cone-shaped, handheld device with a tapered tip, a lemon reamer penetrates the flesh and has furrows that squeeze out the juice from lemons and limes when turned side to side.

Nutmeg grinder Aromatic freshly ground nutmeg adds a special touch to many dishes. Look for a spring-set, crank-driven grinder with top storage compartment for the nutmeg.

Techniques

Here are some helpful hints for using various techniques and ingredients in the preparation of *More Soy Cooking* recipes.

Braising or Stewing

I use a similar technique at the outset of much of my savory food preparation. Basically it is a braising or stewing procedure that is a combination of two cooking techniques. First the pan is greased with a little olive oil or olive oil spray. Initially I might add a small amount of crushed red pepper, dried minced garlic, or grated gingerroot, sometimes all three. The pan is warmed for a minute or two, and then my favorite trilogy is added (fresh minced garlic, some form of onion, and bell pepper or celery) and sautéed just enough to soften, about 3 to 5 minutes. Then I will begin to add the main ingredients, stirring after each addition. At this point, I begin to introduce some form of liquid, perhaps wine, broth, or tomatoes. The heat is reduced and the dish is simmered slowly. I then proceed with the specifics of the particular dish. Using this technique helps to keep the fat profile low because just a touch of oil is enough to lock in the flavor of the ingredients and flavorful liquids keep the dish moist. Braises and stews are almost a complete meal and are ideal company fare because once they are at the simmering stage, they require little attention. You only need to stir occasionally and replenish the liquids from time to time. They also keep well and actually improve in flavor by sitting. To serve, simply reheat.

Baking Without Fat

While there are a few instances where a little olive oil is used, as in a pie crust, you won't find butter or shortening in my kitchen. Fruit purees containing pectins do a terrific job of bonding the ingredients and supporting the structure of the baked product and replacing *all* of the fat.

You can make homemade prune puree in your kitchen: Simply place 2 cups of pitted prunes in a food processor or blender with ¾ cup of water and 4 teaspoons of pure vanilla extract. Blend until smooth, cover, and refrigerate. Because prune puree is very high in sorbitols, a natural preservative, it will keep in the refrigerator for more than two weeks. I prefer to use prune puree for most of my chocolate creations and applesauce when a more delicate flavor is desired.

Lighter Bake, available in supermarkets, is an excellent product made from both apples and prunes and can be substituted one-for-one for prune puree.

These purees work exceptionally well in the amounts required. Be sure to measure accurately.

My baked goods are entirely egg- and dairy-free, as well. Without sacrificing taste, lite silken tofu, enriched soymilk, and EnerG egg replacer powder supplant ingredients that add excessive amounts of fat and cholesterol.

When baking without added fat as I do, it is important to use folding techniques when combining the wet and dry ingredients. If some of the liquid has been set aside to fold in during the mixing process, it is added alternately with the wet and dry ingredients. Work quickly and mix just until moistened, as overbeating will toughen the finished product. When adding dry fruit, nuts, or chocolate pieces, I always add them to the dry ingredients. This is not only helpful in keeping them suspended separately in the batter, it also reduces the amount of mixing needed. Of course, this does not apply to very moist additions such as crushed pineapple or dried fruit stewed in brandy.

Tempeh

Tempeh should be steamed before proceeding with the recipe. Precooking is necessary in order to tenderize the tempeh. Simply cube the tempeh and place it in a steamer over boiling water. Steam for 15 minutes. You may also place 8 ounces of cubed tempeh in 2 cups of water with a tablespoon of tamari and simmer for 20 minutes.

Phyllo Dough

Sometimes spelled filo, this versatile dough is widely available in the freezer section of most supermarkets. Remove the package from the freezer and place it in the refrigerator overnight. Two to four hours before the phyllo is needed, remove the package from the refrigerator and place it on a kitchen counter, unopened, to bring it to room temperature. Remove the number of sheets needed and freeze the remainder, if any.

If you've never worked with these leaves of dough, you might think they are sheets of translucent paper. They are best handled gingerly, as they are very delicate and dry out easily. Work quickly with each individual layer while keeping the remaining leaves covered with a damp cloth. I use a water spritzer, like the typical indoor plant mister, to spray the covering cloth to keep the dough moist. Spray lightly and do not drench the cloth or the dough will become gummy, especially around the edges.

Traditionally, the leaves of dough are brushed with melted butter before placement, to promote flakiness. This procedure alone can add unimaginable fat, calories, and cholesterol. I use an olive oil cooking spray instead.

Always make the filling for phyllo before removing the pastry leaves from the wrapper. If the filling has been cooked, it should be cooled a bit before you mound it onto the prepared layers. I also sprinkle bread crumbs between the layers of phyllo pastry to promote crispness and prevent sogginess.

Pizza Dough

My pizza dough is made with whole wheat flour and fortified with soy flour, flaxseed meal, and cornmeal. The yeast called for is baker's yeast, which is sold in a jar in supermarkets across the country. Red Star and Fleischmann's are two popular brands. Keep yeast in the refrigerator, to extend freshness. I utilize the food processor to make pizza dough. However, if you prefer to make the dough by hand you may proceed with this standard method:

In a small glass measuring cup, warm the water with the sweetener called for to no more than 110° in the microwave. Sprinkle the yeast into the water and set aside to proof. If the yeast is good, it should foam. In a large bowl, stir together the flours and salt. If a cooked potato is called for, it should be riced before adding to the flour. Make a well in the center of the flour and pour in the yeast mixture. Mix well and knead for 10 to 12 minutes, adding more flour, as needed, to make a smooth dough.

To knead by hand, place dough on a lightly floured surface and sprinkle the top lightly with flour. Using the heels of your hands, press down and away, and then fold the dough back onto itself. Repeat this action, turning the dough around a little each time. Add only enough flour to prevent the dough from sticking. When the dough is smooth, elastic, and springy, it is ready to rest. At this point, you may proceed with the recipe.

Pasta Dough

There are six basic steps to making fresh pasta: mixing, kneading, resting, rolling, cutting, and drying. In my kitchen, pasta dough is mixed in the food processor, blending the tofu at the outset and mixing the ingredients. Additionally, this method jump-starts the kneading process. Kneading develops the gluten in the flour and promotes elasticity. Resting the dough is important because it gives the gluten a chance to relax, thereby making the dough more manageable.

Using a hand-cranked pasta machine   Divide the dough into four equal portions. Place one portion on a lightly floured board, and return remaining portions to the covered bowl. To roll dough into sheets, flatten into an oval shape, sprinkle with flour and feed it through the second widest roller setting.

Repeat the rolling process, dusting and folding the dough into thirds. Repeat several times on progressively narrower settings. Continue to feed dough (without folding) until you have a sheet between 16 and 20 inches long. Cut dough crosswise and set sheets aside to dry on lightly floured wax paper covered with a kitchen towel for 30 minutes.

To cut pasta dough by machine, divide the dough into four equal portions, and return remaining portions to the covered bowl. Lightly flour the dough, and cut into desired shape by feeding through wide, thin, or narrow blades. Dry the cut pasta by hanging it on a pasta rack, tossing cut pasta into a loose pile, or laying it flat on wax paper in the open air for at least an hour. This will prevent the pasta from sticking after it has been cut and allow it to remain firm after cooking.

Making pasta dough by hand   Divide the dough into four equal portions. Place one portion on a lightly floured board, and return remaining portions to the covered bowl. Flatten the dough into an oval shape, and roll the dough into an oblong sheet, about 7 inches by 16 inches. Dough should be thin, but not translucent. Divide sheets crosswise and set aside to dry covered, on wax paper or a kitchen towel, in a warm place for about 30 minutes or until it is dry and pliable, but not brittle.

To hand cut pasta into long, thin shapes, such as fettuccini or spaghetti, first sprinkle dough lightly with flour and roll loosely, jelly-roll style. Using a sharp knife, make cuts straight down without dragging the knife through the dough. When cooked, pasta swells to double the width, so make the strips about half the desired width. Allow the cut pasta to dry by tossing into a loose pile or laying flat on wax paper in the open air for at least an hour. This will prevent the pasta from sticking after it has been cut and allow it to remain firm after cooking.

Making filled pasta   Forming ravioli by hand is really quite easy. Fill fresh pasta dough shortly after rolling. There are handy ravioli frames available at gourmet shops and some department stores that are quite easy to use, but they are not necessary. Roll dough for filled pasta to about 1/16 inch, not as thinly as for regular cut shapes. Lay out a sheet of pasta dough and place a rounded teaspoonful of filling at regular intervals along the dough. Cover with a second sheet of pasta dough, and press lightly around the filled mounds. Dip a biscuit cutter or pizza wheel (for square ravioli) in flour; press out or cut the ravioli. I sometimes use a wine glass with a diameter of about 2 inches to cut ravioli. Press the edges closed with a floured fork, allowing about 1/4 inch between the filling and the sealed edge, and cover loosely. Set aside for about 20 minutes.

Filled pasta tastes best when cooked less than an hour after filling. However, you can stuff ravioli in the morning and set it aside to cook just before serving. You can even wrap filled pasta loosely and store in the refrigerator for several days.

Generally, fresh pasta cooks quickly; however, filled pasta can take as long as 20 minutes or more to cook through, depending on the size of the ravioli and thickness of the dough. It is important not to overfill the pan and to check the pasta throughout the cooking process.

Cooking pasta   With the exception of the "no-cook" type of lasagna noodles, pasta is cooked in a large pot of boiling water, using at least 4 quarts per pound. Add a tablespoon of oil and a teaspoon of salt to the water. The oil will discourage the strands from sticking together. Cooking times will vary according to the thickness of the pasta, with filled pastas generally taking longer to cook. It's important to keep a close watch on boiling pasta, and to stir it frequently, taking care not to overcook it. Frequent testing by biting or pinching a test piece is the best method. Pasta has reached what is considered the perfect texture, al dente, when it is firm but flexible; if it is gummy, it's overdone.

Snipping and Slicing

Sometimes a recipe will call for an ingredient to be snipped. I find that in some instances it is easier to use my kitchen shears to cut herbs or dried fruits. For instance, when a recipe calls for snipped fresh basil, stack a few leaves, roll them into a tight cylinder, and cut into strips. With certain dried fruits, such as apricots or sun dried-tomatoes, snip them into halves or thirds, as indicated in each recipe.

Sometimes a recipe calls for a particular ingredient, such as onions or potatoes, to be sliced into half-moons. Simply cut the vegetable in half crosswise, and then laying it cut side down, slice in half again. Then proceed to make thin slices crosswise to produce half-moon slices. In the case of an elongated vegetable such as zucchini, slice in half lengthwise, and then make crosswise cuts to produce half-moons. Half-moon slices add to the quality of the presentation in many dishes.

Dried Fruit

To snip, slice, or chop most dried fruit: Slice with a sharp serrated knife, and then assemble the slices and cut across into pieces. Or snip with kitchen shears. If the knife or scissor blades become sticky, dip in hot water, coat lightly with vegetable oil cooking spray or wipe with oil.

Leeks

Thorough cleaning is essential in order to avoid unpleasant residue, as leeks can be very gritty. They often retain sand beneath their tightly wrapped layers, especially where the white bulb joins the tender green shaft. First, trim the roots and the green leaf ends. Then, without cutting all the way through, slit the leek from top to bottom. Fan the layers open without pulling the leek apart. Rinse the leek thoroughly under cold running water. Finally, soak the rinsed leeks in a large bowl of cold water, changing the water several times, until no grit appears in the bottom of the bowl.

Soy Buttermilk

Adding cider vinegar or lemon juice to 1% fat soymilk creates a low-fat and dairy-free alternative for dairy buttermilk. This wholesome ingredient can be substituted one-for-one in any recipe that calls for dairy buttermilk.

Garlic

The optimal way to mince garlic is to begin by placing an unpeeled clove on a cutting board. Lay the flat side of a large wide-bladed knife over the clove and strike a few times with the heel of your palm. Remove the skin and mince, holding the knife carefully on both ends, using short chopping motions. When a garlic clove is added to a food processor or blender, it need only be peeled before adding.

Avocados

To peel and pit an avocado: Cut the avocado in half lengthwise, down to the pit, and twist the halves to separate. Holding the half with the pit in one hand, use an avocado pitting knife or a tablespoon and scoop the pit out of the center. Slide the avocado knife or spoon between the skin and the flesh and scoop out the flesh in one piece. Place it, cut side down, on a work surface and slice with small knife.

Nutmeats

I generally purchase nutmeats either whole or in large pieces. To chop or crush: Measure the nuts first and then place them in a plastic bag. Place the closed bag on a work surface and rap it with the end of a rolling pin a number of times. This produces crushed nuts that are smaller than those available commercially. I think it makes them go further and seems to increase the volume.

Mushrooms

Mushrooms should be cleaned just before cooking. Remove the grit by wiping the mushrooms with a damp paper towel or a gentle mushroom brush. For a more thorough cleaning, swish the mushrooms very briefly in water, and then pat them dry with paper towels.

Tofu 101

Replacing animal products with soyfoods makes good sense, and tofu plays a major role in that process. There are numerous new and traditional soyfoods available, but none is better known or less understood than tofu. It is characteristically bland, but this very lack of flavor is what gives tofu such well-known versatility. Tofu is extremely adaptable and able to easily absorb a rich marinade or the flavor of other ingredients in a dish.

It is crucial that you use the right kind of tofu for a specific dish. The next time you are at your health food store or supermarket, take a moment to investigate the various textures and seasonings. The fat content of tofu can also vary from one brand to another, averaging about 1.5 grams of fat per 3-ounce serving. Compare this to a 3-ounce serving of chicken breast: 12.9 grams of fat and an additional 63 milligrams of cholesterol. Most varieties of tofu are water packed; some are vacuum packed or aseptically packaged, and there are also organic types. Curdled from hot soy milk in a process similar to the way cheese is made from milk, tofu is solidified using a coagulant, either a mineral derived from sea salt, magnesium chloride (*nigari* in Japanese), or calcium sulfate. *Nigari* produces a tofu that is considered better tasting, but tofu thickened with a calcium-based coagulant will be even higher in calcium.

Tofu is ideal for stir-frys and other medleys, but that's just for openers. Its adaptability makes tofu equally useful in dips, soups, casseroles, desserts, and as a binding agent, replacing eggs in baked goods. Once you try these recipes using the recommended style of tofu, this versatile ingredient is likely to become a regular player in your culinary repertoire.

The key to successful tofu cookery is to understand the differences in styles and textures and the applications suited to each.

Firm tofu   Chinese-style tofu is more compact and solid and is available both extra firm and super firm; the difference in texture depends on how much water is pressed out in processing. It's important to use firm tofu in stir-frys or vegetable medleys where the shape must hold up. Firm, extra firm, and super firm are all excellent choices here, and the degree of density is all a matter of taste.

Silken tofu   This softer Japanese style of tofu is available in regular and lite versions; Japanese-style silken tofu can be found water packed and in the more widely available shelf-stable, aseptic packages that look like large juice boxes. Though never approaching the firmness of other types of tofu, silken tofu is available in varying degrees of firmness, ranging from soft to extra firm. Lite silken tofu is very low in fat and has an ultra-smooth texture and custard-like consistency. While the "regular" silken variety is a bit more dense, it, too, is lower in fat than the more conventional variety. This style of tofu is the optimal choice for dips, dressings, or chilled desserts. It is also an excellent substitute for eggs and dairy products in baked goods and is often preferred in scramblers and eggless egg salad. Aseptically packaged tofu has a long shelf life, can be eaten safely right from the box, and needn't be refrigerated until opened nor steamed before incorporating into uncooked dishes.

When making puddings, dips, sauces, or mixing the liquid ingredients in baking, it is important to blend silken tofu (lite or regular) until smooth, *before* adding other ingredients to the food processor or blender. Drain aseptically packaged tofu by cutting the side flaps where marked and pouring off the liquid. You can wrap the block of tofu in paper towels of double thickness to draw off excess liquid, however, this is not essential. Using a potato masher to break the tofu into "curds" is a quick way to replicate the look of scrambled eggs or egg salad, or ricotta cheese. To measure lite silken tofu by volume, spoon tofu into a liquid measuring cup and stir down with a fork.

Tofu cutlets   Drain lite silken tofu; stand the block on end and divide crosswise into three equal pieces. Lay the tofu down and cut each slice in half lengthwise. You should have six strips 4 inches long and about 1 inch wide. Cover each with plastic wrap so that the tofu is separated. Place wrapped tofu in an airtight plastic freezer bag and freeze for at least 2 days.

Remove from freezer and rinse in cold water. Remove wrap and rinse again. Defrost overnight in the refrigerator, at room temperature for 1 hour, or in microwave on 40 percent power for 4 minutes. Drain and then pat dry with paper towels, gently pressing out as much liquid as possible. Proceed with the recipe.

Precooked tofu   This is a seasoned, baked tofu with a texture and flavor reminiscent of smoked meat or roast duck, while smokehouse-style tofu suggests smoked cheese and is delicious when spread on crackers.

Baked tofu   This is a convenient and ready-to-use component for the busy cook. You may slice or dice baked tofu and add it to salads and sandwiches or to an antipasto straight from the package. A favorite application is to add sliced baked tofu to stir-frys or baked dishes.

Tofu Tips

* Freezing tofu for up to three months will increase the chewy texture. Once defrosted, press out as much excess liquid as possible and proceed with the recipe.

* Another way to solidify tofu and enhance its ability to absorb seasonings and marinades is to cube it and boil in water for 10 minutes and then drain.

* Some cooks prefer vacuum-packed *nigari* firm tofu because of its convenience and noticeably fresh taste.

* If tofu is packed in water, it's a good idea to change the water daily. Tofu stored in this manner can be kept for up to seven days without spoiling. However, it's best to use water-packed tofu as soon as possible for the best flavor and texture. Be sure to check the use-by date and never use tofu with an "off" odor.

* In a hurry? Take advantage of the handy assortment of dry mixes that can transform a box of tofu into a tasty scramble or quick stir-fry. A very popular spice pack (Tofu Hero) can be mixed with lite silken tofu and a few tablespoons of eggless mayonnaise to make a flavorful and authentic-tasting eggless egg salad in less than a minute.

* Tofu, by nature, is mostly liquid. It's sometimes a good idea to draw off some of the water before sautéing to prevent the oil from splattering and to enhance browning. First, pat the tofu dry, wrap it in a clean, dry kitchen towel, and place it in the refrigerator for about an hour. Remove tofu from towel, pat dry, and proceed with the recipe. Vacuum-packed tofu should just be patted dry as it has already been pressed.

Cooking with Spirit!

Wine adds depth of flavor to food, and an unmistakable taste that can be found in no other ingredient. You should never cook with a wine that you wouldn't drink. That is not to say that you would consider reaching for a 25-dollar bottle in order to add a cup of wine to an entrée or soup, but if a wine is okay to drink, it's okay to cook with. Avoid what is called "cooking wine" sold in most supermarkets. This is a poor-quality wine to which salt is added. Shun it even if it means not using wine at all. It is better to purchase a more mainstream wine that will retain the characteristic flavor of the varietal.

There are characteristics that are associated with specific varietals and basic flavors that are common to specific grapes that will vary from one varietal to another. Recipes will generally call for a particular type of wine, like white wine, merlot, sherry, or vermouth. In each case, the characteristic flavor of the wine blends with the other ingredients in a prescribed fashion and is used like any other seasoning. For white wine, use sauvignon blanc, chardonnay, chenin blanc—whatever your personal preference. Chardonnay will add a buttery quality; sauvignon blanc a more herbaceous undertone.

There are some wines that don't fit into the red or white category. Fortified wines such as sherry, port, and vermouth are wines that have a little extra alcohol added before a very long aging. This helps preserve the wine and develop some of the complexities during the extended aging process. Use only dry or very dry vermouth or sherry in savory dishes. Because of their increased aging, these wines develop intense flavors. Some sherries have a nutlike quality. Ports can be sweet and are often used in fruit dishes or desserts. Vermouth differs in that assorted herbs and spices have been steeped in the wine, giving it a unique flavor. I use dry vermouth quite extensively in cooking, but any white wine can be used in its place.

What happens when you cook with wine (or vodka or tequila) depends on when you add the wine and what you do afterward. Heat dissipates the alcohol in wine, which intensifies the flavor and assists in the marriage of the other ingredients. When you deglaze a hot pan with wine, initially more alcohol will evaporate than water. However, as the amount of alcohol decreases in proportion to the water, less alcohol evaporates. Depending on how much you allow the wine to reduce, and whether there is other liquid present, as much as 50 percent of the alcohol could still remain. Prolonged cooking time will decrease the amount of alcohol. For instance, in a braised dish there is a fair amount of liquid, and the lengthy cooking time lets the alcohol evaporate before the liquid is reduced. Therefore the alcohol does not become more concentrated as you cook the wine down. What does become concentrated are the flavors. If in the cooking process the wine is reduced to being "dry" (where no liquid remains, just a syrupy glaze), the alcohol has evaporated. The alcohol, having a lower boiling point, will evaporate before all the liquid is gone.

Special Concerns: Sulfites and Children

For many people sulfites are a problem. There are those who cannot drink wine because they are allergic to the sulfites. Cooking with wine containing sulfites does not concentrate them, as it does flavor; in fact, they evaporate like alcohol. The sulfites go through a conversion in the liquid of the wine to produce sulfur dioxide. This is actually the compound that prevents the oxidation. It is also a gas that when subjected to heat, will dissipate into the air. All that remains are some salts in so minute a quantity that they have no effect on flavor.

If you are concerned about exposing your children to alcohol, the safest bet is to avoid alcohol altogether. In that case you can substitute another liquid, such as broth or apple cider. However, in the most common type of wine cookery, where the wine is reduced, the exposure is greatly diminished. Typically, in a recipe that serves four, you may add ¼ to ½ cup of wine. You are then going to heat this, so some, if not all, of the alcohol evaporates. You will then divide it among four people. Therefore, the amount of alcohol consumed by each person eating the dish is not very large—in fact, there may not be any there at all.

The Recipes

Amazing Appetizers

When entertaining, offering a varied buffet of appetizers encourages your guests to mingle and allows you an opportunity to finalize preparations. As a prelude to the meal, appetizers should be chosen for their complementary appeal. Perhaps there is a theme or common thread that suggests a specific cuisine or style. You will also want your menu selection to reflect the season of the year. For instance, a warm and hearty first course in winter and lighter selections in summer, with holidays suggesting many imaginative themes and traditions.

Consider a balance of flavors, texture, and presentation: hot and cold, finger foods and those that require utensils, highly spiced or mildly so, and so on. For instance, a dinner party buffet might include an elegant phyllo pie, stuffed mushrooms, creamy dips and crudités, and soynuts or edamamé. Many starters in this chapter can be made in advance; indeed, some require time set aside in the refrigerator to fully absorb the flavors. Some might require reheating, whereas others need only be stirred and garnished with herbs or spices and placed in an attractive serving bowl.

Entertaining is an opportunity to share some of our best dishes with family and friends. These easy and elegant dishes are entirely plant-based—created without eggs or dairy or animal products of any kind. When you include these scrumptious dishes in your entertaining repertoire, your guests will be amazed by the authentic flavor, texture, and quality of your culinary creations, all without heavy traditional ingredients.

However, entertaining isn't the only reason to consult this collection of great beginnings. A light meal or snack can also be created by pairing two starters or by adding soup or a salad. Many of the recipes in this section can also be scaled up to make a substantial meal—as a rule of thumb, just double the portion size.

Artichoke-Stuffed Portobellos

*Meaty baby portobello mushrooms are stuffed with
a creamy, rich-tasting artichoke filling for
this delectable appetizer.*

olive oil cooking spray
16 stuffing portobellos, or 1¼
    pounds large stuffing mushrooms
1 12.3-ounce package lite silken tofu
3 cloves garlic, peeled
1 14-ounce can quartered artichoke
    hearts, drained

1 small leek, cleaned and diced
1 20.6-gram package Tofu Hero
    Italian Herb Medley
½ teaspoon dried thyme
⅛ teaspoon coarse black pepper
⅓ cup nutritional yeast
whole wheat bread crumbs

Preheat oven to 350°. Spray baking pan with olive oil cooking spray.

Wipe mushrooms with a damp paper towel and remove
stems, leaving caps intact. Place mushrooms on a baking pan
cavity side up, and set aside.

Place the tofu in food processor and blend. Add peeled
garlic and process. Add artichoke hearts; process. Add the
leeks, seasonings, and yeast; process. Spoon filling into mushroom caps and sprinkle with bread crumbs. Bake for 20 minutes. Serve hot.

PORTOBELLO MUSHROOMS
are actually mature cremini
or Italian brown mushrooms.
As a result of their longer growing period, portobellos develop
much larger caps.

NUTRITION ANALYSIS: PER 3½-OUNCE SERVING (1 STUFFED BABY PORTOBELLO)

Enlightened Artichoke-Stuffed Portobellos
Protein 6 g, carbohydrate 10 g, fiber 2 g, fat 0.5 g,
cholesterol 0 mg, calcium 23 mg, sodium 109 mg
Calories 49: from protein 35%,
from carbohydrate 57%, from fat 8%

Traditional Artichoke-Stuffed Portobellos
Protein 4 g, carbohydrate 6 g, fiber 1 g, fat 10 g,
cholesterol 27 mg, calcium 93 mg, sodium 296 mg
Calories 126: from protein 12%,
from carbohydrate 20%, from fat 68%

"Beef" 'n' Broccoli Roll-Ups

*Sliced roll-ups are a pleasing
addition to a varied buffet.*

olive oil cooking spray

Filling

2 cups TVP, ground beef style
1½ cups beef-flavor vegetarian broth
1½ teaspoons olive oil
¼ teaspoon crushed red pepper
5 cloves garlic, minced
⅓ cup sliced scallions
¼ cup chopped red bell pepper

6 ounces portobello mushrooms, diced
2 cups broccoli florets, cut into bite-size pieces
⅓ cup dry sherry
1 tablespoon tamari
1 teaspoon thyme
½ teaspoon lemon pepper

Pastry

1¼ cups whole wheat pastry flour
½ cup rolled oats
1 tablespoon egg replacer powder
2 teaspoons nonaluminum baking powder
1 cup lite silken tofu

2 tablespoons olive oil
1 tablespoon liquid Fruitsource
1 teaspoon sesame seeds
dash of paprika
1 26-ounce jar fat-free tomato sauce

Preheat oven to 400°. Spray baking pan with olive oil cooking spray.

For the filling: Combine the TVP and broth in a medium bowl and set aside.

In a 5-quart saucepan, heat oil and crushed pepper over medium-high heat for 1 minute. Add the garlic, scallions, and bell pepper and sauté 3 minutes; then add the reconstituted TVP. Cook mixture for 5 minutes, stirring frequently. Reduce heat to low, add mushrooms and broccoli and cook 3 minutes more. Add sherry, tamari, thyme, and lemon pepper. Simmer 5 minutes, stirring occasionally; then set aside to cool.

For the pastry: Place the flour, rolled oats, egg replacer powder, and baking powder in food processor and pulse to mix. Add tofu and process; add oil and Fruitsource and blend until dough forms a ball. Turn dough onto a lightly floured surface, knead lightly, shape into a ball, and divide in two. Cover one half.

Shape the remaining dough into a log. Sprinkle with flour and roll out into a rectangular shape about ¼-inch thick. Place half of the filling along the center of the dough. Roll the dough away from you, tucking in the short ends as you go. Place the roll-up seam side down on prepared baking pan and repeat with remaining ingredients. Lightly spray top of rolls with oil spray and sprinkle the rolls with sesame seeds and paprika. Bake for 30 minutes, or until golden brown. Cool slightly and slice into 1-inch pieces. Serve with tomato sauce.

You may also wrap in foil and refrigerate. Reheat at 325° for 20 minutes.

NUTRITION ANALYSIS: PER 2-SLICE SERVING

Enlightened "Beef" 'n' Broccoli Roll-Ups
Protein 13 g, carbohydrate 30 g, fiber 7 g, fat 4 g,
cholesterol 0 mg, calcium 80 mg, sodium 282 mg
Calories 191: from protein 25%,
from carbohydrate 58%, from fat 17%

Traditional Beef 'n' Broccoli Roll-Ups
Protein 12 g, carbohydrate 26 g, fiber 3 g, fat 19 g,
cholesterol 81 mg, calcium 100 mg, sodium 748 mg
Calories 320: from protein 15%,
from carbohydrate 32%, from fat 52%

Black Bean Dip

*This dip is a delicious blending of creamy black
beans and hearty garbanzo beans.*

*8
Servings*

1 15-ounce can black beans, *not*
   drained
1 15½-ounce can garbanzo beans,
   drained
3 cloves garlic, peeled
1 large shallot, peeled and quartered

¼ cup chopped green bell pepper
¼ cup lemon juice
½ cup coarsely chopped fresh cilantro
1 tablespoon Bragg Liquid Aminos
1 tablespoon balsamic vinegar
¼ cup nutritional yeast

Place beans in food processor and pulse to mix. Add the garlic, shallots, and bell pepper; pulse. Add the remaining ingredients and process until chunky. Cover and refrigerate for several hours. Serve with Savory Pita Crisps (page 78).

NUTRITION ANALYSIS: PER 5-OUNCE SERVING

Enlightened Black Bean Dip
Protein 12 g, carbohydrate 61 g, fiber 7 g, fat 2 g,
cholesterol 0 mg, calcium 35 mg, sodium 255 mg
Calories 135: from protein 16%,
from carbohydrate 80%, from fat 5%

Traditional Black Bean Dip
Protein 10 g, carbohydrate 20 g, fiber 6 g, fat 14 g,
cholesterol 20 mg, calcium 37 mg, sodium 448 mg
Calories 210: from protein 16%,
from carbohydrate 33%, from fat 50%

Cajun Soynuts

*Easy to make in your own kitchen, roasted soynuts
make a great snack with a third less fat than peanuts
and a full measure of phytochemicals.*

Soynuts
1 pound dried soybeans
3 quarts cold water

olive oil cooking spray

Spice Mix
¾ teaspoon lemon pepper
2 teaspoons sea salt
2 teaspoons granulated garlic
1½ teaspoons dried basil
1 teaspoon onion powder

1 teaspoon dried thyme
1 teaspoon chile powder
½ teaspoon coarse black pepper
cayenne to taste

For the soynuts: Rinse beans thoroughly; sort and discard any stones or debris. Place beans in a large bowl, cover with cold water, and soak 3 to 4 hours.

Preheat oven to 350°. Line two baking pans with foil and spray with cooking oil. Drain the beans and place them on the prepared pan in a single layer.

For the spice mix: Place the remaining ingredients in a small bowl and mix thoroughly. Spray the soybeans lightly with oil and sprinkle spice mix evenly over them. Bake 40 to 45 minutes, stirring occasionally, until beans are well browned. Using the foil like a chute, slide beans into a small bowl. After thoroughly cooled, cover and store in the refrigerator.

NUTRITION ANALYSIS: PER 1-OUNCE SERVING

Enlightened Cajun Soynuts
Protein 11 g, carbohydrate 9 g, fiber 2 g, fat 5 g,
cholesterol 0 mg, calcium 77 mg, sodium 250 mg
Calories 122: from protein 32%,
from carbohydrate 29%, from fat 39%

Traditional Cajun Peanuts
Protein 20 g, carbohydrate 15 g, fiber 4 g, fat 28 g,
cholesterol 0 mg, calcium 74 mg, sodium 362 mg
Calories 333: from protein 17%,
from carbohydrate 13%, from fat 70%

Dilled Spinach Dip

This dip is every bit as scrumptious as the popular
Savory Spinach Dip from Soy Cooking.
And it's virtually fat-free.

8
Servings

1 10-ounce package frozen spinach,
   thawed and drained
1 12.3-ounce package lite silken tofu
¼ cup Garlic & Herb Gourmayo
   eggless mayonnaise
4 garlic cloves, peeled
½ cup chopped yellow onion
¼ cup chopped green bell pepper

1 20.6-gram package Tofu Hero
   Italian Herb Medley
2 tablespoons Dijon mustard
2 tablespoons red wine vinegar
1 teaspoon Bragg Liquid Aminos
¼ cup nutritional yeast
2 tablespoons dried dillweed
½ teaspoon lemon pepper

Prepare spinach and set aside. Place tofu in food processor and blend; add the
Gourmayo, garlic, onions, and bell pepper and blend. Add the Tofu Hero and
spinach and pulse to mix. Add the remaining ingredients and process to blend.
Place in a covered container and chill several hours, or overnight for best flavor.
Serve with broccoli florets, baby carrots, and Savory Pita Crisps (page 78).

NUTRITION ANALYSIS: PER 4-OUNCE SERVING

Enlightened Dilled Spinach Dip
Protein 9 g, carbohydrate 21 g, fiber 3 g, fat 1 g,
cholesterol 0 mg, calcium 87 mg, sodium 235 mg
Calories 104: from protein 28%,
from carbohydrate 66%, from fat 6%

Traditional Dilled Spinach Dip
Protein 5 g, carbohydrate 8 g, fiber 2 g, fat 19 g,
cholesterol 41 mg, calcium 115 mg, sodium 543 mg
Calories 216: from protein 9%,
from carbohydrate 14%, from fat 77%

Dilled Spring Asparagus Dip

*This is a velvety smooth dip that will add richness,
color, and the enticing aroma of dill. Delicious!*

¾ pound fresh asparagus
1 12.3-ounce package lite silken tofu
3 cloves garlic, peeled
⅓ cup sliced scallions
¼ cup Soymage cream cheese
2 teaspoons vegetarian Worcestershire
sauce

¼ cup nutritional yeast
1 20.6-gram package Tofu Hero
Italian Herb Medley
1 tablespoon Dijon mustard
1 teaspoon lemon pepper
1 tablespoon dried dill

Trim asparagus spears and cut into 3-inch pieces. Layer asparagus pieces on a
steamer rack with the stalks on the bottom and the delicate tips above. Lightly
steam over medium heat, about 5 minutes, and then plunge into an ice bath.
Set aside.

Place tofu in food processor and blend until smooth. Add the garlic, scallions, "cream cheese," Worcestershire sauce, and yeast. Pulse to mix and then
process to blend. Drain asparagus, add to processor, and blend. Add remaining
ingredients and process. Cover and refrigerate for several hours or, optimally,
overnight. Serve with baby cut carrots and Savory Pita Crisps (page 78).

NUTRITION ANALYSIS: PER 4-OUNCE SERVING

Enlightened Dilled Spring Asparagus Dip
Protein 9 g, carbohydrate 9 g, fiber 2 g, fat 2 g,
cholesterol 0 mg, calcium 49 mg, sodium 186 mg
Calories 75: from protein 43%,
from carbohydrate 40%, from fat 16%

Traditional Dilled Spring Asparagus Dip
Protein 2 g, carbohydrate 4 g, fiber 1 g, fat 11 g,
cholesterol 21 mg, calcium 55 mg, sodium 216 mg
Calories 118: from protein 8%,
from carbohydrate 12%, from fat 80%

Hearty Layered Artichoke Dip

This hearty baked dip can double
as a main course or a side dish.

8
Servings

1⅓ cups beef-flavor vegetarian broth
2 cups TVP, ground beef style
1 12.3-ounce package lite silken tofu
5 cloves garlic, peeled
1 large shallot, peeled and quartered
1 20.6-gram package Tofu Hero
    Italian Herb Medley
1 cup enriched 1% fat soymilk
1 tablespoon cornstarch
½ cup nutritional yeast

1½ teaspoons Bragg Liquid Aminos
½ teaspoon lemon pepper
1 14½-ounce can Mexican-style
    stewed tomatoes
½ cup thinly sliced scallions
1 teaspoon granulated garlic
2 13¾-ounce cans quartered
    artichoke hearts, drained and
    diced
paprika for garnish

Preheat oven to 350°.

Bring broth to a boil and combine TVP granules in a 2-quart baking dish and set aside.

Place tofu in food processor and blend. Add garlic and shallot; process. Add Tofu Hero, soymilk, cornstarch, yeast, liquid aminos, and lemon pepper. Process until smooth and set aside.

Add the stewed tomatoes, scallions, and granulated garlic to the reconstituted TVP and mix thoroughly. Arrange the artichokes over the "ground beef" layer and top with the tofu "cream" sauce. Sprinkle with paprika, cover, and bake for 35 minutes. Serve with Savory Pita Crisps (page 78).

NUTRITION ANALYSIS: PER 9-OUNCE SERVING

Enlightened Hearty Layered Artichoke Dip
Protein 21 g, carbohydrate 41 g, fiber 8 g, fat 1 g,
cholesterol 0 mg, calcium 86 mg, sodium 460 mg
Calories 170: from protein 32%,
from carbohydrate: 63%, from fat 5%

Traditional Hearty Layered Artichoke Dip
Protein 138 g, carbohydrate 13 g, fiber 3 g, fat 26 g,
cholesterol 61 mg, calcium 118 mg, sodium 623 mg
Calories 377: from protein 15%,
from carbohydrate 15%, from fat 69%

"Pepperoni" Roll-Ups

*"Pepperoni" Roll-Ups are just wonderful hot or cold.
This is a dish that can also double as a brunch item or a snack.*

olive oil cooking spray
1 12.3-ounce package lite silken tofu
3 tablespoons eggless mayonnaise
1 17-gram package Tofu Hero
    Eggless Egg Salad
2 cups whole wheat pastry flour
½ teaspoon sea salt
2 teaspoons egg replacer powder
2 teaspoons nonaluminum baking
    powder

3 tablespoons Lighter Bake
2 tablespoons olive oil
1 tablespoon liquid Fruitsource
½ cup enriched 1% fat soymilk
3 to 4 tablespoons Dijon mustard
7½ ounces vegetarian pepperoni,
    sliced thin
¼ cup soy Parmesan cheese
paprika

Preheat oven to 400°. Spray baking pan with olive oil cooking spray.

In a medium bowl, mash tofu with a potato masher. Add eggless mayonnaise and Tofu Hero, mix thoroughly, and set aside.

Place the flour, salt, egg replacer powder, and baking powder in the food processor and pulse to mix. Add Lighter Bake; pulse to mix. Add oil and Fruitsource; blend. While motor is running, pour in soymilk. Mixture will form a dough ball. Turn dough onto a lightly floured surface, pat into a ball, and divide in two. Cover one half and shape the remaining dough into a log. Sprinkle with flour and roll out dough into a rectangular shape about ¼-inch thick. Spread the dough with mustard and place a layer of "pepperoni" slices across the half of the surface closest to you. Top with tofu mixture and sprinkle with soy cheese. Roll the dough away from you, tucking in the short ends as you go. Place the roll-up seam side down on prepared baking pan and repeat with remaining ingredients. Sprinkle the rolls with paprika and bake for 25 minutes,

"Pepperoni" Roll-Ups *(continued)*

or until golden brown. Cool slightly and slice into 1-inch pieces. You may also wrap in foil and refrigerate until ready to serve warm or cold. Reheat, wrapped in foil, at 325° for 15 minutes or until warm.

NUTRITION ANALYSIS: PER 2-SLICE SERVING

Enlightened "Pepperoni" Roll-Ups
Protein 13 g, carbohydrate 26 g, fiber 2 g, fat 5 g,
cholesterol 0 mg, calcium 31 mg, sodium 403 mg
Calories 198: from protein 27%,
from carbohydrate 51%, from fat 22%

Traditional Pepperoni Roll-Ups
Protein 12 g, carbohydrate 14 g, fiber 0 g, fat 35 g,
cholesterol 104 mg, calcium 50 mg, sodium 715 mg
Calories 434: from protein 11%,
from carbohydrate 17%, from fat 72%

Perfectly Pesto Dip

*This tofu-based pesto dip uses a wonderful pesto-flavored eggless
mayonnaise to replace some of the fat usually associated with pesto.*

*Makes over
3 Cups*

1 12.3-ounce package lite silken tofu
⅓ cup Pesto Gourmayo eggless
  mayonnaise
4 cloves garlic, peeled
½ cup sliced scallions
1 20.6-gram packet Tofu Hero Italian
  Herb Medley

1½ tablespoons soy Parmesan cheese
2 tablespoons chopped walnuts
¼ cup chicken-flavor vegetarian
  broth
2 tablespoons nutritional yeast
1 cup firmly packed fresh basil
  leaves

Place tofu in food processor and blend until smooth. Add the mayonnaise, garlic, and scallions; blend. Add Tofu Hero, soy Parmesan, and walnuts; pulse to mix, and then add the remaining ingredients. Process until smooth, but with bits of basil. Cover and refrigerate for several hours or, optimally, overnight. Serve with Garlic and Chive Pita Crisps (page 78).

NUTRITION ANALYSIS: PER 2-OUNCE SERVING

Enlightened Perfectly Pesto Dip
Protein 5 g, carbohydrate 5 g, fiber 1 g, fat 4 g,
cholesterol 0 mg, calcium 29 mg, sodium 162 mg
Calories 69: from protein 26%,
from carbohydrate 26%, from fat 48%*

Traditional Perfectly Pesto Dip
Protein 5 g, carbohydrate 4 g, fiber 0 g, fat 18 g,
cholesterol 15 mg, calcium 85 mg, sodium 121 mg
Calories 181: from protein 10%,
from carbohydrate 8%, from fat 83%

* The percentage of calories from fat seems high because the calories are so low.

Kreatopitta (Phyllo "Meat" Pie)

Olive oil spray is used between the pastry leaves instead of melted butter, and a delicious tempeh filling, dairy-free mushroom gravy, and soy Parmesan cheese replace the ground beef and rich sauce normally found in this elegant Greek-style pie. Serve with whole wheat couscous as an appetizer or entrée.

1 1-pound package phyllo pastry
olive oil cooking spray
2 8-ounce packages tempeh
⅓ cup chicken-flavor vegetarian broth
5 cloves garlic, minced
½ cup chopped yellow onion
2 scallions, sliced
½ pound button mushrooms, sliced
1 medium tomato, chopped

⅓ cup chopped fresh dill
⅓ cup dry sherry
1 tablespoon lite tamari
½ cup frozen peas, thawed
¼ cup soy Parmesan cheese
¼ cup dried dillweed
½ cup bread crumbs, preferably whole wheat
Mushroom Gravy (page 217)

Prepare phyllo pastry (see page 48). Preheat oven to 350°. Spray a 9-by-13-inch baking dish with olive oil cooking spray.

Cube and steam tempeh, and set aside.

In an electric frying pan or 5-quart saucepan, warm the broth over medium heat and add the garlic, onion, scallions, mushrooms, and the tomato. Cook mixture 5 minutes; then crumble the steamed tempeh into the pan and mix thoroughly. Cook mixture 5 minutes; then add the fresh dill, sherry, tamari, peas, and soy Parmesan.

Prepare Mushroom Gravy and add ½ cup to the tempeh mixture, reserving the rest. Reduce heat to low, simmer 5 minutes and set aside to cool.

Lift dampened towel and gently remove one pastry leaf and place it across the bottom of the pan, leaving an overlap. Spray lightly with oil and sprinkle with about ¼ teaspoon of dried dill and about a tablespoon of bread crumbs. Repeat procedure using about 10 leaves of phyllo, or ½ of the package, spraying with oil and sprinkling dill and bread crumbs between each leaf. Spread tempeh filling over the last pastry leaf, and fold the overlapping pastry edges over the filling. Pour the remaining Mushroom Gravy over the filling and top with the remaining pastry—spraying with oil and sprinkling with dried dill and bread crumbs between the leaves as before. Trim the pastry around the edges to a 1-inch overhang and, using a rubber spatula, tuck the top pastry inside the pan. Use a sharp knife to make a diamond pattern, cutting just through the top pastry. Bake for 1 hour and serve warm.

NUTRITION ANALYSIS: PER 5-OUNCE SERVING

Enlightened Kreatopitta
Protein 15 g, carbohydrate 33 g, fiber 2 g, fat 5 g, cholesterol 0 mg, calcium 23 mg, sodium 336 mg
Calories 212: from protein 25%, from carbohydrate 56%, from fat 19%

Traditional Kreatopitta
Protein 15 g, carbohydrate 17 g, fiber 1 g, fat 33 g, cholesterol 104 mg, calcium 123 mg, sodium 576 mg
Calories 434: from protein 14%, from carbohydrate 16%, from fat 70%

Quinoa-Stuffed Portobello Mushrooms

These baby portobello mushrooms stuffed with a delightful orange-quinoa pilaf will brighten the menu whether served as an appetizer or side dish.

9 Servings

olive oil cooking spray
1 cup quinoa
2 cups orange juice
18 baby portobello mushrooms
1½ teaspoons olive oil
2 cloves garlic, minced
⅓ cup sliced scallions

¼ cup chopped red bell pepper
½ cup sliced baby cut carrots
⅓ cup Vegi-Deli pepperoni, Zesty
   Italian flavor
1 cup mushroom broth
¼ cup sliced almonds
¼ cup chopped fresh cilantro

Preheat oven to 400°. Spray baking pan with oil.

Rinse quinoa seeds thoroughly several times, using a wire mesh strainer. Place in a medium saucepan with the orange juice, stir, and bring to a boil. Reduce heat to low and simmer quinoa with pan partially covered, stirring occasionally, for 15 minutes, or until liquid is absorbed. Wipe mushrooms with a damp paper towel and remove stems, leaving caps intact. Place mushrooms on prepared pan cavity side up and set aside.

In a 10-inch frying pan, heat oil, garlic, scallions, bell pepper, carrots, and "pepperoni" over medium-high heat for 5 minutes, stirring frequently. Add cooked quinoa and broth. Reduce heat to medium low and simmer mixture 5 minutes. Add almonds and cilantro and simmer 3 minutes. Spoon filling into mushroom caps and bake 20 minutes. Serve hot.

NUTRITION ANALYSIS: PER 2-MUSHROOM SERVING

Enlightened Quinoa-Stuffed
Portobello Mushrooms
Protein 7 g, carbohydrate 23 g, fiber 2 g, fat 4 g,
cholesterol 0 mg, calcium 38 mg, sodium 78 mg
Calories 148: from protein 19%,
from carbohydrate 60%, from fat 21%

Traditional Quinoa-Stuffed
Portobello Mushrooms
Protein 9 g, carbohydrate 21 g, fiber 2 g, fat 17 g,
cholesterol 29 mg, calcium 30 mg, sodium 467 mg
Calories 265: from protein 13%,
from carbohydrate 32%, from fat 56%

Savory Soynuts

*Easy to make, roasted soynuts are a delicious snack
with about a third less fat than peanuts
and a full measure of phytochemicals.*

Soynuts
  1 pound dried soybeans
  3 quarts cold water

olive oil cooking spray

Spice Mix
  1 teaspoon lemon pepper
  2 teaspoons sea salt
  2 teaspoons granulated garlic

  2½ teaspoons dried chives
  1 teaspoon onion powder

For the soynuts: Rinse beans thoroughly; sort and discard any stones or debris.
Place beans in a large bowl, cover with cold water, and soak 3 to 4 hours.

  Preheat oven to 350°. Line 2 baking pans with foil and spray foil with cooking spray. Drain the beans and place them in a single layer on the prepared
pans.

  For the spice mix: Place the ingredients in a small bowl and mix thoroughly.
Spray the tops of the soybeans with oil and sprinkle spice mix evenly over all.

  Bake 40 to 45 minutes, stirring occasionally, until beans are well browned.
Using the foil like a chute, slide the beans into a small bowl. After thoroughly
cooled, cover and store in the refrigerator.

NUTRITION ANALYSIS: PER 1-OUNCE SERVING

Enlightened Savory Soynuts
Protein 11 g, carbohydrate 10 g, fiber 2 g, fat 5 g,
cholesterol 0 mg, calcium 78 mg, sodium 249 mg
Calories 123: from protein 32%,
from carbohydrate 29%, from fat 39%*

Traditional Savory Peanuts
Protein 8 g, carbohydrate 6 g, fiber 2 g, fat 14 g,
cholesterol 0 mg, calcium 32 mg, sodium 323 mg
Calories 169: from protein 17%,
from carbohydrate 14%, from fat 69%

* The percentage of calories from fat seems high because the calories are so low.

Savory Pita Crisps

*Most commercial crackers are made with hydrogenated fat,
a source of unhealthy trans fatty acids. These easy-to-make pita crisps
are a delicious heart-healthy alternative. Place dip in the
center of a platter or dip tray, surrounded by pita crisps, or serve in a
napkin-lined basket alongside several dips.*

*12
Servings*

Olive oil cooking spray
12 Sahara brand whole wheat pita
    pockets
1 tablespoon granulated garlic

1 tablespoon Gomasio
1 teaspoon onion powder
1 teaspoon lemon pepper
1 tablespoon dried chives

Variation: Garlic and Chive Pita Crisps

12 Sahara brand whole wheat or
    sourdough pita pockets

2 tablespoons granulated garlic
2 tablespoons dried chives

Preheat oven to 400°. Line a baking pan with foil and spray foil with oil. Cut
pita pockets into eighths and place on prepared pan. In a small bowl, mix the
spices together and sprinkle over prepared pitas. Lightly spray top side of pita,
and sprinkle with spice mixture. Bake 10 minutes, or until lightly browned. Set
aside to cool.

NUTRITION ANALYSIS: PER 8 PITA CRISPS (OR 8 CRACKERS)

Enlightened Savory Pita Crisps
Protein 5 g, carbohydrate 26 g, fiber 3 g, fat 2 g,
cholesterol 0 mg, calcium 18 mg, sodium 247 mg
Calories 133: from protein 14%,
from carbohydrate 76%, from fat 10%

Traditional Savory Crackers
Protein 4 g, carbohydrate 29 g, fiber 0 g, fat 11 g,
cholesterol 0 mg, calcium 13 mg, sodium 521 mg
Calories 236: from protein 6%,
from carbohydrate 51%, from fat 43%

Savory Spinach Spread with Crostini

*This wonderful appetizer is served either warm or chilled—
especially good well chilled. The flavor and texture optimize when
made a day in advance and chilled overnight.*

Crostini
   1 sourdough baguette

Spinach Spread
   1 10-ounce package frozen spinach,
      thawed and drained
   1 12.3-ounce package lite silken tofu
   2 15-ounce cans low-sodium
      garbanzo beans
   ¼ cup sesame tahini

   olive oil spray

4 garlic cloves, peeled
1 medium shallot, quartered
½ cup sliced scallions
1 17-gram packet Tofu Hero Eggless
   Egg Salad
1 tablespoon nutritional yeast
1 tablespoon Bragg Liquid Aminos
1 teaspoon dried thyme
paprika

For the crostini: Cut a sourdough baguette into thin slices. Spread on a baking
sheet and spray lightly with oil. Toast until lightly browned, turning once.
   Preheat oven to 350°.
   For the spread: Squeeze excess water from spinach and set aside. Place tofu
in food processor and blend. Add spinach, beans, and next 8 ingredients. Pulse
to mix; then process to blend. Spread mixture in a 2-quart baking dish and
sprinkle with paprika. Bake uncovered 25 minutes.

NUTRITION ANALYSIS: PER 4-OUNCE SERVING

**Enlightened Savory Spinach
Spread with Crostini**
Protein 7 g, carbohydrate 30 g, fiber 3 g, fat 3 g,
cholesterol 0 mg, calcium 65 mg, sodium 128 mg
Calories 97: from protein 15%,
from carbohydrate 69%, from fat 15%

Traditional Savory Spinach Spread with Crostini
Protein 9 g, carbohydrate 15 g, fiber 5 g, fat 11 g,
cholesterol 35 mg, calcium 73 mg, sodium 241 mg
Calories 176: from protein 19%,
from carbohydrate 31%, from fat 50%

Smoky Southwest Dip

*Quick and easy, this dip captures
the flavor of the Old West.*

*12
Servings*

1 12.3-ounce package lite silken tofu
¼ cup Chipotle Gourmayo eggless
    mayonnaise
⅓ cup mesquite barbecue sauce
3 garlic cloves, peeled
½ cup chopped yellow onion
⅓ cup chopped green bell pepper
½ cup nutritional yeast

¼ cup diced canned green chiles
½ cup chopped fresh cilantro
3 tablespoons lime juice
2 teaspoons chili powder
1 teaspoon ground cumin
1 teaspoon dry sherry
½ tablespoon balsamic vinegar

Place tofu in food processor and blend. Add the eggless mayonnaise and barbecue sauce and process. Add the garlic, onions, and bell pepper and blend. Add the remaining ingredients and process to blend.

Place in a covered container and chill several hours, or overnight for best flavor. Serve with baked tortilla chips.

NUTRITION ANALYSIS: PER 3-OUNCE SERVING

Enlightened Smoky Southwest Dip
Protein 7 g, carbohydrate 7 g, fiber 3 g, fat 3 g,
cholesterol 0 mg, calcium 27 mg, sodium 82 mg
Calories 77: from protein 35%,
from carbohydrate 31%, from fat 33%*

Traditional Smoky Southwest Dip
Protein 4 g, carbohydrate 6 g, fiber 0 g, fat 14 g,
cholesterol 25 mg, calcium 110 mg, sodium 210 mg
Calories 161: from protein 9%,
from carbohydrate 15%, from fat 76%

* The percentage of calories from fat seems high because the calories are so low.

Spicy Chipotle Dip

*This creamy dip gets its kick from
the smoky chipotle-spiced Gourmayo.*

1 12.3-ounce package lite silken tofu
¼ cup Chipotle Gourmayo eggless
  mayonnaise
3 cloves garlic, peeled
1 large shallot, peeled and quartered
1 stalk celery, sliced

1 20.6-gram packet Tofu Hero Italian
  Herb Medley
½ cup enriched 1% fat soymilk
½ cup coarsely chopped fresh
  cilantro
⅓ cup nutritional yeast

Place tofu in food processor and blend until smooth. Add eggless mayonnaise,
garlic, shallot, and celery; pulse to mix. Add Tofu Hero, soymilk, cilantro, and
yeast. Process until smooth, but with cilantro bits. Cover and refrigerate for several hours or, optimally, overnight. Serve with Savory Pita Crisps (page 78).

NUTRITION ANALYSIS: PER 2-OUNCE SERVING

Enlightened Spicy Chipotle Dip
Protein 6 g, carbohydrate 5 g, fiber 1 g, fat 3 g,
cholesterol 0 mg, calcium 35 mg, sodium 123 mg
Calories 65: from protein 32%,
from carbohydrate 29%, from fat 39%*

Traditional Spicy Chipotle Dip
Protein 5 g, carbohydrate 3 g, fiber 0 g, fat 15 g,
cholesterol 34 mg, calcium 143 mg, sodium 310 mg
Calories 169: from protein 12%,
from carbohydrate 8%, from fat 80%

* The percentage of calories from fat seems high because the calories are so low.

Stuffed Mushrooms Florentine

You will love these delectable mushrooms with a hearty,
sherry-laced vegetarian sausage and spinach stuffing.

olive oil cooking spray
36 large stuffing mushrooms
1½ teaspoons olive oil
1 tablespoon minced dried garlic
⅓ cup sliced scallions
⅓ cup chopped red bell pepper
1 14-ounce package Gimme Lean,
    sausage style

1 10-ounce package frozen spinach,
    thawed
1 teaspoon lemon pepper
1 teaspoon dried thyme
½ teaspoon onion powder
2 tablespoons nutritional yeast
⅓ cup dry sherry

Preheat oven to 375°. Spray baking pan with oil.

Wipe mushrooms with a damp paper towel and remove stems, leaving caps intact. Chop stems and set aside. Place mushrooms on baking pan cavity side up, and set aside.

In a 4-quart saucepan, heat oil and minced garlic over medium-high heat for 1 minute. Add scallions and bell pepper and sauté mixture 3 minutes. Add veggie sausage, stirring and breaking apart with a fork. Cook 5 minutes or until "sausage" is brown. Add chopped stems and spinach and cook mixture 3 minutes. Add remaining ingredients and cook over medium-low heat 10 minutes, stirring frequently. Spoon filling into mushroom caps and bake for 20 to 25 minutes. Serve hot.

NUTRITION ANALYSIS: PER 3 MUSHROOMS

Enlightened Stuffed Mushrooms Florentine
Protein 9 g, carbohydrate 10 g, fiber 3 g, fat 1 g,
cholesterol 0 mg, calcium 36 mg, sodium 189 mg
Calories 83: from protein 40%,
from carbohydrate 49%, from fat 11%

Traditional Stuffed Mushrooms Florentine
Protein 12 g, carbohydrate 6 g, fiber 2 g, fat 17 g,
cholesterol 50 mg, calcium 169 mg, sodium 367 mg
Calories 221: from protein 22%,
from carbohydrate 10%, from fat 68%

Very Curry Dip

*Make this impressive curried dip the day before to
allow the tofu to absorb the flavorful complexity of the spices.*

1 12.3-ounce package lite silken tofu
½ cup eggless mayonnaise
2 cloves garlic, peeled
1 large shallot, peeled and quartered
¼ cup chopped red bell pepper
¼ cup sliced scallions
1 medium Granny Smith apple,
   peeled and quartered

2½ tablespoons fresh lemon juice
2 teaspoons curry powder
¼ teaspoon turmeric
1 teaspoon ground ginger
3 teaspoons country Dijon mustard
2 teaspoons tamari
1 teaspoon liquid Fruitsource
1 teaspoon dried cilantro

Place tofu in food processor and blend until smooth. Add the eggless mayonnaise, garlic, shallot, bell pepper, scallions, and apple. Pulse to mix. Add remaining ingredients and process. Cover and refrigerate for several hours or, optimally, overnight. Serve with Savory Pita Crisps (page 78).

NUTRITION ANALYSIS: PER 2½-OUNCE SERVING

Enlightened Very Curry Dip
Protein 3 g, carbohydrate 5 g, fiber 0 g, fat 2 g,
cholesterol 0 mg, calcium 21 mg, sodium 140 mg
Calories 52: from protein 20%,
from carbohydrate 37%, from fat 43%*

Traditional Very Curry Dip
Protein 2 g, carbohydrate 6 g, fiber 0 g, fat 11 g,
cholesterol 14 mg, calcium 48 mg, sodium 209 mg
Calories 121: from protein 5%,
from carbohydrate 19%, from fat 77%

* The percentage of calories from fat seems high because the calories are so low.

Sesame Bread Sticks

With wholesome goodness and a minimum of fat,
these bread sticks are really delicious!

olive oil cooking spray
2½ cups whole wheat flour
¼ cup soy flour
2 tablespoons toasted wheat germ
1 teaspoon sea salt
2½ teaspoons quick-rise yeast
   (1 package)

2 teaspoons olive oil
1 tablespoon liquid Fruitsource
¾ cup warm water
¼ cup Gomasio or sesame seeds

Coat the inside of a large bowl with olive oil spray. Place the wheat flour, soy flour, wheat germ, salt, and yeast in food processor and pulse to mix. Add oil and Fruitsource; blend. While motor is running, pour in warm water and process until mixture comes together. Turn dough onto a lightly floured board and knead for 5 minutes. Place in the prepared bowl and turn dough to coat with oil. Cover bowl with plastic wrap and cover with a towel. Place bowl in a warm corner of the kitchen and let rise 30 minutes.

Punch dough down and knead briefly. Return to bowl and cover again with plastic wrap and towel. Let rise for about an hour, or until dough has doubled in size.

Preheat oven to 425°. Spray baking pan with oil.

Place dough on lightly floured board and knead briefly. Divide dough into approximately 18 balls. Roll each ball into about a 6- to 8-inch length. Place on prepared pan, spray lightly with oil, and sprinkle with sesame seeds. Bake 15 to 20 minutes or until crisp and golden. You may also bake the bread sticks plain or sprinkle with Gomasio or poppy seeds or another topping of choice.

NUTRITION ANALYSIS: PER 2 BREAD STICKS

Enlightened Sesame Bread Sticks	Traditional Sesame Bread Sticks
Protein 4 g, carbohydrate 14 g, fiber 2 g, fat 1 g, cholesterol 0 mg, calcium 9 mg, sodium 120 mg Calories 77: from protein 18%, from carbohydrate 69%, from fat 13%	protein 4 g, carbohydrate 18 g, fiber 1 g, fat 7 g, cholesterol 4 mg, calcium 59 mg, sodium 139 mg Calories 153: from protein 9%, from carbohydrate 49%, from fat 42%

The Skinny on
Soups and Salads

Soup can be the most satisfying of comfort foods. A hearty soup can be a nourishing meal created in a single pot, recalling childhood memories of warm kitchens rich with the bouquet of fresh vegetables, grains, herbs, and spices in a simmering broth. The nice thing about soup is that it can lend itself to whatever ingredients you have on hand.

Whether planning a hearty dinner or a lighter, more elegant first course, you will find here many delicious soups rich in flavor and phytochemicals. Choose the hearty Kale and Potato Soup or the distinctive Italian Wedding Soup. Perhaps you are in the mood for something colorful and zesty like the Roasted Corn and Tortilla Soup or the smooth and creamy Great Pumpkin Soup. These soups are among those that can be filling enough to qualify as an entrée.

Soup preparation can sometimes begin with what is called a "mirepoix," a mixture of certain aromatic vegetables sautéed in a separate pan. The vegetables are added to the soup pot and the pan is then deglazed with a liquid. This technique adds richness and complexity, creating a unique depth of flavor. A traditional mirepoix calls for a quarter cup of butter or oil. I find this to be excessive. In my approach, only a tablespoon or two of olive oil are quite sufficient. I finish all of my soups with an enriching miso paste, using light and flavorful miso varieties like mellow white miso and mellow barley miso. This adds not only flavor and character to the soup but also valuable enzymes thought to be health-supporting and an aid to digestion.

Salads can be offered at the beginning or at the end of a meal, adding color and balance. A salad can be quickly assembled from such basics as assorted greens or fresh spinach, a tomato, a cucumber, and sliced mushrooms, garnished with soy bacon bits. The ingredients in salads are generally skinny on the fat—it's the dressings that tip the scales. In this section we will explore ways to cut the fat in dressings, whether creamy or vinaigrette. Buttermilk-Basil and Creamy Dill are just two of the dairy-free classics that can enhance any salad. Whatever your choice, the goodness of soy abounds in these marvelous soups and salads.

SOUPS

"Beef" 'n' Barley Soup

*Just sprinkle the dry TVP into the soup, and the flavorful broth
will transform this versatile soyfood into hearty "ground beef."*

½ cup raw pearl barley
6 cups beef-flavor vegetarian broth
1½ teaspoons olive oil
¼ teaspoon crushed red pepper
8 cloves garlic, minced
1 medium yellow onion, chopped
1½ cups sliced baby-cut carrots
1 small zucchini, sliced
1 cup dry vermouth

1 14½-ounce can Mexican-style
  stewed tomatoes
1 14½-ounce can Italian-style stewed
  tomatoes
¾ cup TVP, ground beef style
½ cup mellow white miso
1½ teaspoons dried thyme
1½ teaspoons dried basil
¾ teaspoon onion powder

Bring 1½ cups of the broth to a boil in a small saucepan and stir in
barley. Bring to a second boil, then reduce heat to low. Simmer for
25 minutes, stirring occasionally, until tender.

In a 5-quart saucepan, warm oil with crushed pepper over
medium-high heat for 1 minute. Add the garlic, onion, carrots, and
zucchini and sauté 5 minutes. Add ¾ cup of the vermouth,
reserving the rest. Add remaining 4½ cups broth. Place the stewed
tomatoes in a food processor and pulse to chop. Add the tomatoes
to the vegetable mixture, then stir in the dry TVP granules and cooked
barley. Reduce the heat to medium and cook the soup 30 minutes, stirring
occasionally.

Finish this and all soups with an enriching miso paste. Be sure to add it at the end of the cooking process.

"Beef" 'n' Barley Soup *(continued)*

In a small bowl, cream the miso paste with the remaining ¼ cup of the vermouth. Add to the soup with the thyme, basil, and onion powder. Simmer 10 minutes, or until ready to serve. Do not boil.

NUTRITION ANALYSIS: PER 16-OUNCE SERVING

Enlightened "Beef" 'n' Barley Soup
Protein 8 g, carbohydrate 32 g, fiber 7 g, fat 2 g,
cholesterol 0 mg, calcium 75 mg, sodium 465 mg
Calories 196: from protein 16%,
from carbohydrate 65%, from fat 7%

Traditional Beef 'n' Barley Soup
Protein 14 g, carbohydrate 25 g, fiber 5 g, fat 23 g,
cholesterol 49 mg, calcium 69 mg, sodium 1,453 mg
Calories 374: from protein 15%,
from carbohydrate 28%, from fat 57%

Butternut Bisque

The flavors of luscious butternut squash,
nutritional yeast, and mellow white miso marry
in this rich, velvet-textured soup.

The Skinny
on Soups
and Salads

89

12
Servings

6 cups water
6 cups peeled and cubed butternut
    squash (about 2½ pounds)
3 cups diced, peeled Yukon gold
    potatoes (about 3 small potatoes)
1 large red onion, chopped
8 cloves garlic, minced
1 14½-ounce can Mexican-style
    stewed tomatoes

¼ cup nutritional yeast
1 teaspoon dried thyme
¼ teaspoon ground sage
⅛ teaspoon white pepper
generous sprinkling of freshly ground
    nutmeg
⅓ cup mellow white miso
¼ cup dry sherry
1 tablespoon tamari lite

Place the water, squash, potatoes, onion, and garlic in a 6-quart saucepan and bring to a boil. Reduce heat to medium and cook 30 to 45 minutes, or until the vegetables are tender. Remove 3 cups of the veggies to the bowl of a food processor, and add the stewed tomatoes and nutritional yeast. Process the mixture to a thick puree. Return the puree to the soup and add the thyme, sage, pepper, and nutmeg.

In a separate bowl, blend the miso with the sherry and add to the bisque with the tamari. Reduce the heat and simmer 5 minutes or just until the bisque begins to bubble. Do not boil. Serve with a crusty whole wheat sourdough bread.

NUTRITION ANALYSIS: PER 12-OUNCE SERVING

Enlightened Butternut Bisque
Protein 5 g, carbohydrate 24 g, fiber 5 g, fat 1 g,
cholesterol 0 mg, calcium 65 mg, sodium 202 mg
Calories 111: from protein 17%,
from carbohydrate 79%, from fat 4%

Traditional Butternut Bisque
Protein 5 g, carbohydrate 29 g, fiber 5 g, fat 11 g,
cholesterol 33 mg, calcium 132 mg, sodium 377 mg
Calories 232: from protein 8%,
from carbohydrate 49%, from fat 43%

Creamy Spinach and Potato Soup

*Extravagantly rich and flavorful, this enticing
creamy soup is dressed to impress!*

*10
Servings*

2 teaspoons olive oil
¼ teaspoon crushed red pepper
1 tablespoon grated fresh gingerroot
6 cloves garlic, minced
¾ cup chopped white onion
1 large shallot, minced
1 large stalk celery, with leaves,
  chopped
1 6-ounce package veggie Canadian
  bacon, diced
3 cups peeled, diced potatoes
⅓ cup plus ¼ cup dry sherry

4 cups chicken-flavor vegetarian
  broth, boiling
1 6-ounce package baby spinach
1 12.3-ounce package lite silken tofu
1 cup enriched 1% fat soymilk
½ cup nutritional yeast
1 tablespoon cornstarch
2 tablespoons cold water
⅓ cup mellow white miso
½ teaspoon dried marjoram
½ teaspoon lemon pepper

In a 5-quart saucepan, warm oil and crushed pepper over medium-high heat for 1 minute. Add gingerroot, garlic, onion, shallot, celery, and veggie bacon. Sauté 5 minutes, stirring frequently. Add the potatoes and cook mixture 8 minutes. Add the ⅓ cup sherry and cook 2 minutes, then add the hot broth and spinach. Reduce heat to medium low and cook 15 minutes, or until the potatoes are tender.

Place the tofu in food processor and blend until smooth. Add soymilk and nutritional yeast and blend.

In a small bowl, mix the cornstarch and water and add to the tofu; process. Add the tofu mixture to the soup, stirring to blend. Simmer 5 minutes.

In a small bowl, cream the miso with the ¼ cup sherry and add with the marjoram and lemon pepper. Simmer soup 5 minutes, or until ready to serve. Do not boil.

NUTRITION ANALYSIS: PER 10-OUNCE SERVING

Enlightened Creamy Spinach and Potato Soup
Protein 16 g, carbohydrate 20 g, fiber 4 g, fat 2 g,
cholesterol 0 mg, calcium 84 mg, sodium 306 mg
Calories 154: from protein 38%,
from carbohydrate 50%, from fat 12%

Traditional Creamy Spinach and Potato Soup
Protein 12 g, carbohydrate 16 g, fiber 2 g, fat 23 g,
cholesterol 45 mg, calcium 157 mg, sodium 952 mg
Calories 314: from protein 15%,
from carbohydrate 20%, from fat 64%

Creamy Asparagus and Pea Soup

This is an elegant soup with a rich velvet texture and an interesting blend of flavors. Be sure to trim the asparagus just above the tough ends.

1½ teaspoons olive oil
¼ teaspoon crushed red pepper
8 cloves garlic, minced
1 medium Vidalia or other sweet
  onion, chopped
1 large shallot, minced
2 stalks celery, with leaves, chopped
4 cups peeled, diced potatoes (about
  1 pound)
4 cups chicken-flavor vegetarian
  broth, boiling
¾ pound fresh asparagus, trimmed
  and cut into 3-inch pieces

1½ cups frozen peas, thawed
1 12.3-ounce package lite silken tofu
1 tablespoon rice butter spread
½ cup nutritional yeast
⅓ cup mellow white miso
¼ cup white wine
1 teaspoon lemon pepper
1 teaspoon granulated garlic
1 teaspoon ground sage
½ teaspoon dried thyme

In a 5-quart saucepan, warm oil and crushed pepper over medium-high heat for 1 minute. Add the garlic, onion, shallot, and celery and sauté 3 minutes before adding the potatoes. Cook mixture 10 minutes, stirring frequently. Add the hot broth, asparagus, and peas. Bring to a boil; then reduce heat to low and simmer about 15 minutes, or until the vegetables are tender. Remove the soup in batches to the food processor and puree each batch. Return the pureed soup to the pot and continue to simmer.

Creamy Asparagus and Pea Soup *(continued)*

Place the tofu in the food processor and blend until smooth; add rice butter and nutritional yeast and blend. Remove 2 cups of puree and add to the tofu mixture. Process with the tofu mixture and return to the pan, stirring to blend.

In a small bowl, blend the miso with the wine and add to the soup along with the spices. Simmer soup 5 minutes, or until ready to serve. Do not boil.

NUTRITION ANALYSIS: PER 12-OUNCE SERVING

Enlightened Creamy Asparagus and Pea Soup	Traditional Creamy Asparagus and Pea Soup
Protein 13 g, carbohydrate 27 g, fiber 5 g, fat 2 g, cholesterol 0 mg, calcium 69 mg, sodium 223 mg	Protein 13 g, carbohydrate 23 g, fiber 4 g, fat 24 g, cholesterol 79 mg, calcium 192 mg, sodium 772 mg
Calories 166: from protein 29%, from carbohydrate 60%, from fat 11%	Calories 363: from protein 15%, from carbohydrate 25%, from fat 60%

Creamy Corn Chowder

Hearty and delightful, this Southwestern favorite is a fusion of flavors and textures in a creamy and rich-tasting broth.

2 teaspoons olive oil
¼ teaspoon crushed red pepper
8 cloves garlic, minced
1 large yellow onion, chopped
1 large stalk celery, with leaves, chopped
1 cup diced hickory baked tofu
1½ cups diced peeled potatoes
½ cup chardonnay, or other white wine
2 cups chicken-flavor vegetarian broth, boiling
1 16-ounce package frozen corn, thawed

1 14½-ounce can creamed corn
1 12.3-ounce package regular silken tofu
1 cup enriched 1% fat soymilk
¾ cup nutritional yeast
2 teaspoons lemon pepper
½ teaspoon ground sage
1 tablespoon tamari
1 teaspoon dried thyme
1 tablespoon cornstarch
2 tablespoons cold water
cayenne
Fire Roasted Salsa (optional)

Warm oil and crushed pepper in a 6-quart saucepan over medium-high heat for 1 minute. Add the garlic, onion, celery, and diced tofu and sauté 3 minutes.

Add potatoes and cook mixture 8 minutes, or until the potatoes are softening. Add wine and broth. Cook mixture, stirring occasionally, 5 minutes. Add thawed corn and creamed corn. Reduce heat to medium low and simmer.

Place silken tofu in food processor; blend, then add the soymilk, yeast, lemon pepper, sage, and tamari and blend until smooth. Add the tofu mixture to the soup along with the thyme and stir to blend.

CHOWDER IS A TERM THAT IS USED TO describe any thick rich soup made with chunks of food. New England–style chowders are traditionally made with milk or heavy cream. In my kitchen lite silken tofu, enriched soymilk, and nutritional yeast are the ingredients that I use to create my delicious, dairy-free interpretations.

Creamy Corn Chowder *(continued)*

In a small bowl, blend cornstarch and cold water. Stir into soup and simmer 10 minutes, stirring occasionally. Add several dashes of cayenne and simmer until ready to serve. Serve with a dollop of salsa, if desired.

NUTRITION ANALYSIS: PER 9-OUNCE SERVING

Enlightened Creamy Corn Chowder
Protein 14 g, carbohydrate 28 g, fiber 8 g, fat 5 g,
cholesterol 0 mg, calcium 60 mg, sodium 288 mg
Calories 178: from protein 29%,
from carbohydrate 57%, from fat 14%

Traditional Creamy Corn Chowder
Protein 9 g, carbohydrate 25 g, fiber 3 g, fat 19 g,
cholesterol 40 mg, calcium 107 mg, sodium 688 mg
Calories 292: from protein 12%,
from carbohydrate 33%, from fat 55%

Great Pumpkin Soup

*Buttery-flavored Yukon Gold potatoes contribute
to the rich texture of this hearty soup when pureed
with flavorful veggies and colorful pumpkin puree.*

2 teaspoons olive oil
¼ teaspoon crushed red pepper
1 medium yellow onion, chopped
2 tablespoons grated fresh gingerroot
1 stalk celery, with leaves, chopped
4 medium Yukon Gold potatoes,
   peeled and diced (4 cups)
2½ cups chicken-flavor vegetarian
   broth, boiling
1 29-ounce can pumpkin puree

1 14½-ounce can Mexican-style
   stewed tomatoes
2 bay leaves
½ cup enriched 1% fat soymilk
⅓ cup nutritional yeast
1½ teaspoons ground sage
½ teaspoon ground nutmeg
½ teaspoon lemon pepper
⅓ cup mellow white miso
¼ cup dry vermouth

Warm the oil and crushed pepper in a 6-quart saucepan over medium-high heat for 1 minute. Add the onion, gingerroot, and chopped celery and sauté 3 minutes. Add potatoes and cook mixture, stirring frequently, for 5 minutes or until the potatoes are beginning to soften. Add boiling broth, reduce heat to medium low, and cook mixture 10 minutes. Stir in pumpkin puree, tomatoes, and bay leaves. Cook, stirring occasionally, 10 minutes.

Remove bay leaves and transfer soup to food processor a few cups at a time, adding the soymilk and yeast to the first batch. Return the puree to the soup pot and add the sage, nutmeg, and lemon pepper.

In a small bowl, cream the miso with the vermouth. Add to the pot and simmer gently until ready to serve. Do not boil.

NUTRITION ANALYSIS: PER 14-OUNCE SERVING

Enlightened Great Pumpkin Soup
Protein 9 g, carbohydrate 36 g, fiber 7 g, fat 2 g,
cholesterol 0 mg, calcium 90 mg, sodium 303 mg
Calories 194: from protein 17%,
from carbohydrate 72%, from fat 11%

Traditional Great Pumpkin Soup
Protein 9 g, carbohydrate 30 g, fiber 6 g, fat 22 g,
cholesterol 45 mg, calcium 174 mg, sodium 730 mg
Calories 354: from protein 10%,
from carbohydrate 34%, from fat 56%

Italian Wedding Soup

I make this delicious soup with the Hot & Spicy style of Vegi-Deli pepperoni for added zest. Considered extravagant by peasant standards because of its costly ingredients, this soup was traditionally saved for special occasions such as weddings.

12
Servings

olive oil cooking spray
1 14-ounce package Gimme Lean,
    ground beef style
6 cloves garlic, minced
1 large yellow onion, chopped
1 stalk celery, with leaves, chopped
4 cups sliced baby-cut carrots
6 cups chicken-flavor vegetarian
    broth
½ 6-ounce package hickory or savory
    baked tofu

⅓ cup diced Vegi-Deli pepperoni
2 14½-ounce cans Italian-style
    stewed tomatoes
1 6-ounce package baby spinach
½ cup mellow white miso
¼ dry vermouth
1 teaspoon dried thyme
1 teaspoon dried basil

Preheat oven to 400°. Spray a baking pan with oil.

Roll the Gimme Lean into about 40 small "meatballs" and place them on the prepared pan. Lightly spray tops with oil. Bake for 5 minutes, then place under broiler until tops are lightly browned. Set aside.

In a 6-quart saucepan, combine the garlic, onion, celery, and carrots with the broth and bring the mixture to a boil. Reduce heat to medium and simmer, stirring occasionally. Slice the tofu on an angle and add to the soup with the diced veggie pepperoni.

Place the stewed tomatoes in a food processor and pulse just until chunky. Add to the soup along with the "meatballs." Cook for 5 minutes, stirring occasionally. Add the spinach and simmer 15 minutes.

Place the miso in a small bowl and blend with the vermouth. Stir into the soup, and add the thyme and basil. Simmer 5 minutes or just until the soup begins to bubble. Do not boil.

NUTRITION ANALYSIS: PER $10^3/4$-OUNCE SERVING

Enlightened Italian Wedding Soup
Protein 10 g, carbohydrate 18 g, fiber 3 g, fat 1 g, cholesterol 0 mg, calcium 53 mg, sodium 562 mg
Calories 124: from protein 35%, from carbohydrate 59%, from fat 6%

Traditional Italian Wedding Soup
Protein 17 g, carbohydrate 8 g, fiber 2 g, fat 23 g, cholesterol 104 mg, calcium 89 mg, sodium 1,152 mg
Calories 355: from protein 19%, from carbohydrate 9%, from fat 58%

Kale and Potato Soup

*This delicious soup gets its zip from sliced vegetarian
Italian sausage, adding an interesting dimension to the
hearty character and rich blend of flavors and textures.*

*12
Servings*

1½ teaspoons plus 1½ teaspoons
　olive oil
1 11.2-ounce package Lean Links
　Italian, cut to ½-inch slices
7 cloves garlic, minced
2 medium leeks, cleaned and sliced
½ cup chopped green pepper
1 pound peeled, diced potatoes
　(4 cups)
1 pound chopped tomatoes (1½
　cups)

1 large head kale, torn into pieces
　(about 8 cups)
7 cups chicken-flavor vegetarian
　broth, boiling
¼ cup nutritional yeast
1 6-ounce can tomato paste
⅓ cup mellow barley miso
½ cup dry sherry
1 teaspoon ground sage
1 teaspoon dried marjoram
1 teaspoon dried thyme

Warm 1½ teaspoons of oil in a 5-quart saucepan over medium-high heat for 1
minute. Sauté the sliced veggie sausage 5 minutes, stirring frequently. Remove
browned "sausage" and add the remaining 1½ teaspoons of oil. Add the garlic,
leeks, and green pepper and sauté 3 minutes. Add the potatoes and cook mixture 8 minutes, stirring frequently. Add the tomatoes and kale; cook mixture 5 minutes or until kale is limp, then add the hot broth, the cooked "sausage," and the nutritional yeast. Reduce heat to medium low and cook 5 minutes. Add the tomato paste, stirring to blend. Simmer the soup 15 minutes.

CRUCIFEROUS VEGETABLES AND LEAFY
greens such as kale are rich in indoles and sul-
foraphanes. These phytochemicals are premier
anticarcinogens, which act as the body's first line of
defense by actually blocking cancer-causing agents
from reaching cells.

In a small bowl, cream the miso with the sherry and stir into the soup with the sage, marjoram, and thyme. Simmer soup 5 minutes, or until ready to serve. Do not boil.

NUTRITION ANALYSIS: PER 12-OUNCE SERVING

Enlightened Kale and Potato Soup
Protein 10 g, carbohydrate 28 g, fiber 4 g, fat 4 g, cholesterol 0 mg, calcium 107 mg, sodium 286 mg
Calories 174: from protein 22%, from carbohydrate 61%, from fat 17%

Traditional Kale and Potato Soup
Protein 11 g, carbohydrate: 23 g, fiber 4 g, fat 15 g, cholesterol 39 mg, calcium 117 mg, sodium 1,170 mg
Calories 264: from protein 16%, from carbohydrate 34%, from fat 50%

Roasted Corn and Tortilla Soup

*Oven- baked tortilla strips and a dollop of
salsa top this Southwestern favorite.*

Soup

2 teaspoons olive oil
¼ teaspoon crushed red pepper
8 cloves garlic, minced
1 medium yellow onion, chopped
1 cup chopped red and green bell
   peppers
1 3-ounce package roasted sweet corn
1 cup sliced baby-cut carrots
3 cups diced, peeled potatoes
½ cup plus ¼ cup dry vermouth

4⅔ cups chicken-flavor vegetarian
   broth, boiling
2 14½-ounce cans Mexican-style
   stewed tomatoes
½ cup chopped fresh cilantro
¼ cup mellow white miso
1 teaspoon ground cumin
1 teaspoon Mexican oregano
½ teaspoon dried thyme
dash hot pepper sauce

Garnish

olive oil cooking spray
1 whole wheat tortilla, cut into
   ¼-inch strips

Fire Roasted Salsa

For the soup: Warm oil and crushed pepper in a 5-quart saucepan over medium-high heat for 1 minute. Add the garlic, onion, bell pepper, corn, and carrots and sauté 3 minutes. Add the potatoes and cook 8 minutes, stirring frequently. Stir in the ½ cup of vermouth, cook 2 minutes, and add the hot broth. Cook mixture 5 minutes.

   Place the stewed tomatoes in food processor and pulse to chop coarsely. Add to soup with the cilantro. Reduce heat and cook for 20 minutes.

In a small bowl, blend the miso with the ¼ cup of vermouth. Add to the soup with the cumin, oregano, thyme, and hot pepper sauce. Simmer 5 minutes, or until ready to serve. Do not boil.

For the garnish: Five minutes before serving, preheat oven to 400°. Spray baking sheet with oil; place tortilla strips on it in a single layer and spray tops lightly. Place on top shelf of oven and bake 5 minutes, or until crisp. Serve soup topped with tortilla strips with a dollop of salsa in the center. Alternately, you can use tortilla chips.

NUTRITION ANALYSIS: PER 10-OUNCE SERVING

Enlightened Roasted Corn and Tortilla Soup
Protein 4 g, carbohydrate 25 g, fiber 4 g, fat 1 g,
cholesterol 0 mg, calcium 44 mg, sodium 312 mg
Calories 136: from protein 11%,
from carbohydrate 74%, from fat 7%

Traditional Roasted Corn and Tortilla Soup
Protein 7 g, carbohydrate 24 g, fiber 3 g, fat 12 g,
cholesterol 29 mg, calcium 92 mg, sodium 563 mg
Calories 239: from protein 12%,
from carbohydrate 41%, from fat 47%

Tuscan White Bean Soup

*Great Northern beans in a chardonnay-laced broth add a
luscious rich flavor and texture to this Northern Italian favorite.*

*Makes over
3 quarts,
12 servings*

1 tablespoon olive oil
⅛ teaspoon crushed red pepper
6 cloves garlic, minced
½ cup chopped yellow onion
1 medium yellow bell pepper,
   chopped (1 cup)
1 cup baby carrots cut into ¼-inch
   pieces
4 slices veggie Canadian bacon, diced
¾ cup plus ¼ cup chardonnay or
   other dry white wine

2 15-ounce cans Great Northern
   beans, with liquid
1 14½-ounce can Mexican-style
   stewed tomatoes
4 cups chicken-flavor vegetarian
   broth
1 teaspoon dried basil
1 teaspoon dried thyme
¼ cup mellow white miso

In 5-quart saucepan, warm oil and crushed pepper for 1 minute, over medium-high heat. Add the garlic, onion, bell pepper, carrots, and diced bacon and sauté 5 minutes. Add the ¾ cup wine, reduce heat to low, and add beans. Place the tomatoes in a food processor or blender and pulse to chop coarsely. Add to bean mixture along with broth, basil, and thyme. Simmer 30 minutes.

In a small bowl, blend miso with ¼ cup wine until smooth; add to soup. Simmer until heated through. Do not boil. Serve with hot pepper sauce.

NUTRITION ANALYSIS: PER 9-OUNCE SERVING

Enlightened Tuscan White Bean Soup
Protein 9 g, carbohydrate 22 g, fiber 5 g, fat 2 g,
cholesterol 0 mg, calcium 74 mg, sodium 286 mg
Calories 147: from protein 26%,
from carbohydrate 64%, from fat 10%

Traditional Tuscan White Bean Soup
Protein 24 g, carbohydrate 19 g, fiber 5 g, fat 10 g,
cholesterol 49 mg, calcium 82 mg, sodium 663 mg
Calories 279: from protein 36%,
from carbohydrate 30%, from fat 34%

Vegetable "Beef" Soup

*In this hearty soup, potatoes, carrots, and fresh green beans
are simmered in a delicious broth with TVP beef chunks.*

8 cups beef-flavor vegetarian broth,
    divided
¾ cup beef chunk-style TVP
8 cloves garlic, minced
1 large yellow onion, chopped
1 stalk celery, with leaves, chopped
4 cups cubed, peeled potatoes
    (1 pound)
1½ cups sliced green beans

1 cup sliced baby carrots
2 14½-ounce cans Italian-style
    stewed tomatoes
1 teaspoon dried oregano
1 teaspoon dried thyme
1 teaspoon lemon pepper
¼ cup chopped fresh basil
½ cup mellow white miso
⅓ cup dry sherry

Bring 1 cup of the broth to a boil, then combine with TVP in a medium bowl
and set aside.

Place the remaining 7 cups of broth in a 6-quart saucepan and add the garlic, onion, celery, potatoes, green beans, and carrots and bring mixture to a boil.
Place the stewed tomatoes in food processor and pulse just until chunky. Add
tomatoes and reconstituted TVP to the pot with the oregano, thyme, lemon
pepper, and basil. Reduce heat to medium low and simmer mixture for 20 minutes, stirring occasionally.

Place the miso in a small bowl and blend with the sherry. Stir into the soup,
and simmer 5 minutes or just until the soup begins to bubble. Do not boil.

NUTRITION ANALYSIS: PER 12-OUNCE SERVING

Enlightened Vegetable "Beef" Soup	Traditional Vegetable Beef Soup
Protein 5 g, carbohydrate 21 g, fiber 4 g, fat 0 g,	Protein 7 g, carbohydrate 17 g, fiber 3 g, fat 14 g,
cholesterol 0 mg, calcium 44 mg, sodium 267 mg	cholesterol 21 mg, calcium 45 mg, sodium 309 mg
Calories 108: from protein 19%,	Calories 219: from protein 12%,
from carbohydrate 77%, from fat 3%	from carbohydrate 30%, from fat 57%

SALADS

"Pepperoni" Caesar Salad

*Vegi-Deli pepperoni adds zest and color to this
plant-based rendition of a classic salad.*

Caesar Salad Dressing
- 6 ounces lite silken tofu
- 2 cloves garlic, peeled
- ½ cup plus ¼ cup enriched 1% fat soymilk
- ⅓ cup chopped shallots
- 3 tablespoons sliced scallions
- 2 tablespoons red wine vinegar
- 2 tablespoons olive oil
- 2 tablespoons Dijon mustard
- 2 tablespoons mellow white miso
- 1 tablespoon vegetarian Worcestershire sauce
- 2 teaspoons lemon pepper
- ¼ cup soy Parmesan cheese

Salad
- 1 large head romaine lettuce, rinsed and dried
- ¼ cup soy Parmesan cheese
- ½ cup Vegi-Deli pepperoni, thinly sliced
- 1½ cups rosemary croutons

For the dressing: Place the tofu in food processor and blend; add garlic and process. Add ½ cup of the soymilk and the shallots, scallions, vinegar, oil, and mustard. Pulse to mix. Place the miso in a small bowl and blend with the reserved ¼ cup of soymilk. Add to the tofu mixture along with the remaining dressing ingredients. Put dressing in a covered jar and place in the refrigerator for at least an hour or, optimally, overnight.

For the salad: Tear romaine leaves into a large bowl. Toss with soy Parmesan cheese; then add a layer of vegetarian pepperoni and top with croutons. Serve with dressing.

NUTRITION ANALYSIS: PER 2 TABLESPOONS

Enlightened Caesar Dressing
Protein 4 g, carbohydrate 5 g, fiber 0 g, fat 3 g,
cholesterol 0 mg, calcium 28 mg, sodium 170 mg
Calories 62: from protein 26%,
from carbohydrate 29%, from fat 45%*

Traditional Caesar Dressing
Protein 4 g, carbohydrate 3 g, fiber 0 g, fat 29 g,
cholesterol 8 mg, calcium 75 mg, sodium 292 mg
Calories 279: from protein 5%,
from carbohydrate 4%, from fat 91%

NUTRITION ANALYSIS: PER 5½-OUNCE SERVING

**Enlightened "Pepperoni" Salad,
Without Dressing**
Protein 15 g, carbohydrate 14 g, fiber 2 g, fat 3 g,
cholesterol 0 mg, calcium 49 mg, sodium 345 mg
Calories 133: from protein 42%,
from carbohydrate 40%, from fat 18%*

Traditional Pepperoni Salad, Without Dressing
Protein 13 g, carbohydrate 21 g, fiber 2 g, fat 20 g,
cholesterol 28 mg, calcium 150 mg, sodium 1,053 mg
Calories 316: from protein 17%,
from carbohydrate 27%, from fat 56%

* The percentage of calories from fat seems high because the calories are so low.

Pasta Salad Primavera

*A creamy pasta salad is made healthy
with delicious dairy-free alternatives.*

1 12.3-ounce package lite silken tofu
3 cloves garlic, peeled
⅓ cup eggless mayonnaise
¾ cup enriched 1% fat soymilk
1 tablespoon balsamic vinegar
1 20.6-gram packet Tofu Hero Italian
  Herb Medley
1 8-ounce package linguini, broken
  into thirds

1½ cups sliced baby-cut carrots,
  lightly steamed
1 cup frozen peas, cooked
⅓ cup thinly sliced scallions
⅓ cup chopped red bell pepper
1 tablespoon dried basil

Place the tofu in food processor and blend until smooth. Add the garlic, mayonnaise, soymilk, vinegar, and Tofu Hero and process. Cook linguini according to package directions and set aside under cold running water. Drain and mix thoroughly with tofu mixture in a large bowl. Stir in carrots, peas, scallions, and bell pepper. Sprinkle generously with basil, cover, and refrigerate. Allow to chill for several hours before serving.

NUTRITION ANALYSIS: PER 7-OUNCE SERVING

Enlightened Pasta Salad Primavera
Protein 9 g, carbohydrate 32 g, fiber 4 g, fat 3 g,
cholesterol 0 mg, calcium 74 mg, sodium 238 mg
Calories 193: from protein 18%,
from carbohydrate 67%, from fat 15%

Traditional Pasta Salad Primavera
Protein 7 g, carbohydrate 32 g, fiber 4 g, fat 36 g,
cholesterol 36 mg, calcium 69 mg, sodium 526 mg
Calories 466: from protein 6%,
from carbohydrate 27%, from fat 67%

Marvelous Macaroni Salad

Make this colorful cold pasta dish with multicolored twists. The rich-tasting dressing is "enlightened" with silken tofu and eggless mayonnaise.

1 12.3-ounce package lite silken tofu
3 cloves garlic, peeled
1 medium shallot, peeled and quartered
½ cup enriched 1% fat soymilk
¼ cup eggless mayonnaise
2 tablespoons nutritional yeast

1 tablespoon red wine vinegar
½ teaspoon sea salt
1 8-ounce package multicolored pasta twists
1 teaspoon dried thyme
1 cup chopped red onion
1 cup frozen peas, cooked

Place the tofu in food processor and blend until smooth. Add the garlic and shallot; blend. Add the soymilk, mayonnaise, yeast, vinegar, and salt; process.

Cook the pasta according to package directions; drain and mix thoroughly with tofu mixture in a large bowl. Stir in the thyme, chopped onion, and peas. Cover and refrigerate for at least an hour before serving.

NUTRITION ANALYSIS: PER 6-OUNCE SERVING

Enlightened Marvelous Macaroni Salad
Protein 9 g, carbohydrate 27 g, fiber 2 g, fat 3 g,
cholesterol 0 mg, calcium 52 mg, sodium 227 mg
Calories 166: from protein 22%,
from carbohydrate 64%, from fat 14%

Traditional Marvelous Macaroni Salad
Protein 6 g, carbohydrate 27 g, fiber 2 g, fat 28 g,
cholesterol 0 mg, calcium 55 mg, sodium 445 mg
Calories 375: from protein 6%,
from carbohydrate 28%, from fat 66%

Hearty Salad with Balsamic Vinaigrette

*Layer the salad greens and colorful ingredients
attractively in this hearty dish, and serve
the tasty vinaigrette on the side.*

*8
Servings*

Salad

½ 6-ounce package baked tofu, hickory or savory style

1 large head of red leaf or romaine lettuce

1 medium tomato, cut into ¼-inch wedges

½ red bell pepper, cut into 2-inch strips

⅓ red onion, thinly sliced

⅓ cup diced Vegi-Deli pepperoni, Original or Hot & Spicy

1 cup garbanzo beans

⅓ cup chopped fresh basil

Balsamic Vinaigrette

⅓ cup extra virgin olive oil

3 tablespoons balsamic vinegar

¼ cup chicken-flavor vegetarian broth

1 clove garlic, minced

1 tablespoon Dijon mustard

1 tablespoon liquid Fruitsource

2 tablespoons chopped scallion

½ teaspoon dried thyme

½ teaspoon dried basil

⅛ teaspoon coarse black pepper

For the salad: Slice the tofu on an angle, laying the knife almost flat against the surface. Tear, wash, and drain lettuce and arrange in salad bowl, layering the remaining ingredients in the order listed. Sprinkle with basil.

For the vinaigrette: In a large liquid measuring cup, whisk together the vinaigrette ingredients, adding them in the order listed. Serve on the side with the salad.

NUTRITION ANALYSIS: PER 6³/4-OUNCE SERVING

Enlightened Hearty Salad
Protein 9 g, carbohydrate 12 g, fiber 3 g, fat 1 g,
cholesterol 0 mg, calcium 59 mg, sodium 124 mg
Calories 91: from protein 37%,
from carbohydrate 50%, from fat 13%

Traditional Hearty Salad
Protein 9 g, carbohydrate 9 g, fiber 3 g, fat 7 g,
cholesterol 21 mg, calcium 56 mg, sodium 310 mg
Calories 151: from protein 22%,
from carbohydrate 25%, from fat 41%

NUTRITION ANALYSIS: PER 2 TABLESPOONS

Enlightened Balsamic Vinaigrette
Protein 0 g, carbohydrate 3 g, fiber 0 g, fat 9 g,
cholesterol 0 mg, calcium 6 mg, sodium 7 mg
Calories 92: from protein 2%,
from carbohydrate 14%, from fat 85%*

Traditional Balsamic Vinaigrette
Protein 0 g, carbohydrate 3 g, fiber 0 g, fat 18 g,
cholesterol 0 mg, calcium 6 mg, sodium 134 mg
Calories 172: from protein 1%,
from carbohydrate 8%, from fat 92%

* The percentage of calories from fat seems high because the calories are so low.

*4
Servings*

Chinese Unchicken Salad

*Lite silken tofu that is frozen and defrosted mimics
the texture of cooked poultry.*

1 12.3-ounce package lite silken tofu,
frozen and defrosted

Marinade

½ cup chicken-flavor vegetarian
broth, boiling
1 tablespoon low-sodium soy sauce

½ tablespoon red wine vinegar
1½ teaspoons granulated garlic

Salad

2 cups loosely packed shredded
cabbage
½ cup canned mandarin orange
sections, drained
½ red bell pepper, sliced into thin
strips

½ yellow bell pepper, sliced into thin
strips
⅓ cup frozen green peas, cooked
½ cup canned water chestnuts,
drained
2 tablespoons chopped fresh cilantro

Dressing

3 tablespoons rice vinegar
2 tablespoons low-sodium soy sauce
1 tablespoon sesame oil

½ teaspoon ground ginger
1 clove garlic, minced
2 tablespoons thinly sliced scallions

Break defrosted tofu into unequal pieces and place in a nonreactive bowl.

For the marinade: Combine the marinade ingredients in a small liquid measuring cup and pour over defrosted tofu. Cover and refrigerate for 1 to 3 hours.

Drain tofu and return to microwave-safe bowl. Cover and cook on full power for 3 minutes; drain thoroughly, pressing gently, and set aside.

For the salad: Place salad ingredients except cilantro in a medium bowl and set aside.

For the dressing: Using a wire whisk, mix the dressing ingredients in a small liquid measuring cup and set aside. Toss ingredients in bowl and top with tofu and cilantro. Pour dressing over all and serve immediately.

NUTRITION ANALYSIS: PER 9⅓-OUNCE SERVING

Enlightened Chinese Unchicken Salad
Protein 9 g, carbohydrate 15 g, fiber 3 g, fat 5 g,
cholesterol 0 mg, calcium 34 mg, sodium 631 mg
Calories 130: from protein 26%,
from carbohydrate 43%, from fat 31%

Traditional Chinese Chicken Salad
Protein 31 g, carbohydrate 12 g, fiber 2 g, fat 13 g,
cholesterol 94 mg, calcium 44 mg, sodium 953 mg
Calories 291: from protein 43%,
from carbohydrate 16%, from fat 41%

Chipotle "Chicken" Salad

*Vegetarian chicken strips, flavored mayonnaise, and silken tofu are
some of the healthy ingredients that provide authentic texture
and creamy flavor in this spiced chicken salad treatment.*

2 7-ounce packages Vegi-Deli
    Chicken Strips
1 stalk celery, chopped
¼ cup Vegi-Deli pepperoni, diced
⅓ cup chopped onion
½ cup dried cranberries
1 medium Granny Smith apple,
    peeled and diced
½ cup chopped fresh cilantro

1 12.3-ounce package lite silken tofu
2 cloves garlic, peeled
¼ cup Chipotle Gourmayo eggless
    mayonnaise
1 teaspoon Bragg Liquid Aminos
1 teaspoon lemon juice
¼ cup nutritional yeast
⅓ to ½ cup sliced almonds
    (optional)

Combine the "chicken" strips with the celery, "pepperoni," onion, cranberries, apple, and cilantro in a medium bowl and set aside.

Place the tofu in food processor and blend; add garlic and process. Add the eggless mayonnaise, liquid aminos, lemon juice, and yeast and process until smooth.

Combine the tofu dressing with the "chicken" strips mixture and mix thoroughly. Top with sliced almonds, cover, and refrigerate for at least an hour. Serve well chilled.

NUTRITION ANALYSIS: PER 4⅓-OUNCE SERVING

Enlightened Chipotle "Chicken" Salad
Protein 21 g, carbohydrate 23 g, fiber 2 g, fat 5 g,
cholesterol 0 mg, calcium 27 mg, sodium 366 mg
Calories 174: from protein 38%,
from carbohydrate 41%, from fat 21%

Traditional Chipotle Chicken Salad
Protein 13 g, carbohydrate 10 g, fiber 1 g, fat 27 g,
cholesterol 54 mg, calcium 21 mg, sodium 466 mg
Calories 327: from protein 15%,
from carbohydrate 12%, from fat 73%

Asparagus and Canadian "Bacon" with Creamy Dill Dressing

Creamy Dill Dressing and lightly steamed asparagus make a lovely presentation. This delicious dish owes its deceptively low-fat profile to plant-based ingredients such as lite silken tofu and veggie bacon.

6
Servings

Creamy Dill Dressing

½ 12.3-ounce package lite silken tofu

1 clove garlic, peeled

1 medium shallot, peeled and quartered

¼ cup chopped red onion

3 tablespoons eggless mayonnaise

⅓ cup chicken-flavor vegetarian broth

1 tablespoon liquid Fruitsource

2 teaspoons cider vinegar

2 teaspoons lite tamari

2 tablespoons nutritional yeast

1 teaspoon dry mustard

½ teaspoon onion powder

⅛ teaspoon coarse black pepper

⅓ cup chopped fresh dill

Salad

1½ teaspoons olive oil

1 6-ounce package veggie Canadian bacon, diced

½ red onion, thinly sliced

2 bunches of asparagus, trimmed and lightly steamed

For the dressing: Place tofu in food processor and blend. Add garlic, shallot, onion, and eggless mayonnaise and process to blend. Add broth, Fruitsource, vinegar, tamari, yeast, dry mustard, onion powder, pepper, and dill. Blend until smooth. Refrigerate at least 1 hour before serving.

For the salad: In a 10-inch frying pan, warm oil over medium-high heat for 1 minute. Cook veggie bacon and onion slices until crisp tender. Plunge steamed asparagus into ice bath, drain, and pat dry. Arrange asparagus on a serving platter, topped with the "bacon" and onions. Drizzle with some of the Creamy Dill Dressing and serve with the remainder on the side.

NUTRITION ANALYSIS: PER 2 TABLESPOONS

Enlightened Creamy Dill Dressing
Protein 4 g, carbohydrate 5 g, fiber 1 g, fat 1 g, cholesterol 0 mg, calcium 18 mg, sodium 118 mg
Calories 47: from protein 32%, from carbohydrate 41%, from fat 27%

Traditional Creamy Dill Dressing
Protein 1 g, carbohydrate 5 g, fiber 0 g, fat 18 g, cholesterol 17 mg, calcium 27 mg, sodium 854 mg
Calories 181: from protein 2%, from carbohydrate 12%, from fat 86%

NUTRITION ANALYSIS: PER 6-OUNCE SERVING

Enlightened Asparagus and Canadian "Bacon"
Protein 11 g, carbohydrate 9 g, fiber 3 g, fat 1 g, cholesterol 0 mg, calcium 28 mg, sodium 276 mg
Calories 81: from protein 49%, from carbohydrate 37%, from fat 14%

Traditional Asparagus and Canadian Bacon
Protein 12 g, carbohydrate 7 g, fiber 3 g, fat 16 g, cholesterol 55 mg, calcium 34 mg, sodium 589 mg
Calories 210: from protein 22%, from carbohydrate 13%, from fat 65%

Marinated "Turkey" on a Bed of Spinach

Following a quick sauté, the succulent marinated vegan "turkey" strips are laid on a bed of spinach with red onion slices and garbanzo beans. Serve with the creamy Buttermilk-Basil Dressing on the side. Great presentation!

6
Servings

Marinade

2 tablespoons low-sodium soy sauce

3 tablespoons tamari

1 tablespoon Dijon mustard

½ tablespoon olive oil

½ cup chicken-flavor vegetarian broth

1 tablespoon liquid Fruitsource

1½ teaspoons granulated garlic powder

1 teaspoon dried chives

2 tablespoons dry vermouth

2 7-ounce packages Vegi-Deli Turkey Strips

Buttermilk-Basil Dressing

½ cup enriched 1% fat soymilk

1 teaspoon cider vinegar

6 ounces lite silken tofu

2 cloves garlic, peeled

1 large shallot, peeled and quartered

⅓ cup chicken-flavor vegetarian broth

1 tablespoon olive oil

1 tablespoon liquid Fruitsource

1 tablespoon balsamic vinegar

3 tablespoons nutritional yeast

1 teaspoon dry mustard

2 teaspoons dried basil

½ teaspoon dried thyme

⅛ teaspoon coarse black pepper

Salad

1½ teaspoons olive oil

1 10-ounce package baby spinach

⅓ medium red onion, thinly sliced

1 cup canned garbanzo beans, drained and rinsed

For the marinade: Combine the marinade ingredients in a 2-cup liquid measuring cup. Place the "turkey" strips in a medium nonreactive bowl and add the marinade, mixing thoroughly. Cover and refrigerate for several hours, stirring occasionally.

For the dressing: Place the soymilk in a small liquid measuring cup and add the cider vinegar. Set aside. Place the tofu in food processor and blend; add the garlic and shallot and process. Add the broth, olive oil, Fruitsource, vinegar, and nutritional yeast and blend. Add the remaining dressing ingredients and process. Place in a covered container and refrigerate several hours.

For the salad: Warm olive oil in an electric or 10-inch frying pan. Remove "turkey" strips from marinade and sauté 10 minutes, or until golden brown. Arrange spinach on a platter and add a generous layer of sliced red onions. Spoon the sautéed "turkey" along the center and sprinkle garbanzo beans around the perimeter. Serve with the dressing on the side.

NUTRITION ANALYSIS: PER 2 TABLESPOONS

Enlightened Buttermilk-Basil Dressing
Protein 4 g, carbohydrate 16 g, fiber 1 g, fat 2 g,
cholesterol 0 mg, calcium 37 mg, sodium 52 mg
Calories 52: from protein 17%,
from carbohydrate 65%, from fat 18%

Traditional Buttermilk-Basil Dressing
Protein 1 g, carbohydrate 5 g, fiber 0 g, fat 16 g,
cholesterol 10 mg, calcium 53 mg, sodium 253 mg
Calories 164: from protein 3%,
from carbohydrate 11%, from fat 85%

NUTRITION ANALYSIS: PER 6-OUNCE SERVING

**Enlightened Marinated "Turkey"
on a Bed of Spinach**
Protein 24 g, carbohydrate 15 g, fiber 5 g, fat 5 g,
cholesterol 0 mg, calcium 53 mg, sodium 635 mg
Calories 209: from protein 49%,
from carbohydrate 28%, from fat 23%

**Traditional Marinated Turkey
on a Bed of Spinach**
Protein 26 g, carbohydrate 13 g, fiber 3 g, fat 18 g,
cholesterol 54 mg, calcium 69 mg, sodium 931 mg
Calories 310: from protein 40%,
from carbohydrate 15%, from fat 45%

"Chicken," Avocado, and Mango Salad with Creamy Cilantro Dressing

*Sautéed and marinated vegetarian chicken strips
join luscious mangoes and avocados.*

Marinade

3 tablespoons tamari
1 tablespoon Dijon mustard
1 teaspoon olive oil
½ cup chicken-flavor vegetarian broth
1 tablespoon liquid Fruitsource

2 teaspoons granulated garlic powder
1 teaspoon dried cilantro
2 tablespoons dry sherry
2 7-ounce packages Vegi-Deli Chicken Strips

Creamy Cilantro Dressing

6 ounces lite silken tofu
2 tablespoons Chipotle Gourmayo eggless mayonnaise
1 clove garlic, peeled
¼ cup sliced scallions
1 stalk celery, with leaves, sliced
⅓ cup chicken-flavor vegetarian broth

1 tablespoon liquid Fruitsource
1 tablespoon rice vinegar
1½ tablespoons lime juice
1 teaspoon Bragg Liquid Aminos
1 teaspoon onion powder
⅓ cup firmly packed fresh cilantro

Salad

1½ teaspoons olive oil
arugula, or assorted greens, washed and stemmed
½ medium red onion, thinly sliced

½ medium avocado, peeled, pitted, and sliced
2 large mangoes, peeled, pitted, and sliced

For the marinade: Combine the marinade ingredients in a 2-cup liquid measuring cup. Place the "chicken" strips in a medium nonreactive bowl and add the marinade, mixing thoroughly. Cover and refrigerate for several hours, stirring occasionally.

For the dressing: Place the tofu and eggless mayonnaise in food processor and blend. Add the garlic, scallions, and celery; process. Add the broth, Fruit-source, rice vinegar, lime juice, liquid aminos, and onion powder and blend. Add the fresh cilantro and process. Place in a covered container and refrigerate several hours.

For the salad: Warm the olive oil in an electric or 10-inch frying pan. Remove "chicken" strips from marinade and sauté 10 minutes, or until golden brown. Arrange arugula on a platter and add a layer of sliced onions. Arrange the avocado and mango slices over the onion; top with sautéed vegetarian chicken. Serve with the dressing on the side.

NUTRITION ANALYSIS: PER 2 TABLESPOONS

Enlightened Creamy Cilantro Dressing
Protein 2 g, carbohydrate 16 g, fiber 0 g, fat 2 g,
cholesterol 0 mg, calcium 19 mg, sodium 84 mg
Calories 40: from protein 8%,
from carbohydrate 72%, from fat 20%

Traditional Creamy Cilantro Dressing
Protein 1 g, carbohydrate 2 g, fiber 0 g, fat 27 g,
cholesterol 18 mg, calcium 19 mg, sodium 407 mg
Calories 247: from protein 1%,
from carbohydrate 3%, from fat 96%

NUTRITION ANALYSIS: PER 6½-OUNCE SERVING

**Enlightened "Chicken," Avocado,
and Mango Salad**
Protein 19 g, carbohydrate 16 g, fiber 4 g, fat 5 g,
cholesterol 0 mg, calcium 43 mg, sodium 507 mg
Calories 172: from protein 43%,
from carbohydrate 34%, from fat 23%

Traditional Chicken, Avocado, and Mango Salad
Protein 17 g, carbohydrate 14 g, fiber 3 g, fat 17 g,
cholesterol 46 mg, calcium 28 mg, sodium 513 mg
Calories 274: from protein 25%,
from carbohydrate 18%, from fat 57%

Enlightened Entrées

&⁂

Many entrées in *More Soy Cooking* are health-supporting reincarnations of hearty traditional fare. Soul-soothing choices like the dairy-free "Chicken" a la King or the richly flavorful vegetarian Swiss "Steak" deliver highly authentic flavor and texture as well as impressive nutrition.

Using an ever-increasing variety of soyfoods and other wholesome kitchen staples and applying simple techniques can transform a heart-heavy meal into heart-healthy fare that is both satisfying and appealing. The key is in replacing high-fat, cholesterol-laden ingredients with easy-to-use and widely available alternatives. Review the "Soyfoods and More" section on page 22 for useful information regarding dependable substitutes.

The recipes that follow provide an extensive selection of international favorites—exotic flavors, textures, and intriguing presentations that can only serve to enhance the dining experience. Richly varied foods are highlighted from cuisines like those of Asia, India, and the Mediterranean. Specific spices sometimes tend to define certain cuisines. For instance, turmeric is easily identified as the spice that gives curries their characteristic brilliant golden orange color. Although they are most common to Indian and Middle Eastern cookery, curries can also be found in many other cuisines, such as Thai, Chinese, and African. Even the English have developed a taste for curries, cultivated during the years when India was a part of the British Empire.

There are also dishes with a Caribbean flavor such as the Caribbean Shepherd's Pie, an intensely flavorful picadillo filling under the traditional mashed potato crust. Updated and enlightened renditions of traditional favorites run the gamut from Sweet and Sour "Meatballs" to Wholesome Waffles, and they have been re-created authentically, healthfully, and delectably.

"Chicken" a la King

Chicken-style seitan, sometimes called wheat meat,
is a most credible meat substitute in this
scrumptious rendition of an American favorite.

6
Servings

1½ teaspoons olive oil
⅛ teaspoon crushed red pepper
1 tablespoon dried minced garlic
   (roasted garlic, if available)
1 large shallot, minced
⅓ cup chopped green bell pepper
1½ cups sliced baby-cut carrots
1 1-pound package chicken-flavor
   seitan (reserve broth)*
8 ounces button mushrooms, sliced
1 13⅓-ounce can quartered artichoke
   hearts, drained

1 cup frozen peas, defrosted
⅔ cup dry vermouth
½ cup plus ¼ cup nutritional yeast
¾ cup enriched 1% fat soymilk
1 tablespoon tamari
1 teaspoon dried marjoram
½ teaspoon dried thyme
3 tablespoons cornstarch
2 tablespoons cold water

Warm oil, crushed pepper, and minced garlic in a large saucepan or electric frying pan over medium-high heat for 2 minutes. Add the shallot, bell pepper, and carrots and sauté 3 minutes. Add seitan and sauté 5 minutes, stirring frequently. Lower heat to medium and add mushrooms, artichoke hearts, and peas; cook mixture 5 minutes. Stir in vermouth and 1 cup of reserved broth.

*This recipe uses chicken-flavor seitan that is packaged in broth. If you are using another type of wheat gluten that is shrink-wrapped and packed without broth, use a 7-ounce package of gluten and simply make 8 ounces of chicken-flavor vegetarian broth.

Whisk ½ cup of the nutritional yeast into the soymilk and add to the pan, stirring to blend. Whisk the remaining ¼ cup of nutritional yeast into the remaining reserved broth and add to the pan with the marjoram and thyme. Lower heat to simmer.

Blend the cornstarch and cold water in a small bowl. Add to mixture and simmer 10 minutes, or until ready to serve.

NUTRITION ANALYSIS: PER 12-OUNCE SERVING

Enlightened "Chicken" a la King
Protein 31 g, carbohydrate 40 g, fiber 15 g, fat 4 g, cholesterol 0 mg, calcium 111 mg, sodium 547 mg
Calories 311: from protein 39%, from carbohydrate 50%, from fat 11%

Traditional Chicken a la King
Protein 24 g, carbohydrate 14 g, fiber 4 g, fat 32 g, cholesterol 143 mg, calcium 59 mg, sodium 609 mg
Calories 457: from protein 22%, from carbohydrate 13%, from fat 65%

"Chicken" Borlotti

*Sometimes called cranberry or Italian beans,
borlotti beans are richly flavorful.*

*6
Servings*

1 ½ teaspoons olive oil
3 cloves garlic, minced
1 medium Vidalia or other sweet
    onion, chopped
2 stalks celery, sliced
1 14-ounce package Vegi-Deli
    Chicken Strips
6 ounces cremini mushrooms, sliced

1 cup chicken-flavor vegetarian
    broth, boiling
1 12.3-ounce jar Italian brown beans
    (borlotti)
1 14½-ounce can Italian-style stewed
    tomatoes
1 teaspoon dried thyme
¼ cup nutritional yeast

Warm oil in a large Dutch oven or electric frying pan and sauté garlic, onion, and celery over a medium-high flame for 3 minutes. Add vegetarian chicken pieces and cook mixture 5 minutes, stirring frequently. Add mushrooms and cook 3 minutes; then add the broth, beans, and tomatoes. Lower heat to medium low and and cook 3 minutes. Add the remaining ingredients and simmer, stirring occasionally, for 15 minutes, or until the sauce cooks down a bit.

NUTRITION ANALYSIS: PER 12-OUNCE SERVING

Enlightened "Chicken" Borlotti
Protein 33 g, carbohydrate 24 g, fiber 9 g, fat 5 g,
cholesterol 0 mg, calcium 76 mg, sodium 787 mg
Calories 255: from protein 50%,
from carbohydrate 35%, from fat 16%

Traditional Chicken Borlotti
Protein 30 g, carbohydrate 16 g, fiber 6 g, fat 26 g,
cholesterol 132 mg, calcium 154 mg, sodium 742 mg
Calories 422: from protein 29%,
from carbohydrate 15%, from fat 56%

"Chicken" Cacciatore

*Flavorful chunks of faux chicken and sausage and
colorful vegetables drenched in a rich tomato sauce make
this easy dish a crowd pleaser. Serve with brown rice.*

1½ teaspoons olive oil
6 cloves garlic, minced
1 cup chopped red onion
1 cup chopped green bell pepper
2 cups sliced baby-cut carrots
8 ounces cremini mushrooms, caps
  sliced and stems chopped
1 7-ounce package Vegi-Deli
  Chicken Strips

1 11.2-ounce package Lean Links
  Italian, cut into 1-inch chunks
¾ cup dry vermouth or white wine
1 14½-ounce can Italian-style stewed
  tomatoes
1 25-ounce jar tomato and basil pasta
  sauce
½ teaspoon dried basil
½ teaspoon dried thyme

In a Dutch oven or large electric frying pan, warm oil over medium-high heat.
Add the garlic, onion, bell pepper, and carrots and sauté 5 minutes. Add mushrooms and cook 3 minutes or until softened; then add the "chicken" strips and
"sausage." Sauté the mixture for 10 minutes, stirring frequently. Add vermouth
and cook 3 minutes; then add the tomatoes, pasta sauce, basil, and thyme.
Reduce heat to medium low and cook, stirring occasionally, for 10 minutes, or
until ready to serve.

NUTRITION ANALYSIS: PER 12-OUNCE SERVING

Enlightened "Chicken" Cacciatore
Protein 12 g, carbohydrate 27 g, fiber 6 g, fat 4 g,
cholesterol 0 mg, calcium 67 mg, sodium 677 mg
Calories 210: from protein 24%,
from carbohydrate 51%, from fat 16%

Traditional Chicken Cacciatore
Protein 25 g, carbohydrate 20 g, fiber 2 g, fat 19 g,
cholesterol 66 mg, calcium 68 mg, sodium 1,194 mg
Calories 337: from protein 29%,
from carbohydrate 23%, from fat 48%

Curried "Chicken" with Basmati Rice

*TVP Chiken Strips add authentic flavor and
texture to this delightful curry dish.*

*8
Servings*

Curry

2½ cups TVP Chiken Strips
2 cups chicken-flavor vegetarian
 broth, boiling
1½ teaspoons olive oil
¼ teaspoon crushed red pepper
2 teaspoons dried minced garlic
1 medium shallot, minced
1 medium red bell pepper, cut into
 1½-inch strips
1 pound fresh green beans, cut into
 2-inch pieces

½ pound portobello mushrooms,
 sliced
1 teaspoon granulated garlic
1 teaspoon ground turmeric
1 teaspoon ground coriander
1 teaspoon curry powder
1 14½-ounce can stewed tomatoes
1 14-ounce can lite coconut milk
1 tablespoon tamari

Basmati Rice

1 cup basmati rice, rinsed
2½ cups chicken-flavor vegetarian
 broth
1 tablespoon grated gingerroot

¼ cup chopped scallions
¼ teaspoon ground turmeric
1 cinnamon stick

For the curry: Place TVP in a medium bowl and stir in boiling broth. Set aside.
In a large Dutch oven or electric frying pan, heat oil with crushed red pepper and minced garlic over medium-high flame for 2 minutes. Add shallot, bell pepper, and beans and sauté 5 minutes, stirring frequently. Add mushrooms and cook 3 minutes; then add TVP. Cook mixture at least 5 minutes and add the remaining curry ingredients.

For the basmati rice: Place all the ingredients in a 2-quart microwave-safe bowl. Stir and cover. Cook at full

TURMERIC IS THE ESSENTIAL
ingredient that imparts the characteristic golden color of curries. This Eastern spice from the ginger family is considered a mild anti-inflammatory.

power for 20 minutes, undisturbed. Fluff gently, remove cinnamon stick, and serve immediately with curry. Alternately, bring the broth to a boil over medium-high heat in a medium saucepan. Add rice, gingerroot, scallions, turmeric, and cinnamon stick. Stir and reduce heat to low. Cover and simmer for 20 minutes. Remove cinnamon stick, fluff with fork, and serve immediately with curry.

NUTRITION ANALYSIS: PER 14-OUNCE SERVING

Enlightened "Chicken" with Basmati Rice
Protein 18 g, carbohydrate 40 g, fiber 9 g, fat 4 g, cholesterol 0 mg, calcium 52 mg, sodium 315 mg
Calories 251: from protein 27%, from carbohydrate 59%, from fat 14%

Traditional Chicken with Basmati Rice
Protein 40 g, carbohydrate 47 g, fiber 3 g, fat 26 g, cholesterol 102 mg, calcium 49 mg, sodium 641 mg
Calories 503: from protein 27%, from carbohydrate 32%, from fat 41%

"Chicken" Teriyaki with Rice and Vegetables

This delicious dish is made with an easy-to-use alternative,
Vegi-Deli Chicken Strips. Serve with hearty brown rice.

Marinade

⅓ cup tamari
¼ cup dry sherry
¼ cup chicken-flavor vegetarian
  broth, boiling
1 tablespoon liquid Fruitsource
1 tablespoon rice vinegar

2 garlic cloves, minced
2 tablespoons sliced scallions
1 teaspoon grated gingerroot

2 7-ounce packages Vegi-Deli
  Chicken Strips

Teriyaki

1½ teaspoons olive oil
¼ teaspoon crushed red pepper
¼ cup chopped shallots
½ cup chopped green bell pepper
1 cup sliced baby carrots
2 cups sliced zucchini
½ pound button mushrooms, caps
  sliced and stems chopped

1 cup frozen peas, thawed
½ cup chicken-flavor vegetarian
  broth, boiling
1 tablespoon cornstarch
2 tablespoons cold water
3 cups cooked brown rice

In a liquid measuring cup, whisk together marinade ingredients. Place chicken strips in a nonreactive 2-quart bowl. Pour marinade over strips and mix thoroughly. Cover and refrigerate for at least 1 hour, stirring halfway through.

In 5-quart saucepan, heat oil and crushed pepper for 1 minute over medium-high heat. Add the shallots and bell pepper and cook 3 minutes. Add the carrots, zucchini, and mushrooms and sauté 5 minutes, or until veggies are crisp-tender. Reserving marinade, add "chicken" strips. Sauté mixture over medium heat, stirring frequently, for 10 minutes. Add thawed peas, ½ cup of the broth, and the reserved marinade. Reduce heat to simmer. Combine cornstarch and water in a small bowl, stirring to form a paste. Add to pan and continue to simmer, stirring frequently, for 10 minutes, or until ready to serve.

NUTRITION ANALYSIS: PER 10-OUNCE SERVING

Enlightened "Chicken" Teriyaki	Traditional Chicken Teriyaki
Protein 22 g, carbohydrate 30 g, fiber 5 g, fat 4 g, cholesterol 0 mg, calcium 31 mg, sodium 907 mg Calories 239: from protein 36%, from carbohydrate 50%, from fat 13%	Protein 18 g, carbohydrate 34 g, fiber 2 g, fat 17 g, cholesterol 68 mg, calcium 37 mg, sodium 1,229 mg Calories 371: from protein 20%, from carbohydrate 38%, from fat 43%

"Chicken" with Roasted Sweet Corn and Sun-Dried Tomatoes

*The marinade serves as the base
for the richly flavored sauce.*

Marinade

1 cup chicken-flavor vegetarian broth
2 tablespoons balsamic vinegar
¼ cup tamari
¼ cup dry vermouth

1 teaspoon olive oil
2 cloves garlic, minced
1 teaspoon dried tarragon
½ teaspoon dried thyme

2 7-ounces packages Vegi-Deli
    Chicken Strips

Sauce

1 cup sliced sun-dried tomatoes, *not*
    packed in oil
1 cup boiling water
1½ teaspoons olive oil
¼ teaspoon crushed red pepper
4 cloves garlic, minced
½ cup sliced scallions
½ cup chopped red bell pepper

1 cup sliced baby carrots
1 medium zucchini, sliced
1 3-ounce package Melissa's roasted
    sweet corn (available in supermar-
    ket produce section)
⅔ cup dry vermouth or white wine
1 cup chicken-flavor vegetarian broth
¼ cup nutritional yeast

For the marinade: Combine the marinade ingredients in a 2-cup glass measuring cup. Place "chicken" strips in a medium nonreactive bowl with marinade. Cover and refrigerate for 2 to 3 hours, turning strips several times during process.

For the sauce: In a medium bowl, stir the sun-dried tomatoes into the boiling water. Set aside.

In a large Dutch oven or electric frying pan, heat oil and crushed pepper over medium-high heat for 1 minute. Add garlic, scallions, bell pepper, carrots, and zucchini and sauté 5 minutes. Reserving marinade, add "chicken" strips to pan. Add roasted sweet corn and the sun-dried tomatoes with the soaking liquid. Cook mixture 3 minutes, stirring frequently; then add vermouth and broth. Reduce heat to medium low and simmer 10 minutes, stirring occasionally. Add reserved marinade and nutritional yeast. Simmer 5 minutes, or until ready to serve.

NUTRITION ANALYSIS: PER 9-OUNCE SERVING

Enlightened "Chicken" with Roasted Sweet
Corn and Sun-Dried Tomatoes
Protein 25 g, carbohydrate 24 g, fiber 6 g, fat 4 g,
cholesterol 0 mg, calcium 31 mg, sodium 780 mg
Calories 237: from protein 44%,
from carbohydrate 42%, from fat 15%

Traditional Chicken with Roasted Sweet
Corn and Sun-Dried Tomatoes
Protein 27 g, carbohydrate 16 g, fiber 2 g, fat 27 g,
cholesterol 111 mg, calcium 45 mg, sodium 1,087 mg
Calories 416: from protein 26%,
from carbohydrate 16%, from fat 59%

"Turkey" and Yams

Marinating Vegi-Deli Turkey Strips really enhances their flavor and texture.

8 Servings

Marinade
¼ cup barbecue sauce
1 tablespoon balsamic vinegar
1 tablespoon tamari
1 tablespoon liquid Fruitsource

1 7-ounce package Vegi-Deli Turkey Strips

1 teaspoon olive oil
1 teaspoon onion powder
1 teaspoon granulated garlic

Sauté
2 teaspoons olive oil
¼ teaspoon crushed red pepper
4 garlic cloves, minced
1 medium yellow onion, thinly sliced
1 cup chopped mixed yellow and red bell peppers
1 large yam, peeled and halved lengthwise and then crosswise into ¼-inch slices
½ cup dry sherry

1 cup chicken-flavor vegetarian broth, boiling
1 cup frozen corn, thawed
1 large fresh tomato, diced
½ cup enriched 1% fat soymilk
3 tablespoons nutritional yeast
1½ teaspoons dried thyme
1 teaspoon dried basil
1 teaspoon dried marjoram

YAMS HAVE A DEEP ORANGE color and are particularly rich in beta-carotene, which, when ingested, converts to vitamin A.

For the marinade: Combine marinade ingredients in a 2-cup glass measuring cup. Place "turkey" strips in a nonreactive 2-quart container. Add marinade and mix thoroughly. Cover and refrigerate for at least 1 hour, stirring occasionally.

For the sauté: In a large electric frying pan or Dutch oven, heat oil and crushed pepper over medium-high flame 1 minute. Add garlic, onion, and bell pepper and sauté 3 minutes. Add yams and cook 5 minutes. Remove "turkey" strips from marinade and add to the sauté. Discard marinade. Cook mixture 8 minutes, stirring frequently. Add sherry, broth, corn, and diced tomato, reduce heat to medium low, and cook 10 minutes, or until yams are softened. Add remaining ingredients and simmer until ready to serve.

NUTRITION ANALYSIS: PER 13-OUNCE SERVING

Enlightened "Turkey" and Yams
Protein 11 g, carbohydrate 56 g, fiber 3 g, fat 3 g, cholesterol 0 mg, calcium 38 mg, sodium 329 mg
Calories 147: from protein 15%, from carbohydrate 77%, from fat 8%

Traditional Turkey and Yams
Protein 19 g, carbohydrate 21 g, fiber 2 g, fat 19 g, cholesterol 79 mg, calcium 44 mg, sodium 840 mg
Calories 340: from protein 23%, from carbohydrate 25%, from fat 52%

"Turkey" Barbecue and Potato Bake

*Deceptively quick and easy, marinating the "turkey" strips imparts
a juicy and flavorful texture to the wheat gluten.*

*6
Servings*

2 7-ounce packages Vegi-Deli Turkey
Strips
½ cup barbecue sauce
1 tablespoon olive oil
4 medium russet potatoes, unpeeled,
cut into 1-inch wedges
1 yellow onion, cut to ¼-inch wedges

½ medium yellow bell pepper, cut
into 3-inch strips
1 tablespoon dried minced garlic
dash paprika
1 tablespoon nutritional yeast

Place "turkey" strips in a nonreactive, 2-quart oven-ready baking pan. Add your
favorite barbecue sauce, cover, and refrigerate for at least 1 hour, stirring occasionally.

Preheat oven to 400°.

Coat a 9-by-13-inch pan with the oil and place potato wedges on it skin side
down. Top with the onion and bell pepper, sprinkle with dried garlic and
paprika, and bake for 25 minutes. At this point, remove marinated strips from
the refrigerator and stir in nutritional yeast. Cover with foil and place casserole
in oven. Bake both dishes for an additional 25 minutes, removing the foil from
the "turkey" during the last 10 minutes. Serve with a crisp tossed salad.

NUTRITION ANALYSIS: PER 9½-OUNCE SERVING

Enlightened "Turkey" Barbecue and Potato Bake
Protein 26 g, carbohydrate 48 g, fiber 8 g, fat 4 g,
cholesterol 0 mg, calcium 11 mg, sodium 454 mg
Calories 329: from protein 31%,
from carbohydrate 57%, from fat 12%

Traditional Turkey Barbecue and Potato Bake
Protein 24 g, carbohydrate 48 g, fiber 2 g, fat 14 g,
cholesterol 67 mg, calcium 39 mg, sodium 481 mg
Calories 410: from protein 24%,
from carbohydrate 46%, from fat 30%

"Turkey" Tetrazzini

*Serve this flavorful dish over
the traditional pasta or rice.*

2 teaspoons olive oil
1 tablespoon dried minced garlic
½ 11.2-ounce package Lean Links
    Italian, sliced
olive oil cooking spray
1 medium yellow onion, chopped
2 stalks celery, sliced
⅓ cup chopped red bell pepper
2 7-ounce packages Vegi-Deli Turkey
    Strips
6 ounces portobello mushrooms,
    sliced

3 tablespoons low-sodium tomato
    paste
¾ cup dry sherry
1 14½-ounce can Mexican-style
    stewed tomatoes
1 cup frozen peas, thawed
⅓ cup nutritional yeast
½ cup enriched 1% fat soymilk
1 teaspoon dried thyme

In a large Dutch oven or electric frying pan, warm oil with minced garlic over medium-high heat for 2 minutes. Add sliced "sausage" links and brown for about 5 minutes. Remove from pan and set aside. Spray pan with oil spray and add onion, celery, and bell pepper. Sauté 3 minutes, add "turkey" strips, and cook 3 minutes, stirring frequently. Return the browned "sausage" to the pan along with mushrooms and cook 3 minutes; then add the remaining ingredients. Reduce heat to low; cover and simmer 10 minutes, stirring occasionally.

NUTRITION ANALYSIS: PER 9-OUNCE SERVING

Enlightened "Turkey" Tetrazzini	Traditional Turkey Tetrazzini
Protein 24 g, carbohydrate 21 g, fiber 6 g, fat 5 g, cholesterol 0 mg, calcium 64 mg, sodium 554 mg Calories 234: from protein 43%, from carbohydrate 37%, from fat 21%	Protein 29 g, carbohydrate 10 g, fiber 2 g, fat 28 g, cholesterol 112 mg, calcium 120 mg, sodium 705 mg Calories 409: from protein 28%, from carbohydrate 10%, from fat 62%

"Turkey" with Rice

*Simple and delicious, this is a one-dish meal made authentic
with veggie Canadian bacon and wheat gluten "turkey" strips.*

1½ teaspoons olive oil
⅛ teaspoon crushed red pepper
1 tablespoon dried minced garlic
1 medium red onion, chopped
1 6-ounce package veggie Canadian
  bacon, diced
1½ cups baby cut carrots, sliced
  lengthwise

2 7-ounce packages Vegi-Deli Turkey
  Strips
⅓ cup dry sherry
1 cup raw white rice
1 cup frozen peas, thawed
4 cups chicken-flavor vegetarian
  broth, boiling
1 tablespoon tamari

In a large Dutch oven or electric frying pan, heat oil with crushed pepper and
dried garlic over medium-high heat for 2 minutes. Add onion, veggie bacon,
and carrots and sauté 5 minutes. Add "turkey" strips and cook mixture 5 minutes, stirring frequently. Add sherry, cook a minute, then stir in rice, and cook
2 minutes before adding the remaining ingredients. Reduce heat to simmer.
Cover and cook 15 to 20 minutes, stirring occasionally, or until rice is tender.

NUTRITION ANALYSIS: PER 11-OUNCE SERVING

Enlightened "Turkey" with Rice
Protein 25 g, carbohydrate 33 g, fiber 4 g, fat 3 g,
cholesterol 0 mg, calcium 30 mg, sodium 732 mg
Calories 270: from protein 38%,
from carbohydrate 51%, from fat 12%

Traditional Turkey with Rice
Protein 30 g, carbohydrate 28 g, fiber 2 g, fat 13 g,
cholesterol 77 mg, calcium 55 mg, sodium 1,255 mg
Calories 362: from protein 34%,
from carbohydrate 32%, from fat 34%

Cajun "Chicken"

*Cajun cookery is a combination of French and Southern
U.S. cuisines. Cajun food takes a robust, country-style
approach that is generous with bell peppers, onions, and
celery and uses a roux to thicken sauces. The roux is
prepared in a separate pan and added toward the end.
Serve with New Orleans Rice Pilaf (page 218).*

Roux

- 2 tablespoons olive oil
- 1 tablespoon dried minced garlic
- 2 tablespoons unbleached flour

- 1 cup reserved broth from seitan package (see below)
- ½ teaspoon vegetarian Worcestershire sauce

Sauté

- 1 teaspoon olive oil
- ¼ teaspoon crushed red pepper
- 6 cloves garlic, minced
- ½ cup chopped red onion
- 1 large stalk celery, with leaves, chopped
- ½ cup chopped red bell pepper
- 2 14-ounce packages Gimme Lean, sausage style

- 1 1-pound package chicken-style seitan (reserve broth)
- 1 14½-ounce can Italian-style stewed tomatoes
- 1 teaspoon dried thyme
- ⅓ cup dry vermouth or white wine

For the roux: In a medium saucepan, warm oil over medium-high heat. Add minced dried garlic and sauté 2 minutes. Stir in flour and cook paste, stirring constantly until brown. Add 1 cup of the reserved broth and the vegetarian Worcestershire sauce, stirring until thickened. Lower heat and simmer 5 minutes. Set aside.

Cajun "Chicken" *(continued)*

For the sauté: In a Dutch oven or large electric frying pan, warm oil and crushed pepper over medium-high heat for 2 minutes. Add the garlic, onion, celery, and bell pepper and sauté 5 minutes. Add the Gimme Lean and cook 10 minutes, stirring frequently to break up "sausage" pieces. Add the seitan and 1 cup of the reserved broth. Add tomatoes and thyme; stir in the roux along with the vermouth. Reduce heat to medium low and simmer, stirring occasionally, for 10 minutes, or until ready to serve.

NUTRITION ANALYSIS: PER 10-OUNCE SERVING

Enlightened Cajun "Chicken"
Protein 25 g, carbohydrate 27 g, fiber 7 g, fat 4 g,
cholesterol 0 mg, calcium 48 mg, sodium 823 mg
Calories 255: from protein 41%,
from carbohydrate 44%, from fat 15%

Traditional Cajun Chicken
Protein 25 g, carbohydrate 9 g, fiber 1 g, fat 38 g,
cholesterol 102 mg, calcium 50 mg, sodium 808 mg
Calories 493: from protein 21%,
from carbohydrate 8%, from fat 71%

Caribbean Shepherd's Pie

Here is an interesting fusion. Two high-fat and heart-heavy dishes are re-created and combined into one delectable entrée. The traditional filling for shepherd's pie is lamb, and the popular Caribbean dish picadillo is traditionally made with ground beef.

6
Servings

Picadillo Filling

1½ teaspoons olive oil
½ medium onion, chopped
¼ cup chopped green bell
    pepper
1 12-ounce package ground beef
    alternative

1 14½-ounce can Mexican-style
    stewed tomatoes
2 tablespoons lime juice
⅓ cup chopped cilantro
½ cup golden raisins
⅛ teaspoon crushed red pepper

Mashed Potato Crust

¾ cup enriched 1% fat soymilk
1 tablespoon lemon juice
1½ cups water
1 tablespoon olive oil

1¾ cups Barbara's Mashed Potatoes
½ teaspoon sea salt
Paprika

Preheat oven to 375°.

For the filling: Place oil in a 2-quart microwave-safe casserole, cover, and microwave 1 minute on full power. Add onion and green pepper, cover, and cook 2 minutes. Stir and add the vegetarian burger and cook 4 minutes. Stir and add remaining filling ingredients and cook 5 minutes, stirring halfway through. Set aside.

For the crust: Combine soymilk and lemon juice in a 2-cup liquid measure and set aside. Place water and olive oil in a medium pan and bring to a boil.

Caribbean Shepherd's Pie *(continued)*

Remove from heat and add the soymilk mixture. Stir in the mashed potato flakes and the salt. Mixture should be thick. Spread mashed potatoes over the picadillo filling and sprinkle with paprika.

Place uncovered casserole in preheated oven. Bake for 25 minutes or until top begins to brown. Serve with Mexicali Brown Rice (page 216).

NUTRITION ANALYSIS: PER 10-OUNCE SERVING

Enlightened Caribbean Shepherd's Pie
Protein 5 g, carbohydrate 22 g, fiber 3 g, fat 4 g,
cholesterol 0 mg, calcium 80 mg, sodium 378 mg
Calories 133: from protein 13%,
from carbohydrate 62%, from fat 24%

Traditional Caribbean Shepherd's Pie
Protein 12 g, carbohydrate 19 g, fiber 2 g, fat 23 g,
cholesterol 64 mg, calcium 40 mg, sodium 789 mg
Calories 338: from protein 15%,
from carbohydrate 22%, from fat 62%

Unchicken Marsala

*Made with wheat gluten (seitan) packed in broth
and veggie bacon, this dish owes its rich, creamy flavor
to soymilk and nutritional yeast.*

½ cup sliced sun-dried tomatoes, *not* packed in oil

1 cup boiling water

1½ teaspoons olive oil

5 cloves garlic, minced

1 medium Vidalia, Maui, or other sweet onion, chopped

⅓ cup chopped yellow bell pepper

3 slices veggie Canadian bacon, diced

6 ounces portobello mushrooms, diced

2 1-pound packages chicken-style seitan, drained

¾ cup marsala

⅔ cup enriched 1% fat soymilk

½ cup nutritional yeast

1 teaspoon chicken-flavor vegetarian broth powder

6 large fresh basil leaves, chopped

1 teaspoon dried marjoram

1 teaspoon lemon pepper

In a small bowl, combine sun-dried tomatoes and boiling water and set aside.

In a Dutch oven or large electric frying pan, warm oil over medium-high heat. Add the garlic, onion, bell pepper, and diced bacon and sauté for 5 minutes. Add mushrooms and cook 3 minutes. Add the seitan and reconstituted tomatoes *with* soaking liquid. Cook the mixture for 3 minutes, and add wine.

In a small bowl, whisk together the soymilk, yeast, and broth powder. Add to pan with the basil, marjoram, and lemon pepper. Lower heat to simmer and cook mixture 10 minutes, stirring occasionally, or until ready to serve.

NUTRITION ANALYSIS: PER 11-OUNCE SERVING

Enlightened Unchicken Marsala
Protein 29 g, carbohydrate 30 g, fiber 12 g, fat 3 g,
cholesterol 0 mg, calcium 91 mg, sodium 408 mg
Calories 252: from protein 45%,
from carbohydrate 46%, from fat 9%

Traditional Chicken Marsala
Protein 29 g, carbohydrate 12 g, fiber 2 g, fat 34 g,
cholesterol 128 mg, calcium 179 mg, sodium 326 mg
Calories 491: from protein 25%,
from carbohydrate 10%, from fat 66%

6
Servings

"Chicken" Stew

*Serve this delightful stew
with rice or potatoes.*

1 tablespoon olive oil
⅛ teaspoon crushed red pepper
6 cloves garlic, minced
1 medium Vidalia or other sweet onion, chopped
½ cup chopped yellow bell pepper
2 cups fresh green beans, cut in 2-inch pieces
1½ cups sliced baby-cut carrots
1 1-pound package chicken-style seitan, drained

½ pound portobello mushrooms, diced
1 large fresh tomato, diced
¾ cup dry sherry
1½ cups chicken-flavor vegetarian broth, boiling
1 teaspoon dried marjoram
1 teaspoon dried thyme
½ tablespoon tamari
2 tablespoons cornstarch
3 tablespoons cold water

In a 5-quart saucepan, warm oil and crushed pepper over medium-high heat for 1 minute. Add the garlic, onion, and bell pepper, and sauté 2 minutes; then add green beans and carrots and cook 5 minutes. Add seitan and continue to cook mixture for 3 minutes, stirring frequently. Add mushrooms, diced tomato, and sherry; cook an additional 5 minutes, stirring occasionally. Add hot broth, marjoram, thyme, and tamari; lower heat and simmer for 5 minutes.

In a small bowl, blend cornstarch with cold water and stir into stew. Simmer until ready to serve, stirring occasionally.

NUTRITION ANALYSIS: PER 12-OUNCE SERVING

Enlightened "Chicken" Stew
Protein 9 g, carbohydrate 22 g, fiber 7 g, fat 2 g,
cholesterol 0 mg, calcium 67 mg, sodium 328 mg
Calories 149: from protein 23%,
from carbohydrate 60%, from fat 10%

Traditional Chicken Stew
Protein 32 g, carbohydrate 20 g, fiber 3 g, fat 19 g,
cholesterol 116 mg, calcium 44 mg, sodium 616 mg
Calories 387: from protein 34%,
from carbohydrate 21%, from fat 45%

Chile Non Carne

*This "meaty" chile owes its authentic texture and flavor
to the coarsely chopped portobello mushrooms and vegetables
as well as the soy-based vegetarian burger.*

1 cup sliced onion
6 cloves garlic, peeled
½ green bell pepper, sliced
1 medium zucchini, sliced
2 cups sliced carrots
6 ounces portobello mushrooms,
  diced
1½ teaspoons olive oil
¼ teaspoon crushed red pepper
2 12-ounce packages ground beef
  alternative
1 15½-ounce can chili beans with
  chipotle peppers

1 14½-ounce can diced tomatoes and
  jalapenos
1 14½-ounce can Mexican-style
  stewed tomatoes
1 tablespoon chili powder
1 teaspoon dried thyme
1 teaspoon dried cilantro
2 teaspoons Mexican oregano
2 teaspoons ground cumin
½ cup snipped fresh cilantro
Cayenne to taste

Place the onion, garlic, and bell pepper in the bowl of food processor and pulse
to chop. Set aside.

Place the zucchini, carrots, and mushrooms in the food processor and pulse
to chop.

In a 5-quart saucepan, heat oil and crushed pepper for 1 minute over
medium-high heat. Add the chopped veggies and sauté 5 to 8 minutes, stirring
frequently. Add the vegetarian beef, chili beans, and tomatoes. Lower heat to
simmer, add remaining ingredients, and cook mixture 20 minutes, or until
ready to serve.

NUTRITION ANALYSIS: PER 12-OUNCE SERVING

Enlightened Chile Non Carne
Protein 10 g, carbohydrate 26 g, fiber 7 g, fat 1 g,
cholesterol 0 mg, calcium 106 mg, sodium 543 mg
Calories 143: from protein 25%,
from carbohydrate 67%, from fat 8%

Traditional Chile Con Carne
Protein 27 g, carbohydrate 25 g, fiber 9 g, fat 38 g,
cholesterol 97 mg, calcium 57 mg, sodium 700 mg
Calories 556: from protein 19%,
from carbohydrate 18%, from fat 63%

Fiesta Fajitas

*These delicious fajitas are made with chicken-style seitan,
hearty potato slices, and colorful vegetables.*

**8
Servings**

1 tablespoon olive oil
¼ teaspoon crushed red pepper
6 cloves garlic, minced
1 large red onion, halved crosswise
 and cut into ⅛-inch wedges
1 green bell pepper, cut into 2-inch
 strips
1 red bell pepper, cut into 2-inch
 strips

4 cups unpeeled russet potatoes, cut
 into ¼-inch wedges
1 cup sliced carrots
2 1-pound packages chicken-style
 seitan (reserve broth)
3 cups broccoli florets
1 teaspoon Mexican oregano
1 tablespoon tamari
8 whole wheat tortillas

Fajitas are great fun to assemble and eat. Add your favorite salsa, jalapeno slices, tomatoes, sliced avocado or guacamole, and crunchy sprouts.

In a large electric frying pan or Dutch oven, warm oil and crushed pepper for 2 minutes, over medium-high heat. Add garlic, onion, and bell peppers and sauté 3 minutes. Add potatoes and carrots and cook mixture 8 minutes, stirring frequently. Add seitan, and cook mixture 5 minutes. Reduce heat to low. Add broth, broccoli, oregano, and tamari. Simmer mixture, stirring occasionally, 10 minutes or until potatoes are cooked through. Warm tortillas covered in tortilla warmer, in oven, or in microwave. Serve with your favorite toppings.

NUTRITION ANALYSIS: PER 1 FAJITA

Enlightened Fiesta Fajitas
Protein 15 g, carbohydrate 49 g, fiber 11 g, fat 2 g,
cholesterol 0 mg, calcium 72 mg, sodium 489 mg
Calories 248: from protein 21%,
from carbohydrate 71%, from fat 8%

Traditional Fiesta Fajitas
Protein 29 g, carbohydrate 42 g, fiber 4 g, fat 17 g,
cholesterol 79 mg, calcium 89 mg, sodium 610 mg
Calories 442: from protein 26%,
from carbohydrate 39%, from fat 35%

Green Beans and "Ham"

*Easy, colorful, and delicious, this dish goes well
with a hearty grain and a crisp salad.*

2 teaspoons olive oil
¼ teaspoon crushed red pepper
4 garlic cloves, minced
1 medium leek, cleaned and sliced
1 stalk celery, sliced
4 cups green beans, cut into 2-inch
   pieces
1 6-ounce package veggie Canadian
   bacon
3 ounces portobello mushrooms,
   diced

½ cup dry vermouth
1 cup beef-flavor vegetarian broth,
   boiling
1 14½-ounce can Mexican-style
   stewed tomatoes
1 tablespoon tamari lite
1 tablespoon nutritional yeast
½ teaspoon dried basil
1 teaspoon dried thyme
⅓ cup chopped fresh cilantro

In a large Dutch oven or electric frying pan, warm oil and crushed pepper over
medium-high heat for 1 minute. Add the garlic, leek, celery, and green beans
and sauté 5 minutes. Add the veggie bacon and mushrooms and cook mixture
5 minutes, stirring frequently. Add the vermouth, cooking for 3 minutes; then
add the broth and tomatoes. Reduce heat to medium low and cook 2 minutes,
stirring occasionally; then add the remaining ingredients. Simmer 10 minutes,
or until ready to serve.

NUTRITION ANALYSIS: PER 10-OUNCE SERVING

Enlightened Green Beans and "Ham"
Protein 12 g, carbohydrate 18 g, fiber 5 g, fat 2 g,
cholesterol 0 mg, calcium 79 mg, sodium 596 mg
Calories 152: from protein 32%,
from carbohydrate 48%, from fat 11%

Traditional Green Beans and Ham
Protein 10 g, carbohydrate 13 g, fiber 5 g, fat 16 g,
cholesterol 23 mg, calcium 95 mg, sodium 800 mg
Calories 225: from protein 16%,
from carbohydrate 22%, from fat 62%

"Ham" Scrambler

*Tofu Hero Garden Scrambler makes this breakfast dish
a "meal in minutes." Round out this delicious scrambler
with Country Potatoes (page 207).*

*4
Servings*

1 26-gram package Tofu Hero
    Garden Scrambler
⅓ cup boiling water
1 12.3-ounce package lite silken tofu,
    drained

2 teaspoons olive oil
4 slices veggie Canadian bacon, diced

Combine Tofu Hero with boiling water and set aside. Mash tofu with a potato masher in a medium bowl and set aside.

Heat oil in a 10-inch frying pan over medium-high heat for 1 minute. Add diced veggie bacon and and cook 3 minutes, stirring frequently. Add mashed tofu to the pan and cook mixture 5 minutes, stirring frequently. Add the Tofu Hero mixture and mix thoroughly. Reduce heat and simmer until ready to serve.

NUTRITION ANALYSIS: PER 5-OUNCE SERVING

Enlightened "Ham" Scrambler
Protein 14 g, carbohydrate 6 g, fiber 1 g, fat 3 g,
cholesterol 0 mg, calcium 51 mg, sodium 456 mg
Calories 106: from protein 53%,
from carbohydrate 23%, from fat 24%

Traditional Scrambled Ham and Eggs
Protein 16 g, carbohydrate 3 g, fiber 0 g, fat 28 g,
cholesterol 283 mg, calcium 54 mg, sodium 864 mg
Calories 326: from protein 20%,
from carbohydrate 3%, from fat 77%

Hearty "Chicken" Fajitas

Sizzling fajitas are a personal favorite. Vegetarian chicken and ham, hearty veggies, and whole wheat tortillas shift the nutritional emphasis from fat, calories, and cholesterol to fiber and complex carbohydrates.

1 tablespoon olive oil
¼ teaspoon crushed red pepper
1 tablespoon dried minced garlic
6 cloves garlic, minced
1 large red onion, halved crosswise and cut into ⅛-inch slices
1 medium red bell pepper, sliced into 2-inch strips
1 6-ounce package veggie Canadian bacon, diced
2 pounds unpeeled russet potatoes, sliced into ¼-inch slices

8 ounces baby portobello mushrooms, sliced
1 medium zucchini, sliced
1 1-pound package chicken-style seitan (reserve broth)
½ cup tequila
1½ cups of reserved seitan broth
½ cup chopped fresh cilantro
1 tablespoon tamari
8 whole wheat tortillas

In a large electric frying pan or Dutch oven, over medium-high heat, heat the oil, crushed pepper, and dried garlic for 2 minutes. Add minced fresh garlic, onion, bell pepper, and diced veggie bacon. Sauté 3 minutes. Add sliced potatoes and cook mixture 8 minutes, stirring frequently. Add mushrooms and zucchini. Cook 5 minutes before adding seitan and remaining ingredients (except for tortillas). Cook mixture 3 minutes, stirring frequently. Reduce heat to medium low and simmer 10 minutes, or until potatoes are cooked through, stirring occasionally. Warm tortillas in oven or microwave, covered. Keep tortillas warm in a tortilla warmer. Serve with salsa, guacamole, and your favorite toppings.

NUTRITION ANALYSIS: PER 1 TORTILLA WITH 1¼ CUPS FILLING

Enlightened Hearty "Chicken" Fajitas
Protein 17 g., carbohydrate 47 g, fiber 9 g, fat 2 g, cholesterol 0 mg, calcium 51 mg, sodium 525 mg
Calories 284: from protein 24%, from carbohydrate 68%, from fat 8%

Traditional Hearty Chicken Fajitas
Protein 26 g, carbohydrate 41 g, fiber 4 g, fat 22 g, cholesterol 73 mg, calcium 81 mg, sodium 786 mg
Calories: 499: from protein 23%, from carbohydrate 35%, from fat 42%

Indian-Spiced Cauliflower

Cauliflower and potatoes are often paired in East Indian cuisine. In India, ghee (clarified butter) is used extensively. I prefer to use just a touch of olive oil and succulent slices of hickory-baked tofu, which lend a heartiness to this enticing dish. Serve with Fragrant Basmati Pilaf (page 211).

*8
Servings*

1½ teaspoons olive oil
¼ teaspoon crushed red pepper
5 cloves garlic, minced
1 medium sweet onion, chopped
2 stalks celery, sliced
1½ tablespoons grated gingerroot
4 medium red-skinned potatoes, cut into ¼-inch wedges
1 6-ounce package hickory baked tofu, sliced

6 ounces cremini mushrooms, sliced
1 small head cauliflower (1¼ pounds), separated into florets
¼ teaspoon turmeric
¼ cup dry sherry
1 14½-ounce can Mexican-style stewed tomatoes
¼ cup chopped fresh cilantro
⅓ cup chicken-flavor vegetarian broth

In an electric frying pan or 5-quart saucepan, warm oil and crushed red pepper over medium-high heat for 1 minute. Add garlic, onion, celery, and gingerroot and sauté 3 minutes. Add the potatoes and cook mixture 8 minutes, or until potatoes are softening. Add the tofu and the mushrooms and cook 3 minutes. Add the cauliflower and cook 5 minutes. Add the turmeric, sherry, tomatoes, cilantro, and broth. Stir to mix thoroughly, reduce heat to medium low, and simmer 10 minutes or until veggies are tender, stirring occasionally.

NUTRITION ANALYSIS: PER 11-OUNCE SERVING

Enlightened Indian-Spiced Cauliflower
Protein 9 g, carbohydrate 27 g, fiber 5 g, fat 2 g, cholesterol 0 mg, calcium 48 mg, sodium 287 mg
Calories 158: from protein 22%, from carbohydrate 68%, from fat 10%

Traditional Indian-Spiced Cauliflower
Protein 11 g, carbohydrate 23 g, fiber 4 g, fat 13 g, cholesterol 52 mg, calcium 50 mg, sodium 400 mg
Calories 256: from protein 18%, from carbohydrate 36%, from fat 46%

Sweet Italian "Sausage" with Peppers

This authentic rendition of a traditional Italian dish is
delicious when served with pasta or sandwiched on a kaiser roll.

1½ teaspoons plus 1 teaspoon olive oil
1 11.2-ounce package Lean Links Italian
3 garlic cloves, minced
1 green bell pepper, sliced into 3-inch strips
1 red bell pepper, sliced into 3-inch strips
1 yellow onion, quartered and cut into ¼-inch wedges
1 cup white wine
1 25-ounce jar fat-free tomato sauce
1 teaspoon dried basil
1 teaspoon dried thyme

In a large nonstick electric frying pan or Dutch oven, warm the 1½ teaspoons of oil over medium-high heat for 1 minute. Brown links in hot oil, turning gently, as they will be fragile until they are browned. Remove from pan, leaving juices, and set aside. Add the remaining teaspoon of oil to the pan and sauté the garlic, bell peppers, and onion for 3 minutes. Return the browned links to the pan and cook 5 minutes. Add the wine, reduce heat to medium low, and cook 2 minutes. Add tomato sauce, basil, and thyme. Reduce heat to low and simmer mixture 10 to 15 minutes, or until ready to serve.

NUTRITION ANALYSIS: PER 9-OUNCE SERVING

Enlightened Sweet Italian "Sausage" with Peppers
Protein 9 g, carbohydrate 23 g, fiber 3 g, fat 5 g,
cholesterol 0 mg, calcium 45 mg, sodium 403 mg
Calories 188: from protein 20%,
from carbohydrate 48%, from fat 22%

Traditional Sweet Italian Sausage with Peppers
Protein 14 g, carbohydrate 14 g, fiber 3 g, fat 25 g,
cholesterol 45 mg, calcium 37 mg, sodium 898 mg
Calories 356: from protein 17%,
from carbohydrate 17%, from fat 66%

Jambalaya

*Jambalaya is a Creole dish with wide variations. This popular
New Orleans dish is traditionally made with cooked rice,
tomatoes, peppers, onions, and almost any kind of meat.*

*8
Servings*

1½ teaspoons olive oil
⅛ teaspoon crushed red pepper
3 large garlic cloves, minced
1 yellow onion, chopped
2 stalks celery, chopped
1 green bell pepper, chopped
1 small zucchini, diced
2 7-ounce packages Vegi-Deli
  Chicken Strips
1 14-ounce package Gimme Lean,
  sausage style

1 large fresh tomato, diced
½ cup dry vermouth
2 cups cooked brown rice
1 cup chicken-flavor vegetarian
  broth, boiling
1 cup frozen white corn, defrosted
1 14½-ounce can stewed tomatoes
½ teaspoon granulated garlic
¼ teaspoon ground cumin
⅛ teaspoon chile powder
cayenne and paprika to taste

Warm oil and crushed pepper in a large Dutch oven or electric frying pan over
medium-high heat for 1 minute. Add the garlic, onion, celery, bell pepper, and
zucchini and sauté 5 minutes. Add the "chicken" strips and Gimme Lean
sausage. Cook mixture 10 minutes, stirring frequently and separating the
"sausage." Add the tomato and vermouth and cook for 3 minutes. Add the
cooked rice, broth, corn, and stewed tomatoes, stirring after each addition.
Reduce heat to low and add remaining ingredients. Simmer, stirring occasionally, 10 minutes, or until ready to serve.

NUTRITION ANALYSIS: PER 12-OUNCE SERVING

Enlightened Jambalaya
Protein 28 g, carbohydrate 36 g, fiber 6 g, fat 4 g,
cholesterol 0 mg, calcium 43 mg, sodium 624 mg
Calories 291: from protein 39%,
from carbohydrate 50%, from fat 11%

Traditional Jambalaya
Protein 28 g, carbohydrate 25 g, fiber 2 g, fat 29 g,
cholesterol 91 mg, calcium 75 mg, sodium 1,613 mg
Calories 492: from protein 24%,
from carbohydrate 21%, from fat 56%

"Lamb" Curry with Broccoli

*Lamb is eaten in some parts of India. In this recipe,
ground beef–style TVP provides background and texture.
Serve with Fragrant Basmati Pilaf (page 211).*

6
Servings

- 1¼ cups TVP, ground beef style
- 1½ cups beef-flavor vegetarian broth, boiling
- 1½ teaspoons olive oil
- ¼ teaspoon crushed red pepper
- 5 cloves garlic, minced
- 1 medium yellow onion, chopped
- ⅔ cup chopped red bell pepper
- 2 stalks celery, sliced
- 1 cup diced carrots
- 4 cups broccoli florets
- ⅓ cup dry sherry
- 1 14½-ounce can Italian-style stewed tomatoes
- 2 tablespoons nutritional yeast
- 1 teaspoon turmeric
- 1 teaspoon ground ginger
- ½ tablespoon Bragg Liquid Aminos

In a medium bowl, combine the TVP with the boiling broth. Set aside.

In a 5-quart saucepan or electric frying pan, heat oil and crushed pepper for 2 minutes over medium-high heat. Add the garlic, onion, bell pepper, and celery, and sauté 3 minutes. Add reconstituted TVP and cook mixture 5 minutes, stirring occasionally. Add the carrots and cook 3 minutes. Add remaining ingredients, reduce heat to low, and simmer 8 to 10 minutes, stirring occasionally.

NUTRITION ANALYSIS: PER 11-OUNCE SERVING

Enlightened "Lamb" Curry with Broccoli
Protein 14 g, carbohydrate 47 g, fiber 8 g, fat 2 g,
cholesterol 0 mg, calcium 77 mg, sodium 274 mg
Calories: 149: from protein 22%,
from carbohydrate 71%, from fat 7%

Traditional Lamb Curry with Broccoli
Protein 28 g, carbohydrate 9 g, fiber 2 g, fat 19 g,
cholesterol 89 mg, calcium 54 mg, sodium 494 mg
Calories 314: from protein 35%,
from carbohydrate 11%, from fat 54%

Louisiana Stuffed Potatoes

*This delightful entrée, which owes its rich and creamy flavor
to nutritional yeast flakes, contains 13 grams of protein
and only 5 grams of fat in each stuffed potato
with sauce. Serve with Cajun "Cream" Sauce (page 232).*

*6
Servings*

6 baking potatoes
1½ teaspoons olive oil
3 garlic cloves, minced
1 medium red onion, chopped
⅓ cup chopped yellow bell pepper
1 stalk celery, chopped
6 ounces cremini mushrooms, sliced

2 medium tomatoes, chopped
2 tablespoons chopped black olives
1 tablespoon balsamic vinegar
1 tablespoon tamari
3 tablespoons nutritional yeast
3 tablespoons chopped fresh basil
hot pepper sauce to taste

Preheat oven to 425°.

Bake potatoes on middle rack of oven 1 hour, or until fork tender.

Heat oil in a 10-inch frying pan and sauté the garlic, onion, bell pepper, and celery for 3 minutes. Add mushrooms, tomatoes, and olives and cook 5 minutes, stirring frequently. Add remaining ingredients and lower heat to simmer until ready to assemble.

When cool enough to handle, cut an **X** into each potato and press sides gently to open. Scoop out 1 tablespoon of pulp from each potato and add to stuffing mixture. Spoon stuffing into and over potatoes. Serve immediately.

NUTRITION ANALYSIS: PER 1 STUFFED POTATO

Enlightened Louisiana Stuffed Potatoes
Protein 10 g, carbohydrate 60 g, fiber 7 g, fat 2 g,
cholesterol 0 mg, calcium 43 mg, sodium 86 mg
Calories 284: from protein 13%,
from carbohydrate 80%, from fat 7%

Traditional Louisiana Stuffed Potatoes
Protein 9 g, carbohydrate 59 g, fiber 7 g, fat 13 g,
cholesterol 33 mg, calcium 122 mg, sodium 464 mg
Calories 372: from protein 9%,
from carbohydrate 61%, from fat 29%

Luscious Layered Polenta

This hearty dish is made easy and healthy using precooked polenta, prepared beans, TVP, and veggie Canadian bacon.

2 cups TVP, ground beef style

1 cup beef-flavor vegetarian broth, boiling

1 cup sliced sun-dried tomatoes, *not* packed in oil

1½ cups boiling water

2 12.3-ounce packages lite silken tofu

1 10-ounce package frozen chopped spinach, thawed and drained

⅓ cup plus 2 tablespoons soy Parmesan cheese

⅓ cup nutritional yeast

1 teaspoon onion powder

½ teaspoon granulated garlic

¼ teaspoon sea salt

1 teaspoon olive oil

1 teaspoon dried minced garlic

⅓ cup chopped red onion

4 slices veggie Canadian bacon, diced

1 13.3-ounce jar borlotti beans or cranberry beans

olive oil cooking spray

1 24-ounce package San Gennaro Basil & Garlic Polenta

1 25-ounce jar fat-free tomato sauce

Preheat oven to 350°.

Combine TVP and boiling broth in a medium bowl and set aside. Place sun-dried tomatoes in a small bowl, add boiling water, and set aside.

Place tofu in a large bowl and mash with a potato masher. Add spinach, ⅓ cup soy Parmesan, yeast, onion powder, granulated garlic, and salt. Mix thoroughly. Set aside.

In a medium saucepan, heat oil and dried minced garlic for 2 minutes over medium-high heat. Add chopped onion and veggie bacon and sauté 3 minutes. Add reconstituted TVP and sun-dried tomatoes with soaking liquid and the beans. Mix well and cook over medium-low heat until ready to assemble.

Spray a 9-by-13-inch baking dish with oil. Divide the polenta roll in half, cut into ½-inch slices, and crumble on bottom of pan, mashing slightly with a fork into an even layer. Cover the polenta with the tofu mixture and spread the

Luscious Layered Polenta *(continued)*

TVP/bean mixture evenly over all. Cut the remaining polenta into very thin slices. Arrange on top of filling, overlapping slightly. Top with tomato sauce and sprinkle with 2 tablespoons soy Parmesan cheese. Cover with foil and bake for 25 minutes. Remove foil and bake an additional 10 minutes. Serve with additional sauce.

NUTRITION ANALYSIS: PER 11-OUNCE SERVING

Enlightened Luscious Layered Polenta
Protein 24 g, carbohydrate 29 g, fiber 8 g, fat 3 g, cholesterol 0 mg, calcium 78 mg, sodium 768 mg
Calories 224: from protein 40%, from carbohydrate 49%, from fat 11%

Traditional Luscious Layered Polenta
Protein 24 g, carbohydrate 25 g, fiber 4 g, fat 31 g, cholesterol 79 mg, calcium 257 mg, sodium 914 mg
Calories 465: from protein 20%, from carbohydrate 21%, from fat 59%

Mexicali Potatoes

Smoky chipotle chiles and hearty tempeh
make this toothsome dish a crowd pleaser!

2 8-ounce packages soy tempeh, cubed
1 tablespoon olive oil
1 tablespoon minced, dried garlic
1 yellow onion, cut into ¼-inch wedges
½ cup thinly sliced scallions
1 large yellow bell pepper, cut into 3-inch strips
2 pounds russet potatoes, cut into ¼-inch wedges

1 or 2 chipotle chiles packed in adobo sauce (reserve 1 teaspoon of adobo sauce)
¼ cup plus ¼ cup dry vermouth
1 14½-ounce can Mexican-style stewed tomatoes
¼ cup chopped fresh cilantro
1 teaspoon dried Mexican oregano
1 tablespoon tamari

Steam tempeh for 15 minutes. Heat the oil and minced garlic in a nonstick electric frying pan or Dutch oven over medium-high heat for 1 minute. Add the onion, scallions, and bell pepper and sauté 3 minutes. Add the potatoes and cook, stirring frequently, for 8 minutes. Crumble the steamed tempeh into the pan. Cook mixture 10 minutes, stirring frequently. Place chipotle chiles (one chile = medium heat, two chiles = getting hot) in a food processor with the 1 teaspoon of adobo sauce and ¼ cup of the vermouth; blend. Add the stewed tomatoes and process; do not puree. Add to the pan along with the cilantro, oregano, and tamari. Then add the remaining ¼ cup of vermouth. Simmer, stirring occasionally, for 8 minutes, or until ready to serve.

NUTRITION ANALYSIS: PER 9-OUNCE SERVING

Enlightened Mexicali Potatoes
Protein 16 g, carbohydrate 35 g, fiber 4 g, fat 5 g,
cholesterol 0 mg, calcium 36 mg, sodium 273 mg
Calories 257: from protein 25%,
from carbohydrate 57%, from fat 18%

Traditional Mexicali Potatoes
Protein 13 g, carbohydrate 26 g, fiber 3 g, fat 24 g,
cholesterol 57 mg, calcium 34 mg, sodium 429 mg
Calories 371: from protein 14%,
from carbohydrate 28%, from fat 58%

"Pepperoni Chicken"

*Chopped Chiken TVP and vegetarian pepperoni
combine to create a fusion of complementary flavors
and textures in this delicious dish.*

*6
Servings*

2½ cups Chopped Chiken TVP
2 cups plus 1 cup chicken-flavor
  vegetarian broth, boiling
1½ teaspoons olive oil
¼ teaspoon crushed red pepper
5 large cloves garlic, minced
1 medium red onion, cut into thin
  wedges

1 stalk celery, sliced
1 cup Vegi-Deli pepperoni, diced
6 ounces cremini mushrooms, sliced
3 medium tomatoes, diced
2 tablespoons tamari
½ cup nutritional yeast
1½ teaspoons dried marjoram

Combine TVP with 2 cups of the boiling broth in a medium bowl and set aside
for 15 minutes.

In a large Dutch oven or electric frying pan, heat oil with crushed pepper
over medium-high heat 2 minutes. Add garlic, onion, and celery and sauté 3
minutes. Add the "pepperoni"; then add mushrooms, tomatoes, and reconstituted TVP, stirring after each addition. Cook mixture 10 minutes, stirring
occasionally. Add remaining 1 cup broth, tamari, yeast, and marjoram. Reduce
heat to low and simmer 10 minutes, or until ready to serve.

NUTRITION ANALYSIS: PER 12-OUNCE SERVING

Enlightened "Pepperoni Chicken"
Protein 40 g, carbohydrate 32 g, fiber 10 g, fat 5 g,
cholesterol 0 mg, calcium 42 mg, sodium 612 mg
Calories 288: from protein 48%,
from carbohydrate 39%, from fat 13%

Traditional Pepperoni Chicken
Protein 53 g, carbohydrate 8 g, fiber 1 g, fat 30 g,
cholesterol 163 mg, calcium 65 mg, sodium 1,134 mg
Calories 520: from protein 41%,
from carbohydrate 6%, from fat 52%

Pineapple "Chicken"

Marinating the "chicken" strips enhances both the flavor and texture. Serve this enticing dish with Tomato and Garlic Couscous (page 226).

Marinade

1 cup chicken-flavor vegetarian broth
2 cloves garlic, minced
¼ cup tamari
1 teaspoon olive oil

1 tablespoon liquid Fruitsource
1 tablespoon lemon juice
½ teaspoon ground ginger
½ teaspoon onion powder

2 7-ounce packages Vegi-Deli Chicken Strips

1 cup sliced baby carrots

Sauté

1½ teaspoons olive oil
4 cloves garlic, minced
1 tablespoon freshly grated ginger-root
1 medium yellow onion
⅓ cup chopped green bell pepper

1 8-ounce can pineapple chunks, drained (reserve syrup)
1 6-ounce package fresh baby spinach
⅓ cup dry sherry
½ cup chopped fresh cilantro
2 tablespoons cornstarch

For the marinade: Combine the marinade ingredients in a 2-cup glass measuring cup. Place "chicken" strips in a medium nonreactive bowl with marinade. Cover and refrigerate for 2 to 3 hours, turning the strips several times during process.

For the Sauté: In a large Dutch oven or electric frying pan heat olive oil and sauté garlic, gingerroot, onion, bell pepper, and carrots over medium-high heat

Pineapple "Chicken" *(continued)*

for 3 minutes. Add veggie chicken to pan, reserving marinade. Add drained pineapple and cook mixture 5 minutes, stirring frequently. Add spinach, reduce heat to medium low, and cook until spinach has softened, about 3 minutes. Add sherry and cilantro and cook 5 minutes, stirring occasionally.

In a small bowl, blend cornstarch and water; stir into the reserved pineapple syrup and set aside.

Pour marinade into pan and add cornstarch mixture. Simmer 5 minutes, or until ready to serve.

NUTRITION ANALYSIS: PER 8-OUNCE SERVING

Enlightened Pineapple "Chicken"
Protein 19 g, carbohydrate 17 g, fiber 3 g, fat 3 g,
cholesterol 0 mg, calcium 46 mg, sodium 758 mg
Calories 173: from protein 43%,
from carbohydrate 39%, from fat 17%

Traditional Pineapple Chicken
Protein 19 g, carbohydrate 16 g, fiber 2 g, fat 23 g,
cholesterol 54 mg, calcium 53 mg, sodium 862 mg
Calories 342: from protein 22%,
from carbohydrate 18%, from fat 60%

"Sausage" 'n' Potatoes

*Bite-size chunks of potatoes simmer with tasty "sausage" balls
in this wholesome and hearty dish.*

1 tablespoon olive oil
1 tablespoon minced, dried garlic
1 yellow onion, cut into ¼-inch
  wedges
1 medium green bell pepper, cut into
  3-inch strips

2 pounds unpeeled russet potatoes,
  cut into ¼-inch wedges
1 14-ounce package Gimme Lean,
  sausage style
4 medium tomatoes, diced
¼ cup chopped fresh basil

Warm the oil and minced garlic in a nonstick electric frying pan or Dutch oven
over medium-high heat for 1 minute. Add the onion and green pepper and
sauté until crisp-tender, 3 minutes. Add the potatoes and cook, stirring frequently, for 8 to 10 minutes. Roll the veggie sausage into small balls and add
to the pan. Cook 5 minutes, or until "sausage" is browning. Add tomatoes and
basil. Reduce heat and simmer, stirring occasionally, 5 minutes, or until ready
to serve.

NUTRITION ANALYSIS: PER 12-OUNCE SERVING

Enlightened "Sausage" 'n' Potatoes
Protein 15 g, carbohydrate 50 g, fiber 6 g, fat 3 g,
cholesterol 0 mg, calcium 30 mg, sodium 356 mg
Calories 278: from protein 21%,
from carbohydrate 70%, from fat 9%

Traditional Sausage 'n' Potatoes
Protein 12 g, carbohydrate 35 g, fiber 4 g, fat 35 g,
cholesterol 66 mg, calcium 51 mg, sodium 516 mg
Calories 495: from protein 10%,
from carbohydrate 28%, from fat 62%

Savory "Sausage" and Rice
with Chardonnay

*Meaty portobellos and fragrant vegetarian sausage combine
in this simple yet elegant rice dish.*

*6
Servings*

1 tablespoon olive oil
½ tablespoon dried minced garlic
1 cup thinly sliced scallions
1 14-ounce package Gimme Lean,
    sausage style
8 ounces portobello mushrooms,
    sliced

½ cup chardonnay
1 cup raw white rice
4 cups chicken-flavor vegetarian
    broth, boiling
3 tablespoons nutritional yeast
1 teaspoon dried marjoram

In a large saucepan, heat oil and minced garlic over medium-high heat for 1 minute. Add scallion and sauté 3 minutes. Add "sausage" and cook 5 minutes, stirring frequently with a large spoon to break up "sausage." Add chardonnay and cook 3 minutes; then stir in rice and add remaining ingredients. Reduce heat to simmer, cover, and cook, stirring occasionally, 20 minutes or until rice is tender.

NUTRITION ANALYSIS: PER 12-OUNCE SERVING

**Enlightened Savory "Sausage" and
Rice with Chardonnay**
Protein 18 g, carbohydrate 41 g, fiber 4 g, fat 3 g,
cholesterol 0 mg, calcium 35 mg, sodium 443 mg
Calories 270: from protein 27%,
from carbohydrate 63%, from fat 10%

**Traditional Savory Sausage and
Rice with Chardonnay**
Protein 13 g, carbohydrate 30 g, fiber 1 g, fat 35 g,
cholesterol 66 mg, calcium 75 mg, sodium 920 mg
Calories 498: from protein 11%,
from carbohydrate 25%, from fat 64%

Savory Stuffed Polenta

Precooked polenta and vegetarian ground beef are ready-to-use ingredients that make this elegant baked entrée a snap to prepare.

1½ teaspoons plus 1½ teaspoons olive oil
¼ teaspoon crushed red pepper
6 garlic cloves, minced
1 cup plus ½ cup Vidalia or other sweet onion, chopped
¼ cup plus ¼ cup green bell pepper, chopped
1 25-ounce jar fat-free tomato sauce
1 14½-ounce can Italian-style diced tomatoes

1 tablespoon dried minced garlic
1 14-ounce package Gimme Lean, ground beef style
6 ounces portobello mushrooms, diced
1 10-ounce package frozen chopped spinach, thawed and drained
olive oil cooking spray
1 24-ounce package San Gennaro Basil & Garlic Polenta
¼ cup soy Parmesan cheese

Preheat oven to 350°.

Over medium-high heat, warm 1½ teaspoons of oil with crushed pepper in a 5-quart saucepan for 1 minute. Add the minced fresh garlic, 1 cup of the chopped onion, and ¼ cup of the green pepper. Sauté 3 minutes; then add the tomato sauce and diced tomatoes. Cover with lid set slightly ajar, and lower heat to simmer, stirring occasionally, until ready to assemble.

In a 10-inch frying pan, heat the remaining 1½ teaspoons oil with the dried minced garlic for 2 minutes over medium heat. Add the remaining chopped onion, bell pepper, and the Gimme Lean and sauté 5 minutes, breaking it up with a fork. Add diced mushrooms and chopped spinach, stirring to mix thoroughly. Lower heat and simmer 10 minutes, stirring frequently. Set aside.

Spray a 9-by-13-inch baking dish with oil. Divide the polenta roll in half; cut one half into ½-inch slices and crumble them on bottom of pan, mashing

Savory Stuffed Polenta *(continued)*

slightly with a fork into an even layer. Top with the veggie beef mixture. Cut the remaining polenta into very thin slices and arrange on top of filling, overlapping slightly. Top with tomato sauce and sprinkle with soy Parmesan cheese. Cover with foil and bake for 20 minutes. Remove foil and bake an additional 5 to 10 minutes. Serve with additional sauce.

NUTRITION ANALYSIS: PER 9-OUNCE SERVING

Enlightened Savory Stuffed Polenta
Protein 11 g, carbohydrate 26 g, fiber 4 g, fat 2 g,
cholesterol 0 mg, calcium 35 mg, sodium 596 mg
Calories 159: from protein 25%,
from carbohydrate 63%, from fat 10%

Traditional Savory Stuffed Polenta
Protein 11 g, carbohydrate 44 g, fiber 4 g, fat 17 g,
cholesterol 42 mg, calcium 74 mg, sodium 663 mg
Calories 272: from protein 12%,
from carbohydrate 48%, from fat 40%

Sweet and Sour "Meatballs"

*Roll the "meatballs" right out of the package and bake
in this delicious fat-free version of a classic.
Sweet and Sour "Meatballs" can be served as an
entrée with rice or noodles, or as an appetizer.*

olive oil cooking spray
2 14-ounce packages Gimme Lean,
   ground beef style
½ teaspoon onion powder
1 14½-ounce can Mexican-style
   stewed tomatoes

1 16-ounce can jellied cranberry
   sauce
1 25-ounce jar fat-free tomato sauce
½ cup barbecue sauce
1 8-ounce can crushed pineapple
   packed in juice

Preheat oven to 400°.

Spray a baking pan with olive oil. Roll the Gimme Lean into balls roughly
1 inch or so in diameter—you should have about 48. Place on prepared pan
and spray tops lightly with oil. Sprinkle with onion powder and bake for 10
minutes. Place pan under the broiler and brown tops. Remove and set aside.

Place the stewed tomatoes and cranberry jelly in a 5-quart saucepan and
heat over medium-high heat, stirring frequently, until the cranberry jelly melts,
about 5 minutes. Add the remaining ingredients and reduce heat to medium.
Cook mixture 5 minutes and add the baked meatballs. Reduce heat to low and
simmer for 20 minutes, or until ready to serve.

NUTRITION ANALYSIS: PER 8-OUNCE SERVING

Enlightened Sweet and Sour "Meatballs"	Traditional Sweet and Sour Meatballs
Protein 12 g, carbohydrate 47 g, fiber 3 g, fat 0 g, cholesterol 0 mg, calcium 11 mg, sodium 612 mg	Protein 13 g, carbohydrate 41 g, fiber 0 g, fat 23 g, cholesterol 58 mg, calcium 11 mg, sodium 777 mg
Calories 250: from protein 20%, from carbohydrate 79%, from fat 1%	Calories 429: from protein 12%, from carbohydrate 39%, from fat 49%

Sweet Corn Veggie Wraps

*Made with delicious veggies wrapped in
wholesome tortillas, this dish is a quick and
easy route to a delightfully healthful meal.*

**4
Servings**

1½ teaspoons olive oil
⅛ teaspoon crushed red pepper
4 cloves garlic, minced
½ cup sliced scallions
⅓ cup chopped green bell pepper
2 medium zucchini, sliced
1 cup Melissa's roasted sweet corn

⅓ cup dry vermouth
1 medium fresh tomato, chopped
⅓ cup chopped fresh cilantro
½ tablespoon Bragg Liquid Aminos
4 whole wheat tortillas
2 tablespoons Creamy Cilantro
    Dressing (page 116)

In a 5-quart saucepan, warm oil and crushed pepper over medium-high heat for
1 minute. Add garlic, scallions, and bell pepper and sauté 3 minutes. Add zucchini and corn and cook mixture 5 minutes. Add vermouth, tomato,
cilantro, and liquid aminos. Reduce heat to medium low and simmer
until ready to serve. Warm tortillas in a tortilla warmer in the oven at
350° for 5 minutes or covered in the microwave for 1 minute. Spread
warmed tortillas with dressing and then spoon in filling. Fold to close,
and serve with Mexicali Brown Rice (page 216).

BE SURE TO READ
the ingredient list when
purchasing tortillas;
many are made with
hydrogenated fat.

NUTRITION ANALYSIS: PER ONE WRAP

Enlightened Sweet Corn Veggie Wraps
Protein 8 g, carbohydrate 78 g, fiber 6 g, fat 3 g,
cholesterol 0 mg, calcium 50 mg, sodium 279 mg
Calories 204: from protein 8%,
from carbohydrate 85%, from fat 7%

Traditional Sweet Corn Veggie Wraps
Protein 7 g, carbohydrate 42 g, fiber 4 g, fat 20 g,
cholesterol 0 mg, calcium 108 mg, sodium 950 mg
Calories 382: from protein 8%,
from carbohydrate 45%, from fat 48%

Sweet Yams and Savory "Sausage"

This hearty and delicious dish is a delightful
mix of interesting flavors and textures.

olive oil cooking spray
1 14-ounce package Gimme Lean,
   sausage style
2 medium yams, peeled and cubed
   (1½ cups cubed)
2 teaspoons olive oil
¼ teaspoon crushed red pepper
4 cloves garlic, minced
1 medium red onion, chopped

1 stalk celery, sliced
2 cups button mushrooms, sliced
⅓ cup dry sherry
1 26-ounce jar fat-free tomato sauce
1 teaspoon dried basil
½ teaspoon dried thyme
½ teaspoon dried marjoram
3 cups cooked brown rice

Preheat oven to 400°. Spray baking pan with oil.

Roll the vegetarian sausage into "meatballs" and place on prepared pan. Bake 5 minutes; then place under broiler until tops are brown. Set aside.

Cook yams in boiling water 15 minutes, or until just cooked through.

In a 5-quart saucepan, warm oil and crushed pepper over medium-high heat for 1 minute. Add the garlic, onion, and celery and sauté 3 minutes. Add mushrooms and cook mixture, stirring frequently, 5 minutes. Add sherry and cook 2 minutes; stir in tomato sauce and add "meatballs" and cooked yams along with the seasonings. Reduce heat to simmer and cook 15 minutes. Serve over brown rice.

NUTRITION ANALYSIS: PER 14-OUNCE SERVING

Enlightened Sweet Yams and Savory "Sausage"
Protein 8 g, carbohydrate 29 g, fiber 3 g, fat 1 g,
cholesterol 0 mg, calcium 15 mg, sodium 292 mg
Calories 159: from protein 21%,
from carbohydrate 73%, from fat 6%

Traditional Sweet Yams and Savory Sausage
Protein 7 g, carbohydrate 26 g, fiber 2 g, fat 20 g,
cholesterol 26 mg, calcium 31 mg, sodium 648 mg
Calories 312: from protein 9%,
from carbohydrate 33%, from fat 57%

Swiss "Steak" with Sautéed Portobello and Cremini Mushrooms

*Sometimes called Salisbury steak,
this hearty entrée presents beautifully.*

2 14-ounce packages Gimme Lean, ground beef style
¼ cup whole wheat bread crumbs
½ teaspoon granulated garlic
⅓ cup fruit-sweetened ketchup
2 tablespoons Dijon mustard
3 tablespoons olive oil, divided
3 large garlic cloves, minced
¾ cup plus ¼ cup Vidalia, Maui, or other sweet onion, chopped
1 stalk celery, chopped
½ cup chopped red bell pepper
3 ounces veggie Canadian bacon, diced
¾ cup plus ¼ cup dry vermouth

1 14½-ounce can Italian-style diced tomatoes
½ cup minced shallots (about 2 to 3 large)
1 6-ounce package baby portobello mushrooms, sliced
2 6-ounce packages cremini mushrooms, sliced
¼ cup balsamic vinegar
1½ tablespoons tamari
½ cup beef-flavor vegetarian broth
3 tablespoons arrowroot
2 tablespoons cold water
½ teaspoon dried thyme
1 teaspoon dried basil

In a large bowl, combine the vegetarian ground beef with the bread crumbs, garlic, ketchup, and mustard. Form mixture into 8 patties. In a large electric frying pan or Dutch oven, brown patties in 1 tablespoon of the oil. Remove from pan and set aside. Add 1 tablespoon oil to pan and sauté the garlic cloves with ¾ cup of the onion, celery, bell pepper and veggie bacon for 5 minutes. Add browned patties and continue to sauté 5 minutes longer. Lower heat to simmer and add ¾ cup vermouth and the tomatoes. Heat remaining table-spoon of oil in a 10-inch frying pan, sauté shallots 2 minutes, and add reserved ¼ cup of onions and the mushrooms. Cook 3 minutes, or until mushrooms are softened. Add the vinegar, tamari, and broth and lower heat to simmer. Dissolve arrowroot in water and stir into mushrooms along with the thyme and basil. Simmer 5 minutes, stirring occasionally. Pour over burgers with remaining ¼ cup vermouth. Simmer until ready to serve.

NUTRITION ANALYSIS: PER 13-OUNCE SERVING

Enlightened Swiss "Steak" with Sautéed Portobello and Cremini Mushrooms

Protein 24 g, carbohydrate 40 g, fiber 4 g, fat 5 g, cholesterol 0 mg, calcium 25 mg, sodium 980 mg
Calories 306: from protein 31%, from carbohydrate 52%, from fat 16%

Traditional Swiss Steak with Sautéed Portobello and Cremini Mushrooms

Protein 20 g, carbohydrate 17 g, fiber 3 g, fat 30 g, cholesterol 76 mg, calcium 38 mg, sodium 1,132 mg
Calories 409: from protein 19%, from carbohydrate 16%, from fat 65%

Tamale Pie

*This enticing dish features a savory filling made with hearty tempeh
and veggie bacon, topped with a golden cornmeal crust.*

*8
Servings*

Filling

olive oil cooking spray
2 8-ounce packages soy tempeh
4 cloves garlic, minced
1 red onion, chopped
1 medium red bell pepper, chopped
1 6-ounce package veggie Canadian
  bacon, diced
¼ teaspoon crushed red pepper
⅓ cup dry sherry

½ cup beef-flavor vegetarian broth,
  boiling
1 14½-ounce can Mexican-style
  stewed tomatoes, diced
⅔ cup frozen white corn, thawed
1 tablespoon chile powder
2 teaspoons dried Mexican oregano
1 teaspoon lemon pepper

Crust

1½ cups yellow cornmeal
¼ teaspoon sea salt
1 tablespoon nonaluminum baking
  powder
1 tablespoon egg replacer powder
2 tablespoons nutritional yeast

½ teaspoon dried marjoram
2 tablespoons rice butter spread
1 tablespoon liquid Fruitsource
¾ cup enriched 1% fat soymilk
dried basil and dried marjoram for
  garnish

Tempeh is high in protein, fiber, calcium, B vitamins, and iron. This nutritional powerhouse is made by introducing a culture to whole cooked soybeans. Fermenting soybeans in this way produces a dense, chewy cake that can be incorporated into many dishes.

Preheat oven to 375°. Spray 9-by-13-inch baking pan with oil.

For the filling: Steam tempeh for 15 minutes and set aside.

Warm a large saucepan that has been generously sprayed with cooking oil. Add the garlic, onion, bell pepper, and diced veggie bacon and cook over medium-high heat for 3 minutes. Crumble the tempeh and add to the pan with the crushed red pepper. Cook mixture 10 minutes, stirring frequently. Add sherry, broth, and remaining filling ingredients. Reduce heat and simmer mixture, stirring occasionally.

For the crust: Place the cornmeal in the bowl of a food processor with the salt, baking powder, egg replacer powder, yeast, and marjoram. Pulse to mix. Add rice butter and Fruitsource and blend. Pour soymilk through feed tube and process until incorporated into the batter.

Spread filling evenly in prepared pan and top with cornmeal batter. Sprinkle with dried basil and marjoram. Bake 30 minutes, or until golden brown.

NUTRITION ANALYSIS: PER 10-OUNCE SERVING

Enlightened Tamale Pie
Protein 24 g, carbohydrate 40 g, fiber 6 g, fat 5 g, cholesterol 0 mg, calcium 205 mg, sodium 601 mg
Calories 298: from protein 32%, from carbohydrate 53%, from fat 16%

Traditional Tamale Pie
Protein 20 g, carbohydrate 25 g, fiber 3 g, fat 34 g, cholesterol 124 mg, calcium 163 mg, sodium 837 mg
Calories 482: from protein 16%, from carbohydrate 21%, from fat 63%

Tequila Fajitas

*Vegetarian Soyrizo and TVP Chiken Strips stand in for
the traditional ingredients in these delicious fajitas.*

*8
Servings*

2 cups TVP Chiken Strips
1½ cups chicken-flavor vegetarian
    broth, boiling
2 teaspoons olive oil
¼ teaspoon crushed red pepper
½ 10-ounce package Soyrizo
    vegetarian chorizo
5 cloves garlic, minced
1 large yellow onion, halved
    crosswise and cut into ⅛-inch
    wedges
1 green bell pepper, cut into 2-inch
    strips

1 yellow bell pepper, cut into 2-inch
    strips
2 cups sliced carrots
3 cups unpeeled red-skinned
    potatoes, cut into ¼-inch wedges
    (3 medium)
1 medium zucchini, sliced lengthwise
    and then crosswise
⅓ cup tequila
½ cup chicken-flavor vegetarian
    broth, boiling
½ cup chopped fresh cilantro
8 whole wheat tortillas

Fajitas originated in Texas as a cowboy snack of grilled meat and veggies wrapped in a flour tortilla.

Place TVP in a medium-size bowl, add 1½ cups boiling broth, stir thoroughly, and set aside.

Heat oil and crushed pepper in a large electric frying pan or Dutch oven over medium-high heat for 2 minutes. Remove casing from the Soyrizo and crumble into pan. Sauté 5 minutes, or until browned, stirring frequently. Add garlic, onion, and bell peppers and sauté 3 minutes. Add carrots and potatoes and and cook mixture 10 minutes, stirring frequently. Add zucchini, tequila, ½ cup boiling broth, and cilantro. Reduce heat to low and simmer mixture, stirring occasionally, 10 minutes, or until potatoes are cooked through. Warm tortillas covered in oven, microwave, or tortilla warmer. Serve with your favorite salsa, sliced tomatoes, and guacamole.

NUTRITION ANALYSIS: PER 11-OUNCE SERVING (1 FAJITA)

Enlightened Tequila Fajitas
Protein 18 g, carbohydrate 50 g, fiber 10 g, fat 2 g,
cholesterol 0 mg, calcium 64 mg, sodium 426 mg
Calories 301: from protein 25%,
from carbohydrate 68%, from fat 7%

Traditional Tequila Fajitas
Protein 27 g, carbohydrate 43 g, fiber 4 g, fat 22 g,
cholesterol 66 mg, calcium 89 mg, sodium 858 mg
Calories 501: from protein 23%,
from carbohydrate 36%, from fat 41%

Zesty Scramble with Country Potatoes

*With the versatile Tofu Hero Garden Scrambler,
lite silken tofu, and Vegi-Deli pepperoni, this quick
and easy brunch is both healthy and delicious.*

Country Potatoes

1½ teaspoons olive oil
1 tablespoon dried minced garlic
½ cup chopped onion
½ cup chopped red bell pepper
3 medium unpeeled russet potatoes,
  halved vertically and cut into
  ¼-inch slices

1 large fresh tomato, chopped
1 teaspoon dried basil
¼ teaspoon paprika
¼ cup dry vermouth
¼ teaspoon sea salt

Scramble

1 26-gram package Tofu Hero
  Garden Scrambler
⅓ cup boiling water

1½ teaspoons olive oil
½ cup Vegi-Deli pepperoni, diced
1 12.3-ounce package lite silken tofu

For the potatoes: Heat olive oil and dried minced garlic in 10-inch frying pan or 5-quart saucepan over medium-high heat for 1 minute. Add onion and bell pepper and cook 2 minutes; then add potatoes. Cook mixture 10 minutes, stirring frequently. Add tomato, basil, and paprika. Cook 3 minutes; then add the vermouth and salt. Cook 5 minutes over medium heat, or until potatoes are tender.

Zesty Scramble with Country Potatoes *(continued)*

For the scramble: While potatoes cook, stir Tofu Hero dry mix into boiling water, and set aside.

Over medium-high heat, heat the olive oil in a 10-inch frying pan. Add diced pepperoni and cook 3 minutes. Drain tofu, place in a medium bowl, and mash with a potato masher; add to the pepperoni. Cook mixture 5 minutes, stirring frequently. Add liquid spice mixture (Tofu Hero) and stir. Lower heat to simmer.

NUTRITION ANALYSIS: PER 8¹/₂-OUNCE SERVING

**Enlightened Zesty Scramble
with Country Potatoes**
Protein 14 g, carbohydrate 37 g, fiber 4 g, fat 4 g,
cholesterol 0 mg, calcium 58 mg, sodium 420 mg
Calories 245: from protein 24%,
from carbohydrate 61%, from fat 16%

**Traditional Zesty Scrambled Eggs
and Country Potatoes**
Protein 13 g, carbohydrate 26 g, fiber 3 g, fat 24 g,
cholesterol 238 mg, calcium 41 mg, sodium 635 mg
Calories 370: from protein 14%,
from carbohydrate 28%, from fat 58%

Pasta and Pizza

Children aren't the only ones who love pasta and pizza. Italian food has consistently been chosen the American "food of choice" when dining out. Pasta is available in a mind-boggling array of shapes and sizes—every conceivable form from the ethereal angel hair to orecchiette (little ears) and from ziti to linguine. They are all pretty much interchangeable. However, when making a primavera, with chunks of fresh cooked veggies, or a cacciatore-style dish with pieces of vegetarian meat, the smaller style like penne, rigatoni, bow ties, or fusilli (twists) would be more suitable.

In this section there are dishes like Penne Vodka and "Chicken" and Pasta in a Tomato-Basil "Cream" Sauce that are entirely dairy- and egg-free. There are several baked, stuffed pasta dishes—classics such as Spinach Lasagna and Manicotti "Bolognese"—and unique creations such as Asparagus Lasagna and Potato Lasagna. Because these rich and flavorful dishes are made without eggs, butter, cream, or other animal products, they are all cholesterol-free and very low in fat. My pasta sauces are equally flavorful, using only a touch of olive oil and taking advantage of the convenience and availability of the wide array of vegetarian alternatives.

Pizza is a wonderful finger food that occupies a special place in the American dining experience. Thought to have evolved from Egyptian flat bread, pizza became popular in the United States after World War II, when soldiers returning from Italy wanted to reproduce the treat they had discovered. Literally translated, "pizza" means pie. A thin crust, olive oil, sauce, various toppings, and cheese are the basic components of a traditional pizza. Variations like deep-dish pizza, with its thick, breadlike crust, and gourmet pizzas with exotic toppings have become quite popular in recent years. In my soy-centered approach to cookery, I take every opportunity to replace unwanted ingredients with those that promote health and well-being. My pizzas are enhanced with ingredients such as veggie pepperoni and soy Parmesan cheese. My pizza crusts are fortified variously with flaxseed meal and nutritious flours like spelt and kamut and, of course, soy flour. So *mangia,* it's good for you!

PASTA DISHES

Fresh Pasta Dough

*This easy pasta dough, made in the food processor,
has a light texture from silken tofu in place of eggs.*

¾ cup lite silken tofu
1 ½ cups semolina flour mix (a blend
    of semolina and kamut flours)
⅓ cup soy flour
½ teaspoon sea salt

1 tablespoon olive oil
1 tablespoon liquid Fruitsource
1 tablespoon enriched 1% fat
    soymilk

Place tofu in food processor and blend. Add semolina and soy flours and salt
and blend. While motor is running, add remaining ingredients. Dough should
form a ball.

Place dough on work surface sprinkled with unbleached flour. Dust dough
lightly with flour and knead 5 minutes, adding flour as needed to produce an
elastic pasta dough. Place dough in floured bowl and cover with plastic wrap. Set
aside to let rest for an hour. Shape dough for spaghetti, fettuccini, or ravioli.

Variations: For delicious variations on this basic pasta recipe, add either 1½
teaspoons dried basil or marjoram or 1 teaspoon granulated garlic or sage when
adding the flours.

NUTRITION ANALYSIS: PER 4-OUNCE SERVING

Enlightened Fresh Pasta Dough
Protein 6 g, carbohydrate 22 g, fiber 2 g, fat 3 g,
cholesterol 0 mg, calcium 21 mg, sodium 156 mg
Calories 135: from protein 18%,
from carbohydrate 63%, from fat 19%

Traditional Fresh Pasta Dough
Protein 8 g, carbohydrate 30 g, fiber 2 g, fat 8 g,
cholesterol 106 mg, calcium 21 mg, sodium 300 mg
Calories 232: from protein 15%,
from carbohydrate 54%, from fat 31%

Fresh Spinach Pasta Dough

*Made with fresh baby spinach leaves, this colorful pasta is a good choice
for ravioli or spinach fettuccini. Served with your favorite tomato sauce.*

*Makes 1 Pound
of Pasta*

⅔ cup lite silken tofu

2 cups firmly packed baby spinach
leaves

1⅓ cups semolina flour mix (a blend
of semolina and kamut flours)

½ cup soy flour

½ teaspoon sea salt

1 tablespoon olive oil

¼ cup unbleached flour
(approximate)

Place tofu in food processor and blend. Add spinach and process. Add semolina
and soy flours, salt, and olive oil; blend. Add unbleached flour 1 tablespoon at
a time, until dough begins to form a ball, blending after each addition. Dough
may be sticky, but will become more cohesive as more flour is added during the
kneading process.

Place dough on work surface sprinkled with unbleached flour. Dust dough
lightly with flour and knead 5 minutes, adding flour as needed to produce an
elastic pasta dough. Place dough in floured bowl and cover with plastic wrap.
Set aside to let rest for an hour. Proceed with recipe.

NUTRITION ANALYSIS: PER 4¼-OUNCE SERVING

Enlightened Fresh Spinach Pasta Dough
Protein 7 g, carbohydrate 19 g, fiber 2 g, fat 3 g,
cholesterol 0 mg, calcium 36 mg, sodium 164 mg
Calories 129: from protein 20%,
from carbohydrate 57%, from fat 22%

Traditional Fresh Spinach Pasta Dough
Protein 8 g, carbohydrate 28 g, fiber 2 g, fat 8 g,
cholesterol 106 mg, calcium 30 mg, sodium 308 mg
Calories 220: from protein 15%,
from carbohydrate 52%, from fat 33%

Asparagus Lasagna

*Delicate spring asparagus in a "ham"-spiked "cream"
sauce enhances this luscious garden lasagna.*

Pasta and
Pizza

ℒ

175

Asparagus Layer

¾ pound fresh asparagus spears,
   trimmed and cut into
   3-inch pieces
3 tablespoons olive oil
5 cloves garlic, minced
½ cup chopped red onion
⅓ cup chopped red bell pepper

1 6-ounce package veggie Canadian
   bacon, diced
3 tablespoons unbleached flour
½ cup dry vermouth
1½ cups enriched 1% fat soymilk
1 teaspoon dried thyme
¼ cup nutritional yeast

Garden Tofu Filling

1 20.6-gram package Tofu Hero
   Italian Herb Medley
½ cup boiling water
3 12.3-ounce packages lite silken
   tofu, drained
3 cloves garlic, minced

½ cup chopped scallions
1 cup finely shredded carrots
1 cup coarsely shredded zucchini
⅓ cup soy Parmesan cheese
½ cup nutritional yeast
2 teaspoons dried oregano

1 26-ounce jar fat-free tomato sauce
¾ of 16-ounce package Barilla
   lasagna noodles
2 fresh tomatoes, thinly sliced

Preheat oven to 350°.

For the asparagus layer: Lightly steam asparagus for 4 minutes; then plunge into ice water to stop cooking. Set aside.

Heat oil in a medium saucepan and sauté the garlic, onion, bell pepper, and veggie bacon over medium-high heat for 5 minutes. Stir in flour and mix thoroughly; add vermouth and reduce heat to medium low. Add soymilk gradually,

Asparagus Lasagna *(continued)*

stirring to blend, while mixture thickens. Stir in thyme and nutritional yeast; cover and set aside.

For the Garden Tofu Filling: Combine Tofu Hero with boiling water and set aside. Place tofu in a large bowl and mash with a potato masher. Add garlic, scallions, and shredded vegetables. Add Tofu Hero mixture, soy Parmesan, nutritional yeast, and oregano. Mix thoroughly and set aside.

To assemble: Spread a layer of tomato sauce evenly along the bottom of a 9-by-13-inch baking pan. Top with a layer of *uncooked* noodles. Add broken noodles around the edges to make an even fit. Layer with ⅔ of the garden filling. Top with a layer of noodles and place tomato slices evenly over noodles. Layer with remaining garden filling and top with steamed asparagus. Cover asparagus with "cream" sauce. Top with a layer of noodles and top noodles with remaining tomato sauce. Cover casserole with foil and bake for 30 minutes. Remove foil and bake an additional 15 minutes. Let lasagna set for 10 to 15 minutes before serving. Reheats very well.

NUTRITION ANALYSIS: PER 9-OUNCE SERVING

Enlightened Asparagus Lasagna
Protein 20 g, carbohydrate 33 g, fiber 4 g, fat 5 g, cholesterol 0 mg, calcium 81 mg, sodium 374 mg
Calories 242: from protein 32%, from carbohydrate 51%, from fat 17%

Traditional Asparagus Lasagna
Protein 17 g, carbohydrate 18 g, fiber 2 g, fat 22 g, cholesterol 55 mg, calcium 314 mg, sodium 556 mg.
Calories 335: from protein 20%, from carbohydrate 21%, from fat 58%

Artichoke-Stuffed Ravioli

*The artichoke filling is rich and creamy-tasting
in this exceptionally delicious dish.*

*Makes
60 Ravioli
(12 Servings)*

1 *double* recipe of Fresh Pasta Dough
(page 173)

Filling:
1 12.3-ounce package lite silken tofu
3 cloves garlic, peeled
1 14-ounce can quartered artichoke
hearts, drained
1 small leek, cleaned and diced

1 12.6-gram package Tofu Hero
Italian Herb Medley
½ teaspoon dried thyme
⅛ teaspoon coarse black pepper
⅓ cup nutritional yeast

olive oil
1 25-ounce jar basil-and-tomato sauce

Prepare fresh pasta dough to the resting stage, and see "Making Filled Pasta," page 50.

Place the tofu in food processor and blend. Add peeled garlic and process. Add artichoke hearts; process. Add the leeks, Tofu Hero, thyme, pepper, and yeast; process.

Fill pasta. Once ravioli have been filled and set aside, bring 3 quarts of salted water in each of two large saucepans to a boil over high heat, adding a tablespoon of olive oil to the water. Divide the ravioli between the two pans and bring to a second boil, reduce heat to medium high, and boil gently for 15 to

Artichoke-Stuffed Ravioli *(continued)*

20 minutes, or until tender, stirring occasionally. Remove ravioli with a slotted spoon and serve with tomato sauce.

Variation: Combine cooked ravioli with tomato sauce in a covered casserole. Sprinkle with soy Parmesan cheese and bake in a preheated 375° oven for 20 minutes. Serve with additional sauce.

NUTRITION ANALYSIS: PER 7-OUNCE SERVING (5 RAVIOLI)

Enlightened Artichoke-Stuffed Ravioli
Protein 6 g, carbohydrate 22 g, fiber 2 g, fat 3 g,
cholesterol 0 mg, calcium 21 mg, sodium 156 mg
Calories 135: from protein 18%,
from carbohydrate 63%, from fat 19%

Traditional Artichoke-Stuffed Ravioli
Protein 8 g, carbohydrate 30 g, fiber 2 g, fat 8 g,
cholesterol 106 mg, calcium 21 mg, sodium 300 mg
Calories 232: from protein 15%,
from carbohydrate 54%, from fat 31%

"Beef" Ravioli

Spinach ravioli with a hearty meatlike filling
is served in a merlot-laced tomato sauce.

Makes
40 Ravioli
(10 Servings)

1 recipe of Fresh Spinach Pasta Dough (page 174)

Filling

olive oil cooking spray
1½ teaspoons olive oil
3 cloves garlic, minced
1 12-ounce package ground beef
   alternative

1 can tomato paste
3 tablespoons dry sherry
1 teaspoon dried thyme
1 teaspoon onion powder
2 tablespoons nutritional yeast

Sauce

½ cup merlot (red wine)
1 25-ounce jar fat-free pasta sauce

¼ cup snipped fresh
basil

THE HEARTY FILLING can be used to stuff basic fresh pasta, herb pasta dough, or mushroom caps.

Prepare Fresh Spinach Pasta Dough to the resting stage.

For the filling: Spray a 10-inch frying pan with oil and add olive oil. Sauté garlic over medium-high heat for 2 minutes and add vegetarian ground beef. Cook 5 minutes, stirring frequently. Stir in 2 tablespoons of tomato paste and the sherry. Reduce heat to medium low and add thyme, onion powder, and 1 tablespoon of the yeast. Simmer 5 minutes, stirring occasionally and set filling aside to cool.

For the sauce: In a medium saucepan, combine the wine and tomato sauce and cook over medium heat 3 minutes. Spoon in the remaining tomato paste and 1 tablespoon yeast, along with the fresh basil. Reduce heat and simmer, stirring occasionally.

Once ravioli have been filled and set aside, add a tablespoons of olive oil to 3 quarts of salted water in a large saucepan and bring to a boil over high heat. Place the ravioli in boiling water, bring to a second boil, reduce heat to medium high, and cook ravioli at a low boil for 15 to 20 minutes, or until tender. Remove ravioli from pan with a slotted spoon and serve with tomato sauce.

NUTRITION ANALYSIS: PER 9-OUNCE SERVING (4 RAVIOLI)

Enlightened "Beef" Ravioli
Protein 12 g, carbohydrate 29 g, fiber 4 g, fat 4 g, cholesterol 0 mg, calcium 54 mg, sodium 407 mg
Calories 192: from protein 24%, from carbohydrate 59%, from fat 17%

Traditional Beef Ravioli
Protein 15 g, carbohydrate 39 g, fiber 2 g, fat 20 g, cholesterol 117 mg, calcium 94 mg, sodium 828 mg
Calories 397: from protein 15%, from carbohydrate 39%, from fat 46%

"Chicken" and Pasta in a Tomato-Basil "Cream" Sauce

Chopped Chiken TVP provides authentic flavor and texture to this delightful dairy-free creamed pasta dish. Reheats well.

12 Servings

2 cups Chopped Chiken TVP
1½ cups chicken-flavor vegetarian broth, boiling
2 teaspoons olive oil
1 tablespoon dried minced garlic
1 medium red onion, cut into ¼-inch wedges
⅓ cup chopped red bell pepper
6 ounces portobello mushrooms, sliced
⅓ cup plus 2 tablespoons dry sherry
1 14½-ounce can Italian-style stewed tomatoes
1½ cups frozen white corn, defrosted

8 ounces medium-wide pasta (½ inch) cooked al dente
1 12.3-ounce package firm regular silken tofu
5 cloves garlic, peeled
1 15-ounce can Great Northern beans
⅓ cup nutritional yeast
1 cup enriched 1% fat soymilk
1 20.6-gram package Tofu Hero Italian Herb Medley
¼ cup mellow white miso
¼ cup chopped fresh basil
2 teaspoons dried basil, divided

Combine Chopped Chiken TVP and boiling broth in a medium bowl and set aside for 15 minutes.

In a large saucepan or electric frying pan, over medium-high heat, warm oil and minced garlic for 1 minute. Add the onion and bell pepper and cook 3 minutes. Add reconstituted TVP and cook 5 minutes, stirring frequently. Add the mushrooms, ⅓ cup sherry, tomatoes, and corn. Cook mixture 3 minutes. Reduce heat to low, add cooked pasta, and simmer, stirring occasionally.

Place tofu in food processor and blend until smooth. Add garlic and process. Add the beans, yeast, soymilk, and Tofu Hero and blend. In a small bowl, cream miso with 2 tablespoons sherry and add to the tofu mixture; process until smooth. Stir tofu mixture into the pan; add fresh basil and 1 teaspoon of dried basil. Simmer mixture, stirring occasionally, 5 minutes, or until ready to serve. Sprinkle with remaining teaspoon of dried basil just before serving.

NUTRITION ANALYSIS: PER 9-OUNCE SERVING

Enlightened "Chicken" and Pasta
in a Tomato-Basil "Cream" Sauce
Protein 19 g, carbohydrate 40 g, fiber 8 g, fat 3 g,
cholesterol 0 mg, calcium 80 mg, sodium 243 mg
Calories 244: from protein 29%,
from carbohydrate 61%, from fat 10%

Traditional Chicken and Pasta
in a Tomato-Basil Cream Sauce
Protein 28 g, carbohydrate 26 g, fiber 2 g, fat 20 g,
cholesterol 97 mg, calcium 218 mg, sodium 400 mg
Calories 390: from protein 28%,
from carbohydrate 26%, from fat 46%

"Chicken," Bow Ties, and Wild Mushrooms

Exotic chanterelles add texture and flavor to this vegetarian chicken and pasta dish. If chanterelles are not available, use any wild mushroom.

8 Servings

1½ teaspoons olive oil
¼ teaspoon crushed red pepper
3 cloves garlic, minced
1 rib celery, chopped
1 medium Vidalia or other sweet onion, chopped
1 1-pound package chicken-style seitan (reserve broth)
1 cup chanterelle mushrooms, drained (or reconstitute 3 ounces dried mushrooms)

½ cup marsala
1 25-ounce jar fat-free tomato sauce
1 14½-ounce can Italian-style stewed tomatoes
1 6-ounce can tomato paste
¾ cup reserved seitan broth
⅓ cup enriched 1% fat soymilk
¼ cup nutritional yeast
1 teaspoon dried thyme
1 teaspoon dried basil
1 8-ounce package bow tie pasta

Warm oil and crushed pepper in a 5-quart saucepan over medium-high heat for 1 minute. Add the garlic, celery, and onion and cook 3 minutes. Add seitan and cook 5 minutes, stirring frequently. Add the mushrooms and wine and cook 3 minutes. Add the tomato sauce and stewed tomatoes. Spoon the tomato paste into the sauce, fill the tomato paste can with the reserved broth and add, stirring to dissolve.

In a small bowl, whisk together the soymilk and yeast and add to the sauce with the thyme and basil. Reduce heat and simmer, stirring occasionally.

Cook pasta according to package directions. Toss cooked pasta with sauce and serve with additional sauce.

NUTRITION ANALYSIS: PER 11-OUNCE SERVING

Enlightened "Chicken," Bow Ties, and Wild Mushrooms
Protein 16 g, carbohydrate 52 g, fiber 11 g, fat 3 g, cholesterol 0 mg, calcium 65 mg, sodium 376 mg
Calories 301: from protein 21%, from carbohydrate 69%, from fat 10%

Traditional Chicken, Bow Ties, and Wild Mushrooms
Protein 25 g, carbohydrate 39 g, fiber 6 g, fat 17 g, cholesterol 70 mg, calcium 112 mg, sodium 874 mg
Calories 403: from protein 25%, from carbohydrate 38%, from fat 38%

Fettuccini with Creamed "Sausage" and Carrots

*Sausage-style Gimme Lean is the key to the
complex blend of flavors and textures in this hearty dish.*

1 tablespoon olive oil
¼ teaspoon crushed red pepper
5 cloves garlic, minced
¾ cup chopped yellow onion
⅓ cup chopped red bell pepper
1⅔ cups coarsely shredded carrots
1 14-ounce package Gimme Lean,
  sausage style
1 14½-ounce can Italian-style stewed
  tomatoes

½ cup white wine
1 12.3-ounce package lite silken tofu
1 cup plus ¼ cup enriched 1% fat
  soymilk
½ cup nutritional yeast
1 teaspoon dried marjoram
1 teaspoon dried basil
2 tablespoons mellow white miso
¼ cup chopped fresh basil
1 pound egg-free fettuccini

Heat 1½ teaspoons oil and crushed pepper in a 5-quart saucepan for 1 minute
over medium-high heat. Add garlic, onion, bell pepper, and carrots and sauté
5 minutes, or until crisp-tender. Add remaining 1½ teaspoons oil and veggie
sausage. Continue to cook mixture 5 minutes, stirring frequently. Add tomatoes and wine, lower heat, and simmer 5 minutes.

In food processor, blend tofu until smooth. Add 1 cup of the soymilk, nutritional yeast, marjoram, and basil. In a small bowl, blend miso with the remaining ¼ cup of soymilk and then add to processor and process until smooth. Add
tofu mixture to saucepan gradually, stirring after each addition. Add chopped
fresh basil and simmer until ready to serve. Cook fettuccini according to package directions and toss with sauce. Serve with additional sauce.

NUTRITION ANALYSIS: PER 9-OUNCE SERVING

Enlightened Fettuccini with Creamed "Sausage" and Carrots	Traditional Fettuccini with Creamed Sausage and Carrots
Protein 18 g, carbohydrate 43 g, fiber 5 g, fat 3 g, cholesterol 0 mg, calcium 81 mg, sodium 307 mg	Protein 11 g, carbohydrate 29 g, fiber 2 g, fat 27 g, cholesterol 84 mg, calcium 77 mg, sodium 295 mg
Calories 266: from protein 27%, from carbohydrate 64%, from fat 9%	Calories 407: from protein 11%, from carbohydrate 29%, from fat 60%

Gnocchi Primavera

*These delicious dumplings are traditionally
made using eggs and/or cheese.*

Gnocchi
6 medium Yukon Gold potatoes,
  peeled and quartered

4 cups semolina flour mix (a blend of
  semolina and kamut flours)

Primavera Sauce
1½ teaspoons plus 1 tablespoon olive
  oil
⅛ teaspoon crushed red pepper
4 cloves garlic, minced
½ cup thinly sliced scallions
¼ cup chopped red bell pepper
1 medium zucchini, cubed
1 26-ounce jar fat-free tomato sauce

1 14.5-ounce can Italian-style diced
  tomatoes
1 6-ounce can tomato paste
⅓ cup white wine
⅔ cup frozen peas, thawed
2 tablespoons capers
1 bay leaf

Place potatoes in a large saucepan with enough salted water to cover. Boil until
tender when pierced, about 20 to 25 minutes. Drain.

In a large stovetop- and oven-safe baking dish, heat 1½ teaspoons oil and
crushed pepper over medium-high heat for 1 minute. Add the garlic, scallions,
bell pepper, and zucchini and sauté 5 minutes. Add the remaining ingredients;
reduce heat to low and simmer, stirring occasionally, until ready to assemble.

Preheat oven to 350°. Transfer potatoes to a large bowl and mash thoroughly. Add 3 cups of the flour and knead in the bowl until dough forms. Add
more flour as necessary until dough is no longer sticky. Divide dough into four
pieces and turn onto a floured surface. With floured hands, roll each piece into

a long cylinder about 2 inches in diameter; then cut each cylinder into 1-inch slices. With a floured fork, make an indentation in the center of each slice and with a gentle rolling motion, flip the dough over to form gnocchi. Set aside on a floured board. Fill a large saucepan with salted water and add 1 tablespoon of oil. Bring to a boil and add gnocchi, using a slotted spoon. Bring water to a second boil and lower heat to simmer. Gnocchi will rise to the top in about 15 minutes. Stir occasionally and simmer 5 minutes. Combine cooked gnocchi with sauce and bake, uncovered, for 15 minutes.

NUTRITION ANALYSIS: PER 11-OUNCE SERVING

Enlightened Gnocchi Primavera
Protein 11 g, carbohydrate 67 g, fiber 6 g, fat 2 g,
cholesterol 0 mg, calcium 33 mg, sodium 297 mg
Calories 325: from protein 14%,
from carbohydrate 82%, from fat 4%

Traditional Gnocchi Primavera
Protein 14 g, carbohydrate 71 g, fiber 5 g, fat 11 g,
cholesterol 39 mg, calcium 114 mg, sodium 759 mg
Calories 433: from protein 12%,
from carbohydrate 65%, from fat 23%

Manicotti "Bolognese"

*The delicious filling in this Italian favorite makes optimal use
of alternative ingredients like textured vegetable protein,
lite silken tofu, soy Parmesan cheese, and nutritional yeast.*

1 cup TVP, ground beef style
¾ cup beef-flavor vegetarian broth,
   boiling
1 12.3-ounce package lite silken tofu,
   drained
3 cloves garlic, minced
½ cup sliced scallions
1 10-ounce package frozen chopped
   spinach, thawed and drained

1 20.6-gram package Tofu Hero,
   Italian Herb Medley
¼ cup soy Parmesan cheese
2 tablespoons nutritional yeast
1 8-ounce package manicotti
1 26-ounce jar tomato sauce

Preheat oven to 350°.

Combine TVP and boiling broth in a medium bowl and set aside.

Place tofu in a large bowl and mash with a potato masher. Add garlic and
scallions and stir in spinach. Add Tofu Hero, soy Parmesan, and nutritional
yeast. Add reconstituted TVP, mix thoroughly, and set aside.

Cook manicotti according to package directions and rinse with cold water.

Spread a thin layer of tomato sauce evenly on the bottom of a 9-by-13-inch
baking pan. Holding each cooked manicotti open gently, stuff with filling. Do
not overfill. Lay filled manicotti in a single layer in pan, top with sauce, and
cover casserole with foil. Place in preheated oven and bake for 30 minutes.
Remove foil, sprinkle with additional soy Parmesan cheese, if desired, and bake
an additional 15 minutes. Let sit for 10 minutes before serving. Reheats very
well.

NUTRITION ANALYSIS: PER 10-OUNCE SERVING

Enlightened Manicotti "Bolognese"
Protein 20 g, carbohydrate 38 g, fiber 6 g, fat 3 g,
cholesterol 0 mg, calcium 72 mg, sodium 594 mg
Calories 242: from protein 31%,
from carbohydrate 60%, from fat 10%

Traditional Manicotti Bolognese
Protein 23 g, carbohydrate 31 g, fiber 4 g, fat 23 g,
cholesterol 97 mg, calcium 242 mg, sodium 661 mg
Calories 419: from protein 22%,
from carbohydrate 30%, from fat 48%

Pasta e Fagiole

*This delicious rustic favorite is "naturally" delicious
when made with healthy ingredients.*

2 teaspoons olive oil
¼ teaspoon crushed red pepper
1½ teaspoons dried minced garlic
½ cup chopped red onion
1 6-ounce package veggie Canadian
    bacon
½ cup dry vermouth
1 25-ounce jar fat-free tomato sauce
1 6-ounce can tomato paste

¾ cup water
1 15-ounce can Great Northern
    beans
¼ cup nutritional yeast
1 bay leaf
⅓ cup chopped fresh basil
1 teaspoons dried thyme
1½ teaspoons dried oregano
1 16-ounce package elbow macaroni

Warm oil, crushed pepper, and dried garlic in a 5-quart saucepan over medium-high heat for 2 minutes. Add the chopped onion and veggie bacon and sauté 3 minutes. Add the vermouth and cook mixture, stirring occasionally, 3 minutes. Add the tomato sauce, spoon the tomato paste into the sauce, fill the tomato-paste can with water, and add to sauce. Stir to blend. Reduce heat to low and add remaining ingredients, except for pasta. Simmer gently, stirring occasionally, for 10 minutes, or until ready to serve. Cook pasta according to package directions and toss with 2 cups of sauce. Serve with additional sauce.

NUTRITION ANALYSIS: PER 9-OUNCE SERVING

Enlightened Pasta e Fagiole
Protein 16 g, carbohydrate 48 g, fiber 6 g, fat 2 g,
cholesterol 0 mg, calcium 51 mg, sodium 348 mg
Calories 274: from protein 23%,
from carbohydrate 71%, from fat 7%

Traditional Pasta e Fagiole
Protein 14 g, carbohydrate 44 g, fiber 5 g, fat 11 g,
cholesterol 18 mg, calcium 122 mg, sodium 820 mg
Calories 332: from protein 17%,
from carbohydrate 53%, from fat 31%

Pasta Twists with "Sausage" and Spinach

*Richly flavorful vegetarian sausage is the healthy
counterpoint to traditional sausage in this delightful dish.*

*12
Servings*

1½ teaspoons plus 1½ teaspoons
  olive oil
1 11.2-ounce package Lean Links
  Italian, cut into 1-inch pieces
3 garlic cloves, minced
½ cup chopped red onion
⅓ cup chopped red bell pepper
⅓ cup dry vermouth
1 25-ounce jar fat-free tomato sauce

1 14½-ounce can Italian-style diced
  tomatoes
1 6-ounce can tomato paste
1 large bay leaf
1 teaspoon dried basil
1 16-ounce package pasta twists
  (fusilli)
2 6-ounce packages baby spinach

Warm 1½ teaspoons oil in a 5-quart saucepan over medium-high heat. Add the veggie sausage and sauté 7 minutes, browning on all sides. Remove from pan and set aside. Add the remaining 1½ teaspoons oil to the pan and add the garlic, chopped onion, and bell pepper. Sauté 3 minutes and add the browned sausage back into the pan; cook 5 minutes. Add vermouth; cook 2 minutes; then add tomato sauce and diced tomatoes. Spoon tomato paste into the sauce, stirring to blend. Add a tomato-paste can of water, bay leaf, and basil. Reduce heat and simmer, stirring occasionally.

  Cook pasta according to package directions, adding spinach in the last 2 minutes of cooking. Drain. Discard bay leaf; toss 1½ cups sauce with pasta and spinach mixture. Serve with additional sauce.

NUTRITION ANALYSIS: PER 10-OUNCE SERVING

Enlightened Pasta Twists with "Sausage" and Spinach	Traditional Pasta Twists with Sausage and Spinach
Protein 11 g, carbohydrate 44 g, fiber 5 g, fat 4 g, cholesterol 0 mg, calcium 68 mg, sodium 420 mg Calories 251: from protein 18%, from carbohydrate 70%, from fat 12%	Protein 15 g, carbohydrate 39 g, fiber 4 g, fat 14 g, cholesterol 25 mg, calcium 122 mg, sodium 908 mg Calories 357: from protein 17%, from carbohydrate: 46%, from fat 37%

Penne Vodka

*In this healthy incarnation, penne pasta is drenched
in a rich, velvety sauce accented with diced veggie bacon.*

Pasta and
Pizza

189

12
Servings

1½ teaspoons olive oil
⅛ teaspoon crushed red pepper
2 teaspoons grated fresh gingerroot
4 garlic cloves, minced
1 medium yellow onion, chopped
1 6-ounce package veggie Canadian
  bacon
1 14½-ounce can Italian-style stewed
  tomatoes
1 12.3-ounce package lite silken tofu
1¼ cups chicken-flavor vegetarian
  broth

½ cup vodka
1 tablespoon cornstarch
⅔ cup nutritional yeast
⅓ cup grated soy Parmesan cheese
1 31.3-gram package Tofu Hero
  Shanghai Stir Fry
⅓ cup boiling water
2 tablespoons chopped fresh cilantro
1 16-ounce package penne pasta

Warm oil, crushed pepper, and grated gingerroot in a 5-quart saucepan over medium-high heat for 2 minutes. Add the garlic, onion, and diced veggie bacon and sauté 5 minutes. Snip stewed tomatoes into smaller pieces and add to the pan. Reduce heat to low and simmer mixture, stirring occasionally.

Place the tofu in food processor and blend. Add broth, vodka, cornstarch, yeast, and soy Parmesan and process. Stir Tofu Hero into boiling water and set aside a minute before adding to the food processor; blend. Add the tofu mixture to the pan with cilantro and stir to blend. Simmer gently, stirring occasionally, until ready to serve. Cook pasta according to package directions and toss with 1½ cups "cream" sauce. Serve with additional sauce.

NUTRITION ANALYSIS: PER 8-OUNCE SERVING

Enlightened Penne Vodka
Protein 22 g, carbohydrate 40 g, fiber 4 g, fat 3 g,
cholesterol 0 mg, calcium 40 mg, sodium 509 mg
Calories 280: from protein 32%,
from carbohydrate 59%, from fat 9%

Traditional Penne Vodka
Protein 14 g, carbohydrate 34 g, fiber 2 g, fat 19 g,
cholesterol 46 mg, calcium 146 mg, sodium 772 mg
Calories 406: from protein 13%,
from carbohydrate 33%, from fat 42%

"Pepperoni" Primavera

*Sauces with chunks of vegetables, like this luscious dish,
are best served with a short noodle pasta like penne or fusilli.
Here we use orecchiette, which means "little ear" in Italian.*

*8
Servings*

1 ½ teaspoons olive oil
¼ teaspoon crushed red pepper
1 tablespoon minced dried garlic
¼ cup chopped red onion
⅓ cup chopped red bell pepper
¼ cup diced Vegi-Deli pepperoni
1 25-ounce jar fat-free tomato sauce
1 14½-ounce can Italian-style stewed
    tomatoes

¼ cup dry vermouth
1 tablespoon capers
1 teaspoon dried thyme
1 teaspoon dried oregano
2 tablespoons nutritional yeast
1 16-ounce package orecchiette
    pasta

Over medium-high heat, warm oil, crushed pepper, and dried garlic in a
5-quart saucepan for 1 minute. Add onion, bell pepper, and veggie pepperoni
and sauté 3 minutes, stirring occasionally. Add tomato sauce and stewed tomatoes; cook 5 minutes and add vermouth. Reduce heat and simmer 3 minutes
before adding capers, thyme, oregano, and nutritional yeast. Simmer until ready
to serve, stirring occasionally.

Cook pasta according to package directions. Toss drained pasta with 1 ½ cups
sauce and serve additional sauce on the side.

NUTRITION ANALYSIS: PER 10 ¾-OUNCE SERVING

Enlightened "Pepperoni" Primavera
Protein 14 g, carbohydrate 58 g, fiber 6 g, fat 3 g,
cholesterol 0 mg, calcium 48 mg, sodium 314 mg
Calories 300: from protein 18%,
from carbohydrate 75%, from fat 7%

Traditional Pepperoni Primavera
Protein 12 g, carbohydrate 43 g, fiber 3 g, fat 15 g,
cholesterol 53 mg, calcium 55 mg, sodium 663 mg
Calories 352: from protein 14%,
from carbohydrate 49%, from fat 37%

Garden "Chicken" with Couscous

Very low in fat and calories, this tempting dish
makes it easy to bring the goodness of soy to the table.

Pasta and
Pizza

191

8
Servings

2 cups TVP Chiken Strips
1 cup chicken-flavor vegetarian
    broth, boiling
1 26-gram package Tofu Hero Gar-
    den Scrambler
⅓ cup boiling water
olive oil cooking spray
3 slices veggie Canadian bacon, diced
1¼ cups sliced baby-cut carrots

¼ cup dry vermouth
1 14½-ounce can Mexican-style
    stewed tomatoes
1¼ cups water
2 teaspoons rice butter spread
1 medium tomato, chopped
¼ teaspoon sea salt
½ cup currants
1 cup whole wheat couscous

Combine the TVP Chiken with the boiling broth in a medium bowl and set aside for 10 minutes. Combine the Tofu Hero mixture with the boiling water and set aside. Spray a 2-quart saucepan or a 2-quart oven-safe casserole with olive oil. Warm the pan and add the diced veggie bacon and sliced carrots. Cook 3 minutes over medium-high heat and add the reconstituted TVP. Cook mixture 5 minutes and add the vermouth and the Tofu Hero mixture. Reduce heat to medium low and add the stewed tomatoes. Cook, stirring occasionally, 10 minutes or until sauce has reduced and thickened.

Combine the water, rice butter, chopped tomato, and salt in a medium saucepan and bring to a boil. Add currants and couscous, stir, cover, and remove from heat. Let stand 5 minutes, fluff with a fork, and serve immediately with "chicken" mixture.

NUTRITION ANALYSIS: PER 8½-OUNCE SERVING

Enlightened Garden "Chicken" with Couscous
Protein 18 g, carbohydrate 40 g, fiber 6 g, fat 1 g,
cholesterol 0 mg, calcium 39 mg, sodium 398 mg
Calories 229: from protein 30%,
from carbohydrate 67%, from fat 3%

Traditional Garden Chicken with Couscous
Protein 25 g, carbohydrate 25 g, fiber 1 g, fat 12 g,
cholesterol 71 mg, calcium 32 mg, sodium 565 mg
Calories 321: from protein 32%,
from carbohydrate 33%, from fat 35%

Potato Lasagna

Potatoes may seem an unlikely addition to lasagna. In this dish, just one cup of diced potatoes in the savory "sausage" filling adds balance, and the flavor and texture of the tofu layer are dramatically enhanced by the addition of Tofu Hero Garden Scrambler.

*16
Servings*

Savory "Sausage" Filling
olive oil cooking spray
3 cloves garlic, minced
⅓ cup sliced scallions
⅓ cup chopped green bell pepper
2 small red-skinned potatoes, diced
 (1 cup, small dice)

1 14-ounce package Gimme Lean,
 sausage style
⅓ cup dry vermouth
¾ teaspoon dried thyme

Tofu Layer
1 26-gram package Tofu Hero
 Garden Scrambler
⅓ cup boiling water
3 12.3-ounce packages lite silken tofu
3 cloves garlic, minced
⅓ cup sliced scallions

⅓ cup chopped green bell pepper
1 teaspoon lemon pepper
¾ teaspoon dried marjoram
1 teaspoon onion powder
¼ cup soy Parmesan cheese

Sauce
¼ teaspoon crushed red pepper
1 25-ounce jar tomato sauce
1 14½-ounce can Mexican-style
 stewed tomatoes

1 6-ounce can tomato paste
¾ cup dry vermouth
1 16-ounce package Barilla lasagna
 noodles

For the filling: Spray a 10-inch frying pan with oil. Warm pan over medium-high heat. Add the garlic, scallions, and bell pepper. Sauté 3 minutes and add diced potatoes. Sauté mixture 5 minutes. Spray with additional oil and add the vegetarian sausage. Cook mixture 8 to 10 minutes, stirring frequently to break up sausage pieces. Add the vermouth and thyme, reduce heat to low, and simmer 5 minutes. Set aside.

For the tofu layer: Combine the Tofu Hero mix with the boiling water and set aside.

Place silken tofu in a large bowl and mash with a potato masher. Add the garlic, scallions, and bell pepper. Add the lemon pepper, marjoram, onion powder, and soy Parmesan. Add the Tofu Hero mixture and and mix thoroughly. Set aside.

For the sauce: Spray a 5-quart saucepan with oil, add the crushed pepper and warm for 1 minute over medium-high heat. Add the tomato sauce and stewed tomatoes. Spoon the tomato paste into the pan, add the vermouth, and stir to blend the tomato paste into the sauce.

To Assemble: Preheat oven to 350°. Spread a layer of tomato sauce evenly along the bottom of a 9-by-13-inch baking pan. Top with a layer of noodles. Add broken noodle pieces around edges to make an even fit. Top with the tofu filling, followed by a layer of noodles, and cover with sauce. Add a layer of savory sausage filling mixture and top with a layer of noodles. Cover noodles with remaining sauce and sprinkle with soy Parmesan cheese. Cover casserole with foil and bake for 45 minutes. Remove foil and bake an additional 15 minutes. Let lasagna sit for 15 minutes before serving. Reheats very well.

NUTRITION ANALYSIS: PER 8½-OUNCE SERVING

Enlightened Potato Lasagna	Traditional Potato Lasagna
Protein 15 g, carbohydrate 33 g, fiber 3 g, fat 1 g, cholesterol 0 mg, calcium 55 mg, sodium 432 mg Calories 215: from protein 29%, from carbohydrate 65%, from fat 6%	Protein 18 g, carbohydrate 29 g, fiber 3 g, fat 24 g, cholesterol 86 mg, calcium 237 mg, sodium 593 mg Calories 412: from protein 18%, from carbohydrate 28%, from fat 53%

"Sausage" and Mushrooms
with Polenta Pasta

*Vegetarian Italian sausage and polenta linguine are
delightful in this delicious wheat-free entrée. Be careful not to
overcook this delicate type of pasta.*

*12
Servings*

2 teaspoons olive oil
¼ teaspoon crushed red pepper
1 11.2-ounce package Lean Links
    Italian, cut into 1-inch pieces
5 cloves garlic, minced
1 medium red onion, cut into wedges
1 medium red bell pepper, chopped
8 ounces mushrooms, sliced
¾ cup dry vermouth

1 14½-ounce can Italian-style stewed
    tomatoes
1 25-ounce jar tomato-basil sauce
2 teaspoons capers
1 teaspoon dried thyme
1 teaspoon dried oregano
2 tablespoons nutritional yeast
1 12-ounce package polenta pasta

Heat oil and crushed pepper in an electric frying pan or Dutch oven for 1 minute over medium-high heat. Add "sausage" pieces and brown, turning frequently. Remove from pan and set aside. Sauté garlic, onion, and bell pepper 5 minutes, stirring occasionally. Return browned "sausage" to pan along with the mushrooms and cook 5 minutes, stirring frequently. Add vermouth, reduce heat, and simmer 3 minutes. Add tomatoes, tomato sauce, capers, thyme, and oregano. Stir in nutritional yeast and simmer until ready to serve. Cook polenta pasta according to package directions. *Do not overcook.* Toss drained pasta with sausage and mushrooms.

NUTRITION ANALYSIS: PER 9-OUNCE SERVING

Enlightened "Sausage" and Mushrooms
with Polenta Pasta
Protein 9 g, carbohydrate 33 g, fiber 4 g, fat 4 g,
cholesterol 0 mg, calcium 44 mg, sodium 380 mg
Calories 214: from protein 18%,
from carbohydrate 65%, from fat 17%

Traditional Sausage and
Mushrooms with Polenta Pasta
Protein 13 g, carbohydrate 32 g, fiber 3 g, fat 19 g,
cholesterol 32 mg, calcium 87 mg, sodium 568 mg
Calories 359: from protein 15%,
from carbohydrate 37%, from fat 49%

Sensational Spinach Lasagna

*This delicious lasagna is easy and healthy when
made with plant-based ingredients such as vegetarian ground beef,
lite silken tofu, and nutritional yeast.*

Tofu-Spinach Filling

1 20.6-gram package Tofu Hero
   Italian Herb Medley

½ cup boiling water

2 12.3-ounce packages lite silken
   tofu, drained

1 10-ounce package frozen chopped
   spinach, thawed and drained

1 teaspoon granulated garlic

¼ cup soy Parmesan cheese

2 tablespoons mellow white miso

2½ tablespoons dry vermouth

⅓ cup nutritional yeast

1 teaspoon dried thyme

1 teaspoon dried basil

"Ground Beef" Layer

1½ teaspoons olive oil

1 tablespoon minced dried
   garlic

2 26-ounce jars fat-free tomato sauce

1 16-ounce package Barilla lasagna
   noodles

¼ teaspoon crushed red pepper

1 12-ounce package vegetarian
   ground beef

½ teaspoon basil (for garnish)

Preheat oven to 350°.

For the filling: Stir Tofu Hero into boiling water and set aside. Place silken tofu in a large bowl and mash with a potato masher. Stir in chopped spinach, Tofu Hero mixture, garlic, and soy Parmesan. In a small bowl, blend miso with vermouth and add to tofu mixture with the yeast, thyme, and basil. Mix thoroughly and set aside.

For the "ground beef": Warm oil, dried garlic, and crushed pepper in a 10-inch frying pan over medium-high heat for 1 minute. Add vegetarian ground beef, reduce heat to medium low, and simmer 10 minutes, stirring frequently. Add 1 cup of tomato sauce. Cover and set aside.

Sensational Spinach Lasagna *(continued)*

To assemble: Spread 1 cup of tomato sauce evenly along the bottom of a 9-by-13-inch baking pan. Top with a layer of noodles. Add broken noodle pieces around edges to make an even fit. Layer with the tofu spinach filling, top with a layer of noodles, and cover with sauce. Layer with "ground beef" mixture and top with a layer of noodles. Cover noodles with remaining sauce and sprinkle with soy Parmesan cheese and dried basil. Cover casserole with foil and bake for 30 minutes. Remove foil and bake an additional 15 minutes. Let lasagna sit for 10 minutes before serving. Reheats very well.

NUTRITION ANALYSIS: PER 11-OUNCE SERVING

Enlightened Sensational Spinach Lasagna
Protein 21 g, carbohydrate 44 g, fiber 6 g, fat 3 g,
cholesterol 0 mg, calcium 107 mg, sodium 538 mg
Calories 266: from protein 30%,
from carbohydrate 62%, from fat 8%

Traditional Sensational Spinach Lasagna
Protein 24 g, carbohydrate 26 g, fiber 3 g, fat 23 g,
cholesterol 95 mg, calcium 317 mg, sodium 564 mg
Calories 397: from protein 23%,
from carbohydrate 25%, from fat 52%

"Chicken" Ziti Parmesan

A hearty dish with a richly flavorful Parmesan-tomato sauce brimming with a delicious fusion of vegetarian chicken and chunky vegetables.

1½ teaspoons olive oil
¼ teaspoon crushed red pepper
4 cloves garlic, minced
1 medium yellow onion, chopped
1 rib celery, sliced
2 7-ounce packages Vegi-Deli Chicken Strips
1 medium zucchini, halved lengthwise and then sliced crosswise
8 ounces button mushrooms, sliced
½ cup dry vermouth
½ cup chicken-flavor vegetarian broth, boiling
2 25-ounce jars basil-tomato sauce
1 6-ounce can tomato paste
1 tablespoon nutritional yeast
2 bay leaves
3 tablespoons soy Parmesan cheese
1 16-ounce package ziti pasta

Warm oil and crushed pepper over medium-high heat in a 5-quart saucepan for 1 minute. Add the garlic, onion, and celery and cook 3 minutes. Add "chicken" strips and cook 5 minutes, stirring frequently. Add the zucchini and mushrooms and cook 3 minutes then add the vermouth and broth. Cook 2 minutes and add the tomato sauce. Spoon the tomato paste into the sauce and stir to dissolve. Add the yeast, bay leaves, and soy Parmesan. Reduce heat and simmer 15 minutes, stirring occasionally. Cook pasta according to package directions. Remove bay leaves from the sauce. Toss cooked pasta with 2 cups sauce and serve with additional sauce.

NUTRITION ANALYSIS: PER 11-OUNCE SERVING

Enlightened "Chicken" Ziti Parmesan
Protein 21 g, carbohydrate 45 g, fiber 5 g, fat 4 g,
cholesterol 0 mg, calcium 17 mg, sodium 656 mg
Calories 298: from protein 28%,
from carbohydrate 60%, from fat 12%

Traditional Chicken Ziti Parmesan
Protein 21 g, carbohydrate 43 g, fiber 4 g, fat 17 g,
cholesterol 61 mg, calcium 101 mg, sodium 1,216 mg
Calories 405: from protein 20%,
from carbohydrate 42%, from fat 38%

PIZZA

Crisp-Crust "Pepperoni" Pizza

*This pizza delivers! Replete with whole-grain goodness,
this tasty pizza has only 5 grams of fat.*

Crust

2 cups plus 2 tablespoons whole
   wheat flour

⅓ cup yellow cornmeal

¼ cup soy flour

2 tablespoons flaxseed meal

1 teaspoon sea salt

2½ teaspoons quick-rise yeast
   (1 packet)

1 tablespoon olive oil

1 tablespoon liquid Fruitsource

¾ cup warm water

olive oil cooking spray

Topping

2 cups tomato sauce

½ cup thinly sliced Vegi-Deli or Yves
   vegetarian pepperoni

½ bell pepper, cut into strips

⅓ cup thinly sliced red onion

2 tablespoons soy Parmesan cheese

For the crust: Place the flour, cornmeal, soy flour, flaxseed meal, salt, and yeast in food processor and pulse to mix. Add oil and Fruitsource; blend. While motor is running, pour in warm water and process until mixture comes together. Turn dough onto a lightly floured board and knead for 5 minutes. Lightly spray a large bowl with oil. Place dough in bowl and turn to coat dough with oil. Cover bowl with plastic wrap and cover with a towel. Place in a warm corner of the kitchen and let rise 30 minutes. Punch dough down and knead briefly; then cover again with plastic wrap and towel. Let rise for about an hour, or until dough has doubled in size.

Preheat oven to 425°. Lightly spray pizza pan with oil. Place dough on lightly floured board and knead briefly. Roll dough out into a circle between 12 and 16 inches in diameter, depending upon the size of your pan.

To assemble: Press dough into pan. Pour tomato sauce evenly over crust and arrange suggested toppings in the order listed, or choose from your favorite topping combinations. Bake for 20 minutes.

NUTRITION ANALYSIS: PER SLICE OF PIZZA (⅛ OF PIE)

Enlightened Crisp-Crust "Pepperoni" Pizza
Protein 14 g, carbohydrate 40 g, fiber 6 g, fat 5 g, cholesterol 0 mg, calcium 27 mg, sodium 254 mg
Calories 244: from protein 21%, from carbohydrate 62%, from fat 17%

Traditional Pepperoni Pizza
Protein 16 g, carbohydrate 40 g, fiber 3 g, fat 17 g, cholesterol 33 mg, calcium 172 mg, sodium 800 mg
Calories 383: from protein 17%, from carbohydrate 43%, from fat 40%

Hearty Deep-Dish Pizza

Deep-dish pizza allows room for creating
delicious, hearty topping combinations.

Crust

2¼ cups kamut flour
¼ cup yellow cornmeal
3 tablespoons soy flour
2 tablespoons flaxseed meal
1 tablespoon vital wheat gluten
1 teaspoon sea salt

2½ teaspoons quick-rise yeast
   (1 packet)
1 teaspoon olive oil
1 tablespoon liquid Fruitsource
¾ cup plus 2 tablespoons warm water
olive oil cooking spray

Topping

1 cup TVP, ground beef style
1¼ cup beef-flavor vegetarian broth,
   boiling
2 cups tomato sauce
½ cup thinly sliced red onion
1 cup sliced mushrooms

½ bell pepper, cut into strips
1 13½-ounce can quartered
   artichokes, drained
2 tablespoons soy Parmesan cheese
1 teaspoon dried basil
1 teaspoon dried thyme

For the crust: Place the kamut flour, cornmeal, soy flour, flaxseed meal, wheat gluten, salt, and yeast in food processor and pulse to mix. Add oil and Fruitsource; blend. While motor is running, pour in warm water and process until mixture comes together. Turn dough onto a lightly floured board and knead for 5 minutes. Lightly spray a large bowl with oil. Place dough in the bowl and turn to coat dough with oil. Cover bowl with plastic wrap and cover with a towel. Place bowl in a warm corner and let rise 30 minutes. Punch dough down and knead briefly; then cover again with plastic wrap and towel. Let rise for about an hour, or until dough has doubled in size.

Preheat oven to 425°. Lightly spray a large round or oblong baking pan with 2-inch-high sides. Combine the TVP and boiling broth in a medium bowl and set aside. Place dough on lightly floured board, knead briefly, and then roll out into a rectangle or circle a little larger than your pan.

To assemble: Press dough into pan and along sides to about 1 inch from top edge. Prick the dough with a fork and spray lightly with oil. Spread sauce over the dough and top with reconstituted TVP. Arrange the remaining toppings in the order listed and sprinkle with soy Parmesan, basil, and thyme. Bake for 20 to 25 minutes.

NUTRITION ANALYSIS: PER SLICE OF PIZZA (⅛ OF PIE)

Enlightened Hearty Deep-Dish Pizza	Traditional Hearty Deep-Dish Pizza
Protein 15 g, carbohydrate 47 g, fiber 10 g, fat 3 g, cholesterol 0 mg, calcium 20 mg, sodium 274 mg	Protein 24 g, carbohydrate 42 g, fiber 3 g, fat 31 g, cholesterol 76 mg, calcium 243 mg, sodium 686 mg
Calories 254: from protein 22%, from carbohydrate 68%, from fat 10%	Calories 544: from protein 18%, from carbohydrate 31%, from fat 51%

Select Sides

Dishes that complement the entrée are chosen for their ability to bring a certain symmetry to the meal. Potatoes can take the role of supporting player in so many dishes. Yukon Gold, russet, red-skinned, or yams; wedged, sliced, baked, boiled, or mashed—potatoes present a wonderful opportunity to round out a dish with hearty texture. Twice-Baked Potatoes present beautifully and can be offered with any number of dishes. Enticing and colorful with jellied cranberry sauce, Yam Good Potatoes! is delicious when served as an alternative to the usual holiday sweet potato casserole.

Grains have been an essential part of cuisines for thousands of years, highly valued for their ease of preparation and nutritional value. Rice is as ubiquitous as potatoes in the kitchen, and varieties of fragrant rice, such as delicate basmati and jasmine rice, round out an Asian or Indian meal like no other. Although new to North Americans, quinoa (pronounced keen'wa) has been cultivated in the South American Andes since 3000 B.C. High in protein, calcium, and iron, the ancient Incas called quinoa "the Mother Grain." These interesting grains will please the palate and boost the nutritional bottom line. Be sure to rinse basmati rice, jasmine rice, and quinoa thoroughly before proceeding with the recipe. It's a good idea to double the recipe when cooking grains like brown rice. With the addition of a few staples, the busy cook can easily transform leftover dishes into delicious new incarnations. For example, beans mixed with a leftover rice dish makes a quick, healthy meal.

Need something quick? Try the delightful Tomato and Garlic Couscous. Ready in 5 minutes, couscous is easy to prepare and widely available. Whether taking advantage of flavored varieties, such as Roasted Garlic & Olive Oil or Wild Mushroom, or using plain whole wheat couscous, you can easily customize this light and fluffy side dish.

Here are stuffings and sauces, hearty squash, potatoes, and pilafs as well— all designed to lighten the heart and entice the palate.

Butternut Squash Bake

*Also known as pumpkin squash, butternut squash
is one of the most popular of the winter varieties.*

1 tablespoon olive oil
⅛ teaspoon crushed red pepper
6 large cloves garlic, minced
1 medium shallot, minced
1 medium yellow onion, chopped
⅓ cup chopped green bell pepper
1 medium butternut squash, cubed
   (about 5 cups)

2 cups sliced carrots
½ cup chicken-flavor vegetarian
   broth, boiling
1 14½-ounce can Mexican-style
   stewed tomatoes
1 teaspoon dried basil
½ cup nutritional yeast
1 tablespoon tamari

To PEEL AND CUBE BUTTERNUT squash: Cut the squash in half lengthwise with a heavy knife. If the skin is very firm, tap the inserted knife with a kitchen mallet. Using a sharp-edged spoon, scrape out the seeds and fibers. Use a paring knife or vegetable peeler to remove the skin. Cube the flesh by making first crosswise and then lengthwise cuts.

Preheat oven to 350°.

In 5-quart stovetop- and oven-safe baking dish, warm oil and crushed pepper for 1 minute over medium-high heat. Add garlic, shallot, onion, and bell pepper and sauté 3 minutes. Add squash and carrots and cook 8 minutes, stirring frequently. Add broth and tomatoes and reduce heat to medium low. Add remaining ingredients and simmer 5 minutes, stirring occasionally. Cover and bake for 15 minutes.

NUTRITION ANALYSIS: PER 7-OUNCE SERVING

Enlightened Butternut Squash Bake
Protein: 7 g, carbohydrate 20 g, fiber 5 g, fat 2 g,
cholesterol 0 mg, calcium 70 mg, sodium 172 mg
Calories 109: from protein 22%,
from carbohydrate 65%, from fat 13%

Traditional Butternut Squash Bake
Protein 4 g, carbohydrate 16 g, fiber 4 g, fat 10 g,
cholesterol 18 mg, calcium 101 mg, sodium 348 mg
Calories 159: from protein 9%,
from carbohydrate 38%, from fat 53%

Cauliflower with Sun-Dried Tomatoes

*Sun-dried tomatoes and portobello mushrooms join
with succulent cauliflower in this enticing dish.*

6
Servings

1 3-ounce package sun-dried
tomatoes, *not* packed in oil
1⅓ cups boiling water
2 teaspoons olive oil
1 tablespoon dried minced garlic
½ cup chopped red bell pepper
1 medium leek, cleaned and sliced
2 cups baby-cut carrots, sliced
vertically

3 ounces portobello mushrooms,
diced
1 medium head cauliflower, cut into
florets
⅓ cup mirin
1 tablespoon tamari
3 tablespoons nutritional yeast
1½ teaspoons dried thyme

Combine sun-dried tomatoes and boiling water in medium bowl.
Set aside.

Warm oil and garlic in a large saucepan over medium-high heat
for 1 minute. Add the bell pepper, leek, and carrots and cook 5
minutes, stirring frequently. Add the mushrooms, cauliflower, and
sun-dried tomatoes with soaking liquid. Cook 5 minutes; then add
remaining ingredients. Lower heat and simmer 5 minutes, stirring
occasionally.

CAULIFLOWER IS A
member of the cabbage
family, a cruciferous vegetable. Like broccoli and
brussels sprouts, it contains
powerful anticarcinogens,
among them a phytochemi-
cal called sulforaphane.

NUTRITION ANALYSIS: PER 9½-OUNCE SERVING

Enlightened Cauliflower with
Sun-Dried Tomatoes
Protein 10 g, carbohydrate 26 g, fiber 7 g, fat 2 g,
cholesterol 0 mg, calcium 62 mg, sodium 211 mg
Calories 146: from protein 24%,
from carbohydrate 63%, from fat 12%

Traditional Cauliflower with
Sun-Dried Tomatoes
Protein 10 g, carbohydrate 20 g, fiber 6 g, fat 18 g,
cholesterol 43 mg, calcium 184 mg, sodium 655 mg
Calories 227: from protein 14%,
from carbohydrate 28%, from fat 58%

Cornbread 'n' Cranberry Stuffing

*Diced smoked tofu adds flavor and Red Star nutritional yeast adds
a particularly creamy texture to this wholesome and delicious
cornbread stuffing. Beyond replacing unhealthy traditional ingredients,
the bonus here is the boost in protein, calcium, and vitamin B_{12}.*

*12
Servings*

1 teaspoon olive oil
⅛ teaspoon crushed red pepper
1 tablespoon dried minced garlic
1 medium yellow onion, chopped
2 stalks celery, sliced
1 6-ounce package hickory smoked
   tofu, diced
¼ cup rice butter spread

½ cup dried cranberries
2 8-ounce packages cornbread
   stuffing mix
6 cups chicken-flavor vegetarian
   broth, boiling
1½ teaspoons Bragg Liquid Aminos
½ cup nutritional yeast

Preheat oven to 350°.

In a 5-quart stovetop- and oven-safe casserole dish, warm oil, crushed pepper, and garlic over medium-high heat for 1 minute. Add onion, celery, and
diced tofu and sauté 3 minutes. Add rice butter and cranberries and reduce heat
to medium low. Stir in cornbread and add boiling broth, liquid aminos, and
nutritional yeast, stirring to mix thoroughly. Cover and bake 20 minutes.

NUTRITION ANALYSIS: PER 7½-OUNCE SERVING

Enlightened Cornbread 'n' Cranberry Stuffing
Protein 11 g, carbohydrate 57 g, fiber 3 g, fat 3 g,
cholesterol 0 mg, calcium 31 mg, sodium 375 mg
Calories 203: from protein 14%,
from carbohydrate 76%, from fat 10%

Traditional Cornbread 'n' Cranberry Stuffing
Protein 7 g, carbohydrate 40 g, fiber 1 g, fat 12 g,
cholesterol 33 mg, calcium 23 mg, sodium 743 mg
Calories 253: from protein 10%,
from carbohydrate 55%, from fat 35%

Country Potatoes

*Here we have a dish that could be bulked up
with calories and fat, but not in my kitchen!*

1 tablespoon olive oil
1 tablespoon dried minced garlic
½ cup chopped onion
½ cup chopped red bell pepper
3 medium unpeeled russet potatoes,
    halved vertically, and cut into
    ¼-inch slices

1 large fresh tomato, chopped
1 teaspoon balsamic vinegar
¼ cup dry vermouth
2 tablespoons nutritional yeast
½ tablespoon tamari
1 teaspoon dried basil
¼ teaspoon paprika

Warm oil and garlic in a 10-inch frying pan over medium-high heat for 2 minutes. Add onion and bell pepper and sauté 3 minutes. Add potatoes and cook 10 minutes, stirring frequently. Add tomato, vinegar, and vermouth and reduce heat to low. Add remaining ingredients and simmer 5 minutes, stirring occasionally, or until potatoes are tender.

POTATOES GET A BAD rap. A complex carbohydrate, the potato is a delicious vegetable that is low in both calories and fat! It is what people tend to put with them that adds unnecessary fat, cholesterol, and calories.

NUTRITION ANALYSIS: PER 6-OUNCE SERVING

Enlightened Country Potatoes
Protein 6 g, carbohydrate 32 g, fiber 4 g, fat 3 g,
cholesterol 0 mg, calcium 25 mg, sodium 80 mg
Calories 174: from protein 13%,
from carbohydrate 73%, from fat 14%

Traditional Country Potatoes
Protein 4 g, carbohydrate 31 g, fiber 3 g, fat 14 g,
cholesterol 20 mg, calcium 36 mg, sodium 373 mg
Calories 261: from protein 5%,
from carbohydrate 47%, from fat 48%

Orzo and Chile Beans

*Orzo in Italian means "barley," but it is actually tiny,
rice-shaped grains of pasta—wonderful in soup and also a welcome
change when served in place of rice. In this dish, orzo adds a
light and creamy balance to the heat of the chile beans.*

*6
Servings*

2 tablespoons pine nuts
¾ cup raw orzo
1 teaspoon olive oil
1 teaspoon dried minced garlic
¼ cup chopped red onion
3 slices veggie Canadian bacon, diced

1 15½-ounce can chile beans with
    chipotle peppers
1 medium tomato, chopped
¼ cup nutritional yeast
¼ cup chopped fresh cilantro
¼ teaspoon lemon pepper

Warm a dry frying pan over medium heat for 1 minute. Add pine nuts and raise heat to medium high. Toast nuts while shaking pan, being careful not to scorch nuts, about 2 to 3 minutes. Set aside.

Cook orzo according to package directions. Drain in a wire mesh colander and set aside.

In a 2-quart saucepan, heat oil and minced garlic for 1 minute. Add onion and veggie bacon and sauté 3 minutes. Add beans and orzo and cook 3 minutes, stirring frequently. Add tomato, yeast, and cilantro, reduce heat, and simmer 5 minutes. Add toasted pine nuts and lemon pepper and serve.

NUTRITION ANALYSIS: PER 6½-OUNCE SERVING

Enlightened Orzo and Chile Beans
Protein 13 g, carbohydrate 33 g, fiber 6 g, fat 4 g,
cholesterol 0 mg, calcium 48 mg, sodium 418 mg
Calories 211: from protein 23%,
from carbohydrate 60%, from fat 17%

Traditional Orzo and Chile Beans
Protein 11 g, carbohydrate 29 g, fiber 4 g, fat 23 g,
cholesterol 35 mg, calcium 50 mg, sodium 747 mg
Calories 354: from protein 12%,
from carbohydrate 32%, from fat 57%

Creamed Asparagus and Rice Pilaf

*A savory brown rice pilaf bakes under lightly steamed asparagus
in a bubbly "cream" sauce in this luscious and attractive side dish.*

---

1 pound fresh asparagus spears,
    trimmed and cut into 2-inch
    pieces
1½ teaspoons olive oil
⅛ teaspoon crushed red pepper
1 tablespoon dried minced garlic
3 cups cooked brown rice
1 cup frozen white corn, thawed
2 medium tomatoes, diced

⅔ cup beef-flavor vegetarian broth,
    boiling
1 tablespoon tamari
1 cup enriched 1% fat soymilk
2 tablespoons Dijon mustard
⅓ cup nutritional yeast
1 teaspoon granulated garlic
1 teaspoon dried marjoram
1 teaspoon lemon pepper

Preheat oven to 400°.

Steam asparagus 5 minutes, plunge into ice water, and set aside.

In a 4-quart, stovetop- and oven-safe casserole, warm oil, crushed pepper,
and garlic over medium-high heat for 1 minute. Add cooked rice and corn.
Cook 3 minutes and add the tomatoes, broth, and tamari. Reduce heat to
medium low and cook mixture 10 minutes, stirring occasionally.

Place soymilk in a large glass measuring cup (2 cups or more) and whisk in
the remaining ingredients. Arrange the asparagus on top of the rice mixture and
pour sauce over all. Bake uncovered for 15 minutes.

NUTRITION ANALYSIS: PER 9-OUNCE SERVING

Enlightened Creamed Asparagus and Rice Pilaf
Protein 9 g, carbohydrate 29 g, fiber 5 g, fat 3 g,
cholesterol 0 mg, calcium 60 mg, sodium 125 mg
Calories 161: from protein 21%,
from carbohydrate 66%, from fat 13%

Traditional Creamed Asparagus and Rice Pilaf
Protein 6 g, carbohydrate 31 g, fiber 2 g, fat 21 g,
cholesterol 68 mg, calcium 71 mg, sodium 457 mg
Calories 335: from protein 7%,
from carbohydrate 37%, from fat 56%

Creamy Black Beans with Rice

*Black beans are rich-tasting on their own and
don't need to be weighed down with unhealthy fat and
cholesterol. In this tasty dish black beans are nestled
in a creamy sauce and served over brown rice.*

*8
Servings*

1½ teaspoons olive oil
¼ teaspoon crushed red pepper
½ cup sliced scallions
2 large garlic cloves, minced
1 15-ounce can black beans (do *not* drain)
1 large fresh tomato, chopped

1 tablespoon Bragg Liquid Aminos
¼ cup chopped fresh cilantro
1 teaspoon Mexican oregano
½ teaspoon ground cumin
⅓ cup nutritional yeast
3 cups cooked brown rice

In a medium saucepan, warm oil and crushed pepper over medium-high heat for 1 minute. Add scallions and garlic and sauté 3 minutes. Add beans, tomato, and liquid aminos; reduce heat to low and simmer 5 minutes. Add cilantro, oregano, cumin, and yeast. Simmer 5 minutes, or until ready to serve, stirring occasionally. Spoon over brown rice.

NUTRITION ANALYSIS: PER 5½-OUNCE SERVING

Enlightened Creamy Black Beans with Rice
Protein 10 g, carbohydrate 67 g, fiber 6 g, fat 2 g,
cholesterol 0 mg, calcium 22 mg, sodium 255 mg
Calories 156: from protein 12%,
from carbohydrate 82%, from fat 7%

Traditional Creamy Black Beans with Rice
Protein 10 g, carbohydrate 30 g, fiber 4 g, fat 10 g,
cholesterol 19 mg, calcium 118 mg, sodium 506 mg
Calories 238: from protein 16%,
from carbohydrate 47%, from fat 37%

Fragrant Basmati Pilaf

*Simple and delicious, this dish delights
the senses with the enticing fragrance of
basmati rice and Indian spices.*

1 cup basmati rice
2½ cups beef- or chicken-flavor
   vegetarian broth, boiling
1 cinnamon stick
1 bay leaf

1 cup frozen peas, thawed
½ teaspoon turmeric
1 teaspoon onion powder
1 teaspoon Bragg Liquid Aminos
2 tablespoons chopped cashews

Place the rice in a wire mesh colander and rinse thoroughly. Set aside.

Bring the broth, cinnamon stick, and bay leaf to a boil in a medium saucepan. Add drained rice, thawed peas, tumeric, onion powder, and liquid aminos. Bring to a second boil, cover, and lower heat. Simmer for 20 minutes. Fluff gently with a fork, remove bay leaf and cinnamon stick, sprinkle with cashews, and serve immediately.

NUTRITION ANALYSIS: PER 5³/₄-OUNCE SERVING

Enlightened Fragrant Basmati Pilaf
Protein 5 g, carbohydrate 46 g, fiber 2 g, fat 1 g,
cholesterol 0 mg, calcium 15 mg, sodium 82 mg
Calories 155: from protein 9%,
from carbohydrate 85%, from fat 6%

Traditional Fragrant Basmati Pilaf
Protein 5 g, carbohydrate 31 g, fiber 2 g, fat 12 g,
cholesterol 22 mg, calcium 15 mg, sodium 171 mg
Calories 254: from protein 8%,
from carbohydrate 48%, from fat 43%

Green Beans Italian

*Nutritional yeast and soy Parmesan cheese impart
an authentic creaminess and flavor to this dish.*

*6
Servings*

1½ teaspoons olive oil
3 cloves garlic, minced
½ medium red bell pepper,
  chopped
1 stalk celery with leaves, sliced
1 pound fresh green beans, cut into
  2-inch pieces
6 ounces portobello mushrooms,
  diced
½ cup dry vermouth

1 14½-ounce can Italian-style stewed
  tomatoes
10 fresh basil leaves, chopped
1 bay leaf
¼ cup beef-flavor vegetarian broth,
  boiling
⅓ cup nutritional yeast
1 teaspoon dried thyme
1 teaspoon dried oregano
2 tablespoons soy Parmesan cheese

In a medium saucepan, warm oil over medium-high heat and sauté the garlic,
bell pepper, and celery 3 minutes. Add the green beans and cook 5 minutes or
until the beans are crisp-tender, stirring occasionally. Add the mushrooms and
cook 3 minutes; add the vermouth and cook 2 minutes longer. Reduce heat to
medium low and add the remaining ingredients. Simmer, stirring occasionally,
5 minutes, or until ready to serve.

NUTRITION ANALYSIS: PER 8⅓-OUNCE SERVING

Enlightened Green Beans Italian
Protein 11 g, carbohydrate 18 g, fiber 6 g, fat 3 g,
cholesterol 0 mg, calcium 74 mg, sodium 260 mg
Calories 139: from protein 31%,
from carbohydrate 56%, from fat 16%

Traditional Green Beans Italian
Protein 4 g, carbohydrate 15 g, fiber 5 g, fat 16 g,
cholesterol 50 mg, calcium 111 mg, sodium 285 mg
Calories 228: from protein 7%,
from carbohydrate 27%, from fat 66%

Herbed "Cream" Sauce

*No butter, greasy chicken broth, or dairy ingredients in this velvety rich
"cream" sauce. This sauce is a nice addition to steamed vegetables like
asparagus or broccoli, or serve with Savory "Sausage" and
Rice with Chardonnay (page 158).*

*Makes about
2½ Cups*

---

2 tablespoons olive oil
1 teaspoon dried minced garlic
3 tablespoons unbleached flour
⅓ cup dry vermouth
1⅓ cups chicken-flavor vegetarian
   broth, boiling

½ cup nutritional yeast
3 tablespoons enriched 1% fat
   soymilk
1 teaspoon dried basil
½ teaspoon dried marjoram

Warm oil and dried garlic in a medium saucepan for 1 minute over medium-high heat. Whisk in flour and form a paste. Whisk vermouth into paste; when smooth, add the hot broth. Reduce heat to simmer and add yeast, stirring until blended. Add remaining ingredients and continue to simmer until thickened, or until ready to serve.

NUTRITION ANALYSIS: PER 2⅔-OUNCE SERVING (MORE THAN ⅓ CUP)

Enlightened Herbed "Cream" Sauce
Protein 8 g, carbohydrate 7 g, fiber 2 g, fat 4 g,
cholesterol 0 mg, calcium 17 mg, sodium 97 mg
Calories 94: from protein 32%,
from carbohydrate 30%, from fat 38%*

Traditional Herbed Cream Sauce
Protein 3 g, carbohydrate 3 g, fiber 0 g, fat 13 g,
cholesterol 42 mg, calcium 85 mg, sodium 380 mg
Calories 140: from protein 8%,
from carbohydrate 9%, from fat 83%

* The percentage of calories from fat seems high because the calories are so low.

Potato Latkes

These positively perfect potato pancakes can be served as an entrée or a side dish with applesauce or vegan sour cream on the side. Latkes are traditionally made with eggs and fried in lots of oil. The enlightened version is very low in fat and without cholesterol because of the clever use of alternative ingredients.

8
Servings

4 cups grated potatoes (about
    4 medium)
1 medium yellow onion, grated
½ 12.3-ounce package lite silken tofu
¼ cup nutritional yeast
2½ tablespoons whole wheat flour
2 tablespoons yellow cornmeal
1 tablespoon egg replacer powder

1 teaspoon nonaluminum baking
    powder
1 teaspoon sea salt
½ cup enriched 1% fat soymilk
½ cup Barbara's Potato Flakes
olive oil cooking spray
1 tablespoon olive oil

POTATO LATKES AND sour cream are traditionally served on Hanukkah, the Festival of Lights, which is a Jewish holiday.

Preheat oven to 200°.

Place the grated potatoes on several thicknesses of paper towels or a clean kitchen towel to drain. Then place grated potatoes and onions in a large bowl and set aside.

Put the tofu in food processor bowl and process until smooth. Add the yeast, flour, cornmeal, egg replacer powder, baking powder, and salt. While processing, and with motor running, add soymilk.

In a large bowl, combine the tofu mixture with the grated veggies and add the potato flakes. Mix thoroughly.

Spray electric frying pan or 10-inch frying pan with olive oil cooking spray; place over medium-high heat and add olive oil. Using a ⅓-cup measure, drop batter onto hot pan and cook pancakes, browning on both sides. Place cooked pancakes on a baking sheet and keep warm in preheated oven while cooking remaining batter, and until ready to serve.

NUTRITION ANALYSIS: PER 5¾-OUNCE SERVING (2½ PANCAKES)

Enlightened Potato Latkes
Protein 8 g, carbohydrate 27 g, fiber 4 g, fat 3 g,
cholesterol 0 mg, calcium 76 mg, sodium 220 mg
Calories 153: from protein 20%,
from carbohydrate 66%, from fat 14%

Traditional Potato Latkes
Protein 5 g, carbohydrate 20 g, fiber 2 g, fat 18 g,
cholesterol 85 mg, calcium 48 mg, sodium 440 mg
Calories 267: from protein 8%,
from carbohydrate 31%, from fat 61%

Japanese Eggplant Medley

Easy and delectable, this dish is wonderful either as a side or light main course. The baked tofu is a credible stand-in for the pork usually found in Asian dishes.

2 teaspoons olive oil
¼ teaspoon crushed red pepper
4 cloves garlic, minced
½ cup chopped red bell pepper
2 cups thinly sliced baby-cut carrots
1 6-ounce package hickory baked tofu, sliced on an angle
6 medium Japanese eggplants, thinly sliced
1 15-ounce can whole baby corn, drained and sliced

½ cup dry sherry
1 cup cooked pearl barley
1½ cups chicken-flavor vegetarian broth, boiling
3 tablespoons tamari
2 tablespoons rice vinegar
2 teaspoons liquid Fruitsource
3 drops hot pepper sauce
1 tablespoon cornstarch
2 tablespoons cold water
⅓ cup chopped fresh cilantro

In a medium saucepan, warm oil and crushed pepper over medium-high heat for 1 minute. Add the garlic, bell pepper, carrots, and tofu and sauté 3 minutes. Add the eggplant and baby corn and cook 5 minutes, stirring occasionally. Reduce heat to low and add the sherry; simmer 2 minutes, stir, and add the cooked barley.

In a large liquid measuring cup, combine the broth, tamari, vinegar, Fruitsource, and hot pepper sauce. In a small bowl blend the cornstarch and cold water and add to the broth mixture. Stir the sauce into the veggies and add the cilantro. Simmer 8 minutes, or until ready to serve, stirring occasionally.

NUTRITION ANALYSIS: PER 9-OUNCE SERVING

Enlightened Japanese Eggplant Medley
Protein 8 g, carbohydrate 22 g, fiber 6 g, fat 2 g,
cholesterol 0 mg, calcium 32 mg, sodium 471 mg
Calories 142: from protein 22%,
from carbohydrate 64%, from fat 14%

Traditional Japanese Eggplant Medley
Protein 11 g, carbohydrate 17 g, fiber 5 g, fat 10 g,
cholesterol 23 mg, calcium 28 mg, sodium 657 mg
Calories 202: from protein 22%,
from carbohydrate 34%, from fat 44%

Mexicali Brown Rice

Wholesome brown rice with a Spanish flavor,
this dish is creamy and rich without cheese or excess fat.

1 cup raw brown rice
2½ cups chicken-flavor vegetarian
    broth, boiling
¼ cup sliced scallions
1 medium tomato, chopped

1½ tablespoons lime juice
1½ teaspoons tamari lite
1 tablespoon nutritional yeast
1 teaspoon dried cilantro

Combine rice with boiling broth in a medium saucepan. Stir, bring to a second boil, reduce heat, cover, and simmer for 35 minutes, stirring occasionally. Add remaining ingredients and continue to simmer mixture 8 to 10 minutes, or until broth is absorbed and rice is tender.

NUTRITION ANALYSIS: PER 5¾-OUNCE SERVING

Enlightened Mexicali Brown Rice
Protein 4 g, carbohydrate 27 g, fiber 2 g, fat 1 g,
cholesterol 0 mg, calcium 15 mg, sodium 97 mg
Calories 131: from protein 12%,
from carbohydrate 80%, from fat 8%

Traditional Mexicali Rice
Protein 6 g, carbohydrate 21 g, fiber 0.5 g, fat 12 g,
cholesterol 31 mg, calcium 137 mg, sodium 602 mg
Calories 217: from protein 11%,
from carbohydrate 39%, from fat 49%

Mushroom Gravy

Select
Sides

217

Flavorful and very easy, this sauce is made without butter and is ready in minutes. Serve with potatoes, rice, or steamed vegetables.

*Makes
2 Cups*

2 tablespoons olive oil
3 tablespoons unbleached flour
1⅔ cups Pacific mushroom broth

⅓ cup nutritional yeast
¼ teaspoon dried thyme
¼ teaspoon granulated garlic

Warm oil in a medium saucepan over medium-high heat for 1 minute. Whisk in flour to form a paste. Whisk in the mushroom broth. Reduce heat to medium low and add yeast, stirring until blended. Add remaining ingredients and continue to simmer, whisking or stirring occasionally until thickened, or ready to serve.

NUTRITION ANALYSIS: PER 2⅓-OUNCE SERVING (⅓ CUP)

Enlightened Mushroom Gravy
Protein 3 g, carbohydrate 3 g, fiber 1 g, fat 4 g,
cholesterol 0 mg, calcium 5 mg, sodium 57 mg
Calories 56: from protein 22%,
from carbohydrate 18%, from fat 60%*

Traditional Mushroom Gravy
Protein 1 g, carbohydrate 2 g, fiber 0 g, fat 15 g,
cholesterol 23 mg, calcium 33 mg, sodium 228 mg
Calories 148: from protein 3%,
from carbohydrate 4%, from fat 93%

* The percentage of calories from fat seems high because the calories are so low.

New Orleans Rice Pilaf

This very festive dish is simple, creamy,
and delicious without excess fat, sodium, and calories.

8
Servings

1 cup raw white rice
3 cups chicken-flavor vegetarian
   broth, boiling
¼ cup sliced scallions
1 medium tomato, diced

⅓ cup chopped fresh basil leaves
3 tablespoons nutritional yeast
1 teaspoon lemon pepper
¼ teaspoon sea salt
dash or two hot pepper sauce

Stir rice into boiling broth in a medium saucepan. Bring to a second boil, reduce heat, cover, and simmer for 15 minutes, stirring occasionally. Add remaining ingredients and continue to simmer 5 minutes, or until broth is absorbed and rice is tender.

NUTRITION ANALYSIS: PER 5-OUNCE SERVING

Enlightened New Orleans Rice Pilaf
Protein 5 g, carbohydrate 22 g, fiber 1 g, fat 1 g,
cholesterol 0 mg, calcium 17 mg, sodium 120 mg
Calories 107: from protein 17%,
from carbohydrate 79%, from fat 4%

Traditional New Orleans Rice Pilaf
Protein 5 g, carbohydrate 21 g, fiber 0.5 g, fat 13 g,
cholesterol 47 mg, calcium 99 mg, sodium 416 mg
Calories 221: from protein 8%,
from carbohydrate 38%, from fat 54%

Pinquito Potatoes

*Pinquito beans are small, tender, pink, and very flavorful. Veggie bacon
and mushroom broth enhance this dish with a minimum of fuss.*

1 tablespoon olive oil
¼ teaspoon crushed red pepper
1 tablespoon dried minced
 garlic
1½ tablespoons grated fresh
 gingerroot
1 medium yellow onion, chopped
½ cup chopped sweet red bell
 pepper
1 6-ounce package veggie Canadian
 bacon, diced

2 pounds potatoes, peeled, halved
 lengthwise, and cut into ¼-inch
 slices
1 cup dry vermouth
1 14½-ounce can Mexican-style
 stewed tomatoes
1 15-ounce can pinquito beans
⅓ cup chopped fresh cilantro
2 cups mushroom broth
½ teaspoon lemon pepper
1 teaspoon Mexican oregano

In a large electric frying pan or Dutch oven, warm oil, crushed pepper, and
dried garlic over medium-high heat for 1 minute. Add the gingerroot, onion,
bell pepper, and diced veggie bacon and sauté 3 minutes. Add sliced potatoes
and cook 10 minutes, stirring frequently. Add vermouth and tomatoes and
reduce heat to medium low. Add pinquito beans and cilantro. Add the mushroom broth, lemon pepper, and oregano and cook 15 minutes, or until potatoes are tender, stirring frequently.

NUTRITION ANALYSIS: PER 8-OUNCE SERVING

Enlightened Pinquito Potatoes
Protein 8 g, carbohydrate 23 g, fiber 4 g, fat 1 g,
cholesterol 0 mg, calcium 36 mg, sodium 392 mg
Calories 145: from protein 24%,
from carbohydrate 67%, from fat 9%

Traditional Pinquito Potatoes
Protein 9 g, carbohydrate 21 g, fiber 4 g, fat 8 g,
cholesterol 16 mg, calcium 37 mg, sodium 547 mg
Calories 197: from protein 18%,
from carbohydrate 45%, from fat 36%

Quinoa Pilaf

This dish is simple to prepare and can be the perfect complement to a hearty soup and colorful salad. The quinoa is cooked separately, added to the sauté, and finished with a touch of vermouth and hot broth.

6
Servings

1 cup quinoa, rinsed
2 cups water
2 teaspoons olive oil
¼ teaspoon crushed red pepper
4 cloves garlic, minced
⅓ cup sliced scallions
1 stalk celery, chopped
⅓ cup diced Vegi-Deli pepperoni, Zesty Italian flavor

1 6-ounce package hickory baked tofu, sliced
⅓ cup dry vermouth
⅓ cup chicken-flavor vegetarian broth, boiling
1 cup frozen peas, thawed

Using a narrow-weave wire mesh strainer, rinse the quinoa several times before combining with water in a medium saucepan. Bring to a boil, stir, and reduce heat to low. Cover and simmer for 15 minutes, or until liquid is absorbed.

Heat olive oil and crushed pepper in a 10-inch frying pan for 1 minute. Add garlic, scallions, and celery and sauté for 3 minutes. Stir in the pepperoni and sliced tofu. Cook 3 minutes and stir in the vermouth. Cook 3 minutes longer; then add the cooked quinoa, broth, and peas. Simmer 10 minutes, or until ready to serve.

NUTRITION ANALYSIS: PER 8-OUNCE SERVING

Enlightened Quinoa Pilaf
Protein 14 g, carbohydrate 28 g, fiber 2 g, fat 4 g,
cholesterol 0 mg, calcium 41 mg, sodium 284 mg
Calories 214: from protein 28%,
from carbohydrate 55%, from fat 17%

Traditional Quinoa Pilaf
Protein 14 g, carbohydrate 22 g, fiber 1 g, fat 21 g,
cholesterol 56 mg, calcium 47 mg, sodium 366 mg
Calories 341: from protein 17%,
from carbohydrate 27%, from fat 57%

Quinoa Vegetable Medley

*A delightful treatment that complements
this delicate and very nutritious grain.*

1 cup quinoa
2 cups water
2 teaspoons olive oil
¼ teaspoon crushed pepper
1 teaspoon minced dried garlic
½ cup sliced scallions
1½ cups sliced baby-cut carrots
1 10-ounce package fresh baby
   spinach

¼ cup dry sherry
1 medium tomato, diced
⅓ cup chicken-flavor vegetarian
   broth, boiling
2 tablespoons nutritional yeast
¼ cup chopped fresh basil

Using a small wire mesh strainer, rinse the quinoa several times before placing in a medium saucepan with cold water. Bring to a boil, stir, and reduce heat to low. Cover and simmer gently for 15 minutes, or until liquid is absorbed.

Heat olive oil and crushed pepper in a 10-inch frying pan over medium-high heat for 1 minute. Add garlic, scallions, and carrots and sauté for 5 minutes. Add the spinach and cook mixture 3 minutes, stirring occasionally. Reduce heat and add the sherry and tomato. Cook 3 minutes, then add the cooked quinoa and the broth. Stir in the yeast and basil and simmer 8 minutes, or until ready to serve.

NUTRITION ANALYSIS: PER 9-OUNCE SERVING

Enlightened Quinoa Vegetable Medley
Protein 8 g, carbohydrate 26 g, fiber 3 g, fat 4 g,
cholesterol 0 mg, calcium 95 mg, sodium 69 mg
Calories 165: from protein 19%,
from carbohydrate 62%, from fat 18%

Traditional Quinoa Vegetable Medley
Protein 7 g, carbohydrate 25 g, fiber 2 g, fat 13 g,
cholesterol 31 mg, calcium 138 mg, sodium 102 mg
Calories 243: from protein 12%,
from carbohydrate 41%, from fat 47%

Saffron Pommes de Terre

*In this hearty dish succulent savory baked tofu mimics sautéed duck,
nestled in a delicious saffron-laced sauce with red bliss potatoes.*

*10
Servings*

½ cup dry vermouth
¼ teaspoon saffron threads
1 tablespoon olive oil
1 tablespoon dried minced garlic
1 large yellow onion, halved crosswise and cut into ⅛-inch wedges
½ cup chopped green bell pepper
8 cups unpeeled red bliss potatoes,
  cut into ¼-inch slices

1 6-ounce package savory baked tofu
2 medium fresh tomatoes, diced
1 cup chicken-flavor vegetarian
  broth, boiling
2 tablespoons tamari
2 tablespoons nutritional yeast

Combine vermouth and saffron threads in a small bowl and set aside. Warm oil
and dried minced garlic in a large electric frying pan or Dutch oven over
medium-high heat for 2 minutes. Add onion wedges and green pepper and
sauté 3 minutes. Add sliced potatoes and tofu and cook 10 minutes, stirring frequently. Add tomatoes and broth and reduce heat to low. Add tamari, yeast,
and saffron with soaking liquid. Simmer mixture 10 minutes, or until potatoes
are cooked through, stirring occasionally.

NUTRITION ANALYSIS: PER 9-OUNCE SERVING

Enlightened Saffron Pommes de Terre
Protein 9 g, carbohydrate 35 g, fiber 4 g, fat 2 g,
cholesterol 0 mg, calcium 23 mg, sodium 294 mg
Calories 200: from protein 18%,
from carbohydrate 72%, from fat 10%

Traditional Saffron Pommes de Terre
Protein 15 g, carbohydrate 37 g, fiber 4 g, fat 23 g,
cholesterol 62 mg, calcium 31 mg, sodium 361 mg
Calories 418: from protein 15%,
from carbohydrate 36%, from fat 49%

Stuffed Acorn Squash

Luscious acorn squash and a toothsome "sausage" and apple stuffing are featured in this hearty dish. Serve with whole-berry cranberry sauce.

---

3 medium acorn squash, halved and seeded
1 medium Granny Smith apple, peeled and diced
1 teaspoon lemon juice
2 teaspoons olive oil
3 cloves garlic, minced
⅓ cup sliced scallions

1 14-ounce package Gimme Lean, sausage style
⅓ cup dried currants, raisins, or cranberries
¼ cup dry sherry
1 tablespoon rice butter spread
paprika for garnish

Preheat oven to 350°.

Place squash halves cut side down in a 9-by-13-inch baking pan; add 1 inch of water. Bake in preheated oven 1 hour.

Drizzle the diced apple with lemon juice and set aside. In a 10-inch frying pan, heat olive oil and sauté the garlic and scallions for 3 minutes over medium-high heat. Add the vegetarian sausage and sauté 5 minutes, stirring to separate the mixture into chunks, until brown. Add apples and currants and cook 3 minutes, stirring frequently. Add sherry, reduce heat to low, and simmer 3 minutes, stirring occasionally.

Leaving oven on, remove the cooked squash from baking pan and discard water. Return squash to pan cut side up and moisten the flesh with the rice butter spread, including the outer edge. Spoon the stuffing into each cavity and sprinkle lightly with paprika. Cover pan loosely with foil and bake 20 minutes.

NUTRITION ANALYSIS: PER STUFFED SQUASH HALF

Enlightened Stuffed Acorn Squash
Protein 14 g, carbohydrate 53 g, fiber 12 g, fat 3 g, cholesterol 0 mg, calcium 122 mg, sodium 368 mg
Calories 274: from protein 19%, from carbohydrate 73%, from fat 8%

Traditional Stuffed Acorn Squash
Protein 11 g, carbohydrate 44 g, fiber 11 g, fat 38 g, cholesterol 56 mg, calcium 126 mg, sodium 491 mg
Calories 541: from protein 8%, from carbohydrate 31%, from fat 61%

Superb No-Bake Stuffing

*Add brandied raisins, chopped apples, and diced veggie bacon
to packaged stuffing mix for a delicious healthy alternative to
the usual meat-based and butter-drenched stuffing.*

*12
Servings*

1 cup golden raisins
¼ cup ginger brandy
2 teaspoons olive oil
5 cloves garlic, minced
½ cup sliced scallions
1 medium shallot, minced
¼ cup chopped red bell pepper
3 slices veggie Canadian bacon, diced
3 tablespoons rice butter spread

1 12-ounce package herb bread
  stuffing
4 cups chicken-flavor vegetarian
  broth, boiling
1 medium Granny Smith apple
1 teaspoon dried chives
2 teaspoons dried thyme
2 teaspoons ground sage

WHEN PURCHASING prepared stuffing, make sure to read the ingredient list for any mention of hydrogenated fats. Choose the one without hydrogenated fat.

Combine raisins and brandy in a small saucepan and heat over medium heat for 5 minutes, or until liquid is absorbed. Set aside. In a 5-quart saucepan, heat oil over medium-high heat and sauté garlic, scallions, shallot, and bell pepper for 3 minutes. Add the veggie bacon and cook 5 minutes, stirring frequently. Add the rice butter and cook, stirring frequently, until rice butter is melted, about 2 minutes. Reduce heat and add stuffing cubes; stir to mix and add the hot broth, raisins, and apple. Mix thoroughly, adding the chives, thyme, and sage. Cover and simmer, stirring occasionally, for 15 minutes, or until ready to serve. Moisten with additional broth if stuffing seems dry.

NUTRITION ANALYSIS: PER 6¾-OUNCE SERVING

Enlightened Superb No-Bake Stuffing
Protein 6 g, carbohydrate 40 g, fiber 3 g, fat 2 g,
cholesterol 0 mg, calcium 52 mg, sodium 606 mg
Calories 214: from protein 13%,
from carbohydrate 80%, from fat 7%

Traditional Superb No-Bake Stuffing
Protein 6 g, carbohydrate 38 g, fiber 3 g, fat 11 g,
cholesterol 21 mg, calcium 48 mg, sodium 986 mg
Calories 286: from protein 9%,
from carbohydrate 56%, from fat 35%

Sweet Beans in "Cream" Sauce

*Look in the supermarket freezer for shelled green soybeans,
sometimes called sweet beans. They add hearty flavor
and valuable whole soy goodness to any dish.*

1 recipe Herbed "Cream" Sauce
  (page 213)
olive oil cooking spray
⅛ teaspoon crushed red pepper
⅓ cup sliced scallions

2 cups sliced baby-cut carrots
¾ cup cooked sweet beans
¼ cup vegetable broth
3 cups cooked brown rice
⅔ cup dried cranberries

Make cream sauce and set aside.

Spray a medium saucepan generously with cooking oil spray, warm the pan, and add crushed pepper, scallions, and carrots. Cook over medium-high heat for 5 minutes. Add the prepared sweet beans and broth. Cook 3 minutes; then add the rice and cranberries. Lower heat and simmer 5 minutes; then add "cream" sauce. Continue to simmer until ready to serve, stirring occasionally.

NUTRITION ANALYSIS: PER 8-OUNCE SERVING

Enlightened Sweet Beans in "Cream" Sauce
Protein 12 g, carbohydrate 35 g, fiber 5 g, fat 5 g,
cholesterol 0 mg, calcium 56 mg, sodium 156 mg
Calories 233: from protein 20%,
from carbohydrate 59%, from fat 21%

Traditional Sweet Beans in Cream Sauce
Protein 7 g, carbohydrate 30 g, fiber 2 g, fat 16 g,
cholesterol 43 mg, calcium 129 mg, sodium 424 mg
Calories 289: from protein 10%,
from carbohydrate 41%, from fat 49%

Tomato and Garlic Couscous

*Couscous is a delightful change from rice
or pasta, and so quick to the table!*

*4
Servings*

1 ¼ cups water
1 tablespoon rice butter spread
1 cup chopped fresh tomato

1 5.8-ounce package roasted-garlic-
    and-olive-oil-flavored couscous

Place water, rice butter spread, spice pack from the couscous package, and chopped tomato in a medium saucepan. Bring mixture to a boil and stir in couscous. Cover pan, remove from heat, and let stand 5 minutes. Fluff with a fork and serve immediately.

NUTRITION ANALYSIS: PER 7½-OUNCE SERVING

Enlightened Tomato and Garlic Couscous
Protein 6 g, carbohydrate 33 g, fiber 2 g, fat 2 g,
cholesterol 0 mg, calcium 16 mg, sodium 389 mg
Calories 166: from protein 13%,
from carbohydrate 76%, from fat 10%

Traditional Tomato and Garlic Couscous
Protein 6 g, carbohydrate 32 g, fiber 2 g, fat 7 g,
cholesterol 16 mg, Calcium 6 mg, sodium 417 mg
Calories 207: from protein 10%,
from carbohydrate 60%, from fat 29%

Twice-Baked Potatoes

*Use russet (sometimes called Idaho) potatoes
for this easy and delicious side dish.*

4 baking potatoes (about 3¼
   pounds)
olive oil cooking spray
1 tablespoon olive oil
1 tablespoon dried minced garlic
   (minced roasted garlic, if
   available)

½ cup enriched 1% fat soymilk
⅓ cup nutritional yeast
½ teaspoon sea salt
½ teaspoon dried marjoram
¼ teaspoon coarse black pepper
paprika

Preheat oven to 425°.

Bake potatoes on middle rack for 1 hour, or until fork-tender. Leaving oven on, remove potatoes and set aside. When cool enough to handle, cut potatoes lengthwise and scoop flesh into a medium bowl, leaving ¼-inch-thick shells. Place the shells on a baking sheet and spray them lightly with oil. Return to oven and bake 15 minutes.

In a medium saucepan, warm oil with minced garlic over medium heat for 1 minute (do not brown). Using a potato masher, mash the potato flesh and add to the pan. Add the soymilk, yeast, salt, marjoram, and pepper and simmer 5 minutes, stirring frequently. Spoon mashed potato mixture into shells and sprinkle with paprika. Bake 10 minutes, or until golden brown.

NUTRITION ANALYSIS: PER ONE STUFFED POTATO HALF

Enlightened Twice-Baked Potatoes
Protein 6 g, carbohydrate 31 g, fiber 1 g, fat 2 g,
cholesterol 0 mg, calcium 6 mg, sodium 142 mg
Calories 164: from protein 15%,
from carbohydrate 73%, from fat 12%

Traditional Twice-Baked Potatoes
Protein 6 g, carbohydrate 27 g, fiber 1 g, fat 10 g,
cholesterol 78 mg, calcium 93 mg, sodium 268 mg
Calories 222: from protein 11%,
from carbohydrate 49%, from fat 40%

Yam Good Potatoes!

Serve this luscious fusion of dried apricots, veggie bacon, and sweet yams with jellied cranberry sauce. Holiday yams were never this good!

8 Servings

1 tablespoon olive oil
⅛ teaspoon crushed red pepper
4 cloves garlic, minced
⅓ cup sliced scallions
⅓ cup chopped yellow bell pepper
1 6-ounce package veggie Canadian
    bacon, diced
2 pounds yams, peeled, halved
    lengthwise, and then cut into
    ¼-inch-thick slices

1 cup snipped dried apricots
⅓ cup mirin
1 large fresh tomato, diced
1 cup chicken-flavor vegetarian
    broth, boiling
¼ cup nutritional yeast
1 teaspoon dried marjoram

Preheat oven to 400°.

In a 5-quart stovetop- and oven-safe casserole, warm oil and crushed pepper over medium-high heat for 1 minute. Add the garlic, scallions, bell pepper, and veggie bacon and sauté 5 minutes, stirring frequently. Add the yams and apricots; cook another 5 minutes. Stir in mirin, tomato, and hot broth; reduce heat to medium and cook 5 minutes, stirring occasionally. Cover and bake for 25 minutes. Stir in yeast and marjoram, cover, and return to oven for 5 minutes.

NUTRITION ANALYSIS: PER 10-OUNCE SERVING

Enlightened Yam Good Potatoes!
Protein 11 g, carbohydrate 26 g, fiber 4 g, fat 2 g,
cholesterol 0 mg, calcium 15 mg, sodium 296 mg
Calories 148: from protein 26%,
from carbohydrate 62%, from fat 12%

Traditional Yam Good Potatoes!
Protein 7 g, carbohydrate 13 g, fiber 0 g, fat 12 g,
cholesterol 32 mg, calcium 28 mg, sodium 788 mg
Calories 195: from protein 16%,
from carbohydrate 28%, from fat 57%

Savory Spiced Potatoes

Hearty potato slices, spiced stewed tomatoes, and veggie
Canadian bacon make this microwave-quick dish a crowd pleaser.

2 teaspoons olive oil
⅛ teaspoon crushed red pepper
1 teaspoon dried minced garlic
⅓ cup chopped red onion
⅓ cup chopped green bell pepper
3 slices veggie Canadian bacon, diced
4 medium unpeeled russet potatoes,
    cut into ¼-inch slices (about 4
    cups)

1 14½-ounce can Italian-style stewed
    tomatoes
1 teaspoon dried thyme
⅛ teaspoon coarse ground black
    pepper

In microwave, warm oil, crushed pepper, and minced garlic in a covered 2-quart microwave-safe casserole for 2 minutes at full power. Add onion, bell pepper, and diced "bacon"; cover and microwave 3 minutes. Add sliced potatoes, stir mixture, and cook 5 minutes more. Stir in remaining ingredients and cook mixture for 15 minutes more, stirring at 5-minute intervals, until potatoes are cooked through and sauce is thickened.

NUTRITION ANALYSIS: PER 9-OUNCE SERVING

Enlightened Savory Spiced Potatoes
Protein 8 g, carbohydrate 43 g, fiber 5 g, fat 3 g,
cholesterol 0 mg, calcium 42 mg, sodium 277 mg
Calories 217: from protein 14%,
from carbohydrate 79%, from fat 7%

Traditional Savory Spiced Potatoes
Protein 9 g, carbohydrate 42 g, fiber 5 g, fat 17 g,
cholesterol 27 mg, calcium 40 mg, sodium 587 mg
Calories 347: from protein 10%,
from carbohydrate 47%, from fat 42%

Potato Gratin with Green Chilies

*This enticing dish is a fusion of flavors,
textures, and aromas. So delicious!*

*8
Servings*

2 teaspoons olive oil
¼ teaspoon crushed red pepper
5 cloves garlic, minced
1 medium red onion, chopped
1 stalk celery, sliced
2 pounds potatoes, peeled, halved
    lengthwise, and cut into ¼-inch
    slices (about 5 cups)
3 whole green chilies (canned), diced
1 14½-ounce can Mexican-style
    stewed tomatoes
1½ cups enriched 1% fat soymilk

⅓ cup nutritional yeast
⅓ cup shallots, minced
1 teaspoon dried Mexican oregano,
    plus a pinch for garnish
½ teaspoon dried thyme
1 tablespoon cornstarch
1 teaspoon tamari
¼ cup chopped fresh cilantro
2 tablespoons whole wheat bread
    crumbs
3 tablespoons soy Parmesan cheese

"GRATIN" IS A
French word for a
baked dish that is
topped with buttered
breadcrumbs or grated
cheese.

Preheat oven to 425°.

    In a 4-quart stovetop- and oven-safe casserole, warm oil and crushed pepper over medium-high heat for 1 minute. Add the garlic, onion, and celery and sauté 3 minutes. Add sliced potatoes and cook 5 minutes, stirring frequently; add chilies.

    Place tomatoes in food processor; pulse to chop coarsely. Add tomatoes to potato mixture and reduce heat to medium low.

    Place soymilk, yeast, shallots, oregano, thyme, cornstarch, and tamari in food processor and blend. Add to the potato mixture along with the cilantro. Remove from heat and top with bread crumbs and soy Parmesan. Sprinkle with additional Mexican oregano and bake, uncovered, for 25 minutes.

NUTRITION ANALYSIS: PER 9½-OUNCE SERVING

Enlightened Potato Gratin with Green Chilies
Protein 11 g, carbohydrate 35 g, fiber 5 g, fat 3 g,
cholesterol 0 mg, calcium 88 mg, sodium 575 mg
Calories 185: from protein 21%,
from carbohydrate 67%, from fat 12%

Traditional Potato Gratin with Green Chilies
Protein 7 g, carbohydrate 34 g, fiber 3 g, fat 13 g,
cholesterol 37 mg, calcium 136 mg, sodium 796 mg
Calories 275: from protein 10%,
from carbohydrate 48%, from fat 41%

Yams and "Bacon" Medley

*Veggie Canadian bacon and yams are a natural
in this easy, colorful, delicious, and nutritious dish.*

2 teaspoons olive oil
⅛ teaspoon crushed red pepper
1 tablespoon dried minced garlic
1½ cups chopped red onion
½ cup chopped red bell pepper
1 6-ounce package veggie Canadian
   bacon, diced

2 cups peeled and cubed yams
¼ cup dry sherry
1 cup chicken-flavor vegetarian
   broth, boiling
2 cups broccoli florets
1 teaspoon dried thyme

In a large electric frying pan, warm oil, crushed pepper, and minced dried garlic over medium-high heat for 1 minute. Add the onion, bell pepper, and veggie bacon and sauté 3 minutes, stirring frequently. Add the yams and cook 8 minutes. Stir in sherry and hot broth. Reduce heat to medium and add broccoli and thyme. Cover and simmer for 10 minutes, or until veggies are cooked through. Good served with brown rice.

NUTRITION ANALYSIS: PER 12-OUNCE SERVING

Enlightened Yams and "Bacon" Medley
Protein 5 g, carbohydrate 11 g, fiber 1 g, fat 1 g,
cholesterol 0 mg, calcium 15 mg, sodium 184 mg
Calories 75: from protein 28%,
from carbohydrate 61%, from fat 11%

Traditional Yams and Bacon Medley
Protein 6 g, carbohydrate 11 g, fiber 0 g, fat 6 g,
cholesterol 21 mg, calcium 17 mg, sodium 446 mg
Calories 119: from protein 20%,
from carbohydrate 36%, from fat 43%

Cajun "Cream" Sauce

*This elegant sauce is rich-tasting and flavorful
without heavy cream or butter. Serve with Louisiana Stuffed
Potatoes (page 150) or over rice or steamed vegetables.*

*6
Servings*

2 teaspoons olive oil
⅛ teaspoon crushed red pepper
1 clove garlic, minced
1½ tablespoons unbleached flour
⅓ cup enriched 1% fat soymilk

1⅓ cups mushroom broth, heated
¾ cup nutritional yeast
1 teaspoon Bragg Liquid Aminos
½ teaspoon dried chives

Warm oil, crushed pepper, and minced garlic in a medium saucepan for 2 minutes over medium-high heat. Add flour, stirring until mixture forms a paste. Using a small wire whisk, gradually add the soymilk and hot broth. Reduce heat to simmer and add yeast, whisking until blended. Add liquid aminos and chives and continue to simmer until sauce begins to thicken, or until ready to serve. Sauce will thicken further as it sits.

NUTRITION ANALYSIS: PER 2½-OUNCE SERVING

Enlightened Cajun "Cream" Sauce
Protein 3 g, carbohydrate 20 g, fiber 1 g, fat 2 g,
cholesterol 0 mg, calcium 23 mg, sodium 87 mg
Calories 37: from protein 10%,
from carbohydrate 74%, from fat 16%

Traditional Cajun Cream Sauce
Protein 3 g, carbohydrate 5 g, fiber 0 g, fat 11 g,
cholesterol 34 mg, calcium 80 mg, sodium 292 mg
Calories 127: from protein 7%,
from carbohydrate 14%, from fat 78%

Delightful Desserts

Whether desserts are grand creations with sensational presentations or simple treats, they tend to be notoriously high in fat, calories, and cholesterol. Should the health-conscious cook abandon rich-tasting desserts? Should dessert lovers avoid chocolate altogether? Should we give up the festive finale to a holiday meal? Not if you follow my lead. Replace the high-fat and cholesterol-laden ingredients normally found in luscious desserts with my easy alternatives, and you *can* have your cake and eat it, too! You can enjoy delectable desserts such as Fudge Glazed Chocolate Almond Brownies and the outrageous Sweet Potato Pie. How about a warm and wonderful Strawberry Mango Cobbler? These luscious treats are completely egg- and dairy-free. You can enjoy all these and more with a healthier bottom line.

There is a better way to produce rich-tasting, sweet, and delicious desserts. The focus is on the ingredients used to replace eggs, refined sugar, butter, and dairy products. I recommend using fruit purees to replace fat. Prune puree, applesauce, and Lighter Bake do an excellent job of bonding the structure of the baked product without sacrificing taste. Each of these purees has its own application, and it's important not to use too much, or the result could be a mealy texture. Lite silken tofu and egg replacer powder are my binding agents of choice, and enriched 1% fat soymilk is used in place of cow's milk. These are just some of the wholesome ingredients that I have used very successfully to create these enchanting desserts. Check the Resource Guide on page 285 for information regarding these ingredients.

Perhaps the easiest desserts in my kitchen are my rich-tasting puddings. Prepared in the traditional fashion, a simple pudding can be the source of quite a bit of excess fat and calories. Make my Orange Apricot Pudding or Chocolate Rice Pudding, and you will marvel at the rich flavor and creamy texture you have produced, completely dairy- and cholesterol-free! I take my desserts very seriously and enjoy creating scrumptious desserts that will surprise and satisfy. It's really so easy to do—healthfully!

Almond Cranberry Mocha Cake

*This cake has a brownielike texture enhanced by
chocolate chips that actually disappear into the cake.*

olive oil cooking spray
2¼ cups whole wheat pastry flour
1 cup unsweetened cocoa powder
1 teaspoon baking soda
1 teaspoon nonaluminum baking
    powder
1 teaspoon ground cinnamon
½ cup dairy-free chocolate chips

½ cup dried cranberries
1 12.3-ounce package lite silken tofu
⅔ cup prune puree
2 cups evaporated cane juice
¾ cup strong brewed coffee
1 tablespoon pure vanilla extract
⅓ cup sliced almonds

Preheat oven to 350°. Spray a 9-cup tube pan with oil.

Mix together the pastry flour, cocoa, baking soda, baking powder, cinnamon, chocolate chips, and dried cranberries in a large bowl. Set aside.

Place tofu in food processor and blend. Add prune puree and evaporated cane juice; blend. Add coffee and vanilla and process until smooth. Make a well in the center of the dry ingredients and quickly fold in the tofu mixture. Pour into prepared pan, and top generously with sliced almonds. Bake 50 minutes, or until tester comes out clean. Serve with Hip Whip.

NUTRITION ANALYSIS: PER 4½-OUNCE SERVING

Enlightened Almond Cranberry Mocha Cake
Protein 8 g, carbohydrate 56 g, fiber 6 g, fat 4 g,
cholesterol 0 mg, calcium 67 mg, sodium 272 mg
Calories 280: from protein 10%,
from carbohydrate 76%, from fat 13%

Traditional Almond Cranberry Mocha Cake
Protein 7 g, carbohydrate 64 g, fiber 4 g, fat 20 g,
cholesterol 84 mg, calcium 61 mg, sodium 460 mg
Calories 444: from protein 6%,
from carbohydrate 55%, from fat 39%

Apricot Butter

*My friend Mimi Clark, the Vegetarian Gourmet
Cooking Class instructor in Virginia, gave me
the initial recipe for this velvety, rich-tasting spread.
I added the brandy for more depth of flavor.
It's great for toast, muffins, waffles, or pancakes.*

*Makes
3 Cups*

1½ cups chopped dried apricots
2 tablespoons apricot brandy
(optional)

1½ cups natural apple juice

Place apricots and brandy in a small saucepan and cook 1 minute over medium-high heat. Reduce heat to low and add apple juice. Simmer, stirring frequently, 25 minutes, or until liquid has been absorbed. Set aside to cool. Puree mixture in food processor or blender. Spoon into a sterilized jar, place a circle of parchment paper under the lid, and store in the refrigerator.

NUTRITION ANALYSIS: PER 2 TABLESPOONS

Enlightened Apricot Butter
Protein 1 g, carbohydrate 21, fiber 2 g, fat 0 g,
cholesterol 0 mg, calcium 0 mg, sodium 6 mg
Calories 88: from protein 5%,
from carbohydrate 94%, from fat 1%

Traditional Apricot Butter
Protein 2 g, carbohydrate 35 g, fiber 3 g, fat 7 g,
cholesterol 19 mg, calcium 2 mg, sodium 5 mg
Calories 196: from protein: 3%,
from carbohydrate 67%, from fat 30%

Baked Butterscotch Pudding

Baking this dairy-free pudding gives the texture
a certain density that intensifies the rich flavors.

3 tablespoons rice butter spread
1½ cups plus ½ cup firmly packed
 brown sugar
1 cup enriched vanilla 1% fat
 soymilk
1 12.3-ounce package lite silken tofu
1 medium banana
¼ cup strong coffee

2 tablespoons liquid Fruitsource
1 tablespoon cornstarch
2 tablespoons pure vanilla extract
⅛ teaspoon ground allspice
ground cinnamon and ground nutmeg for garnish

Preheat oven to 350°.

In a medium saucepan, melt rice butter spread over moderate heat, and stir in the 1½ cups of brown sugar. Cook mixture until smooth and bubbling, stirring frequently, about 5 minutes.

Warm soymilk in microwave and add to sugar mixture, stirring until sugar has dissolved, about 2 minutes.

Place tofu in food processor and blend; add remaining ½ cup of brown sugar and process. Break banana into pieces and add with the sugar/soymilk mixture; blend about 2 minutes. Add remaining ingredients and process until smooth. Pour into a 2-quart oven-proof bowl, sprinkle with cinnamon and nutmeg, and place in preheated oven. Bake 30 minutes. Serve warm, or chill several hours or overnight.

ALL TOFU HAS A very high liquid content, and these puddings tend to separate a bit when stored in the refrigerator. Not to worry—the flavor is not affected. Briefly stir the pudding, and it will be restored to its original luxurious texture.

NUTRITION ANALYSIS: PER 5½-OUNCE SERVING

Enlightened Baked Butterscotch Pudding
Protein 4 g, carbohydrate 46 g, fiber 0 g, fat 1 g,
cholesterol 0 mg, calcium 102 mg, sodium 116 mg
Calories 219: from protein 8%,
from carbohydrate 86%, from fat 6%

Traditional Baked Butterscotch Pudding
Protein 4 g, carbohydrate 34 g, fiber 0 g, fat 24 g,
cholesterol 169 mg, calcium 128 mg, sodium 175 mg
Calories 362: from protein 5%,
from carbohydrate 36%, from fat 59%

Banana Fudge Pudding

It's richly delectable! Chill several hours or
overnight to allow the flavors to meld.

2 12.3-ounce packages lite silken tofu
2 medium bananas
1½ tablespoons lemon juice
⅓ cup plus 2 tablespoons unsweet-
    ened cocoa

1 cup liquid Fruitsource
2 tablespoons pure vanilla extract

Place tofu in food processor and blend. Break banana into pieces and add to the tofu with the lemon juice.

Place cocoa in a medium bowl. Place Fruitsource in a glass measuring cup and microwave for 60 seconds or until hot—be careful not to let Fruitsource boil over. Or heat in saucepan for 2 minutes over medium-low heat. Whisk hot Fruitsource into cocoa powder and add to tofu mixture along with vanilla; blend. Pour into a 2-quart bowl, cover, and refrigerate at least 1 hour (best to allow flavors to develop overnight). Serve with Hip Whip.

NUTRITION ANALYSIS: PER 4¹/₃-OUNCE SERVING

Enlightened Banana Fudge Pudding
Protein 5 g, carbohydrate 31 g, fiber 2 g, fat 1 g,
cholesterol 0 mg, calcium 34 mg, sodium 57 mg
Calories 150: from protein 13%,
from carbohydrate 82%, from fat 5%

Traditional Banana Fudge Pudding
Protein 4 g, carbohydrate 33 g, fiber 1 g, fat 11 g,
cholesterol 74 mg, calcium 97 mg, sodium 130 mg
Calories 239: from protein 6%,
from carbohydrate 54%, from fat 40%

Cherry Cobbler

*Dark sweet cherries, crushed pineapple, and
golden raisins fill this luscious cobbler. The healthy topping
is made with soy grits, kamut flour, and Sucanat.*

Cobbler

1 16-ounce package frozen pitted
    dark cherries
1 20-ounce can crushed pineapple
1 cup golden raisins
¼ cup ginger brandy
¾ cup liquid Fruitsource

1 tablespoon pure vanilla extract
¼ teaspoon almond extract
2 teaspoons lemon juice
1 tablespoon cornstarch
1 tablespoon cold water

Almond Crunch Topping

⅔ cup rolled oats
¼ cup kamut flour
3 tablespoons soy grits
¼ cup whole almonds
½ cup Sucanat or brown sugar

½ teaspoon ground cinnamon
¼ teaspoon ground nutmeg
3 tablespoons Lighter Bake
2 tablespoons rice butter spread

Preheat oven to 350°.

For the cobbler: Place the cherries and crushed pineapple in a stovetop- and oven-safe 5-quart casserole over medium heat and warm, stirring occasionally, until cherries are thawed.

Place the raisins in a small saucepan with the brandy and cook over medium-low heat 5 minutes, or until the liquid is absorbed. Add the Fruitsource, vanilla and almond extracts, and lemon juice. Cook mixture over medium heat for 5 minutes, stirring frequently.

In a small bowl, blend the cornstarch and water. Reduce heat to low and add the cornstarch paste to the fruit. Simmer 5 minutes and set aside.

Cherry Cobbler *(continued)*

For the topping: Place the oats, flour, soy grits, almonds, Sucanat, cinnamon, and nutmeg in food processor and pulse to mix, keeping the almonds chunky. Add Lighter Bake and rice spread and process until mixture is crumbly but holding together. Sprinkle over top of filling and bake, uncovered, for 25 minutes.

NUTRITION ANALYSIS: PER 5-OUNCE SERVING

Enlightened Cherry Cobbler
Protein 3 g, carbohydrate 42 g, fiber 3 g, fat 4 g,
cholesterol 0 mg, calcium 35 mg, sodium 37 mg
Calories 244: from protein 5%,
from carbohydrate 68%, from fat 13%

Traditional Cherry Cobbler
Protein 5 g, carbohydrate 44 g, fiber 4 g, fat 14 g,
cholesterol 18 mg, calcium 46 mg, sodium 186 mg
Calories 343: from protein 5%,
from carbohydrate 51%, from fat 36%

Cherry Noodle Kugel

*My friend Gail Storch asked me to "enlighten" her family kugel recipe.
This delectable noodle pudding makes a beautiful presentation.*

Pudding

2 tablespoons lemon juice

1 cup enriched 1% fat soymilk

8 ounces eggless fettuccine, broken
in half

3 12.3-ounce packages regular silken
tofu

¼ cup Soymage cream cheese

1 cup evaporated cane juice

2 tablespoons Soyco rice butter
spread

1 tablespoon egg replacer powder

1 tablespoon pure vanilla extract

Topping*

1 16-ounce can unsweetened pie
cherries (or cherry pie filling)

1 cup chopped dried apricots

¾ cup evaporated cane juice

¼ teaspoon almond extract

1 tablespoon cornstarch

1 tablespoon cold water

Preheat oven to 350°.

For the pudding: Add lemon juice to soymilk and set aside.

Cook noodles according to package directions. Rinse thoroughly with cold
water, and set aside, rinsing from time to time, until ready to assemble.

Place tofu in food processor and blend until smooth. Add cream cheese and
evaporated cane juice and process. Add remaining pudding ingredients and
blend until smooth. Pour mixture into 9-by-13-inch glass baking dish; add
cooked noodles and mix thoroughly. Cover with foil and bake for 30 minutes.

For the topping: Place cherries and apricots in a medium saucepan over
medium heat. Add evaporated cane juice and almond extract and bring the

* Alternately, you may substitute prepared cherry pie filling for the topping.

Cherry Noodle Kugel *(continued)*

mixture to a low boil, stirring occasionally.

In a small bowl, blend cornstarch with water; add to cherry mixture. Reduce heat and simmer for 10 minutes.

Uncover pudding and spread fruit mixture evenly over top. Return to oven and bake, uncovered, an additional 15 minutes. Serve warm or cover and refrigerate.

NUTRITION ANALYSIS: PER 6-OUNCE SERVING

Enlightened Cherry Noodle Kugel
Protein 8 g, carbohydrate 41 g, fiber 2 g, fat 3 g,
cholesterol 0 mg, calcium 51 mg, sodium 57 mg
Calories 213: from protein 14%,
from carbohydrate 73%, from fat 13%

Traditional Cherry Noodle Kugel
Protein 7 g, carbohydrate 32 g, fiber 1 g, fat 19 g,
cholesterol 66 mg, calcium 100 mg, sodium 147 mg
Calories 324: from protein 9%,
from carbohydrate 39%, from fat 52%

Chocolate Chip Bundt Cake with Orange Blossom Glaze

Whole-grain yellow cornmeal enhances the texture and crust in this cake.

olive oil cooking spray

Cake

3 cups whole wheat pastry flour
½ cup yellow cornmeal
1½ teaspoons baking soda
2 teaspoons nonaluminum baking powder
1 teaspoon ground cinnamon
½ cup dairy-free chocolate chips

⅓ cup chopped almonds
1 12.3-ounce package lite silken tofu
½ cup unsweetened applesauce
1½ cups evaporated cane juice
½ cup enriched vanilla rice milk
1 teaspoon almond extract

Glaze

¾ cup sifted powdered sugar
1½ to 2 tablespoons orange juice

⅛ teaspoon orange blossom water
⅛ teaspoon almond extract

Preheat oven to 350°. Spray 10-inch Bundt pan with oil.

For the cake: Combine the flour, cornmeal, baking soda, baking powder, cinnamon, chocolate chips, and almonds in a large bowl and set aside.

Place tofu in food processor and blend. Add applesauce and evaporated cane juice; blend. Add rice milk and almond extract and process until smooth. Make a well in the center of the dry ingredients and quickly fold in the tofu mixture. Pour into prepared pan. Bake 40 minutes, or until tester comes out clean. Cool in pan 15 minutes; then turn onto cooling rack. Set aside.

For the glaze: Sift powdered sugar into a medium bowl. Add 1½ tablespoons orange juice and the remaining ingredients and stir to blend. If the glaze is too thick, add a little more orange juice, measured by the teaspoon. Drizzle glaze on cooled cake.

Popular in Mediterranean cuisine, orange blossom water is sometimes called orange flower water. It is a perfumy distillation of bitter orange flowers and is used as a flavoring in baked goods and in savory dishes.

NUTRITION ANALYSIS: PER 4¼-OUNCE SERVING

Enlightened Chocolate Chip Bundt Cake with Orange Blossom Glaze
Protein 8 g, carbohydrate 54 g, fiber 4 g, fat 4 g, cholesterol 0 mg, calcium 86 mg, sodium 350 mg
Calories 275: from protein 11%, from carbohydrate 76%, from fat 13%

Traditional Chocolate Chip Bundt Cake with Orange Blossom Glaze
Protein 8 g, carbohydrate 67 g, fiber 3 g, fat 16 g, cholesterol 65 mg, calcium 104 mg, sodium 494 mg
Calories 434: from protein 7%, from carbohydrate 60%, from fat 33%

Chocolate Almond Brownies

*Luscious, fudge-glazed chocolate brownies that are
low in fat and calories and rich in phytochemicals are
easy to make when using wholesome ingredients.*

*40
Brownies*

olive oil cooking spray

Brownies
2⅓ cups whole wheat pastry flour
2 cups Wonderslim cocoa
2 tablespoons soy flour
1 teaspoon baking soda
1 teaspoon nonaluminum baking
   powder
1½ teaspoons ground cinnamon
½ teaspoon sea salt
⅓ cup chopped almonds

½ cup dairy-free chocolate chips
1 12.3-ounce package lite silken tofu
1 cup prune puree
2 cups evaporated cane juice
2 teaspoons pure vanilla extract
½ teaspoon almond extract
1 cup enriched vanilla 1% fat
   soymilk

Frosting
1 12.3-ounce package lite silken tofu
½ cup evaporated cane juice
⅓ cup Wonderslim cocoa
1 tablespoon cornstarch

1 cup liquid Fruitsource
1½ tablespoons pure vanilla extract
¼ cup sliced almonds

Preheat oven to 350°. Spray 11-by-17-inch jelly roll pan with oil.

For the brownies: In a large bowl, combine flour, cocoa, soy flour, baking soda, baking powder, cinnamon, and salt. Stir in chopped almonds and chocolate chips and set aside.

Place tofu in food processor and blend until smooth. Add prune puree and blend. Add the evaporated cane juice, vanilla and almond extracts, and soymilk and process until smooth. Make a well in the dry ingredients and fold tofu mixture in quickly. Do not overbeat. Pour batter into the prepared pan and bake for 30 minutes, or until tester comes out clean.

For the frosting: Place tofu in food processor and blend until smooth. Add evaporated cane juice and process.

Mix cocoa and cornstarch in a medium bowl and set aside.

Heat Fruitsource in microwave 60 seconds, or until hot, being careful not to boil over. Or heat in saucepan over low heat, 2 minutes. Whisk the Fruitsource into the cocoa mixture until a smooth syrup has formed. Add to the tofu mixture along with vanilla and process until smooth. Spread evenly over brownies and top with sliced almonds. Place in refrigerator to set.

NUTRITION ANALYSIS: PER 2-BY-2-INCH BROWNIE

Enlightened Chocolate Almond Brownies
Protein 4 g, carbohydrate 21 g, fiber 1 g, fat 2 g,
cholesterol 0 mg, calcium 36 mg, sodium 96 mg
Calories 117: from protein 14%,
from carbohydrate 71%, from fat 15%

Traditional Chocolate Almond Brownies
Protein 4 g, carbohydrate 25 g, fiber 1 g, fat 18 g,
cholesterol 48 mg, calcium 46 mg, sodium 112 mg
Calories 259: from protein 5%,
from carbohydrate 37%, from fat 58%

Chocolate Banana Cake

*This delicious textured cake
is nutritious and caffeine-free.*

olive oil cooking spray
2 cups spelt flour
¼ cup soy flour
⅔ cup Wonderslim cocoa
2 tablespoons flaxseed meal
2 tablespoons cornstarch
1 teaspoon baking soda
1 teaspoon nonaluminum baking
    powder

1 teaspoon ground cinnamon
½ teaspoon sea salt
1 12.3-ounce package lite silken tofu
¼ cup Lighter Bake
¾ cup mashed bananas (2 medium)
1¼ cups evaporated cane juice
½ cup enriched 1% fat soymilk
1 tablespoon pure vanilla extract

Preheat oven to 350°. Spray a 9-by-13-inch baking pan with oil.

In a large bowl, combine the spelt flour, soy flour, cocoa, flaxseed meal, cornstarch, baking soda, baking powder, cinnamon, and salt. Set aside.

Place tofu in food processor and blend. Add Lighter Bake and mashed bananas; blend. Add the remaining ingredients and process thoroughly. Make a well in the dry ingredients and fold in the liquid mixture without overbeating. Pour into prepared pan and bake 35 minutes, or until tester comes out clean. Set aside to cool. Serve with Hip Whip or a dusting of powdered sugar.

NUTRITION ANALYSIS: PER 2¾-OUNCE SERVING

Enlightened Chocolate Banana Cake
Protein 6 g, carbohydrate 31 g, fiber 3 g, fat 1 g,
cholesterol 0 mg, calcium 45 mg, sodium 202 mg
Calories 148: from protein 14%,
from carbohydrate 78%, from fat 8%

Traditional Chocolate Banana Cake
Protein 3 g, carbohydrate 36 g, fiber 1 g, fat 10 g,
cholesterol 58 mg, calcium 39 mg, sodium 260 mg
Calories 241: from protein 6%,
from carbohydrate 58%, from fat 37%

Chocolate Chip Walnut Bread

This quick bread is hearty,
sweet, and delicious.

Servings

olive oil cooking spray
2½ cups spelt flour
¼ cup soy flour
2 tablespoons toasted wheat germ
2 tablespoons flaxseed meal
1 teaspoon baking soda
1 teaspoon nonaluminum baking
    powder
1 teaspoon ground cinnamon
½ teaspoon sea salt

¼ teaspoon ground allspice
⅛ teaspoon ground nutmeg
⅓ cup chopped walnuts
⅓ cup espresso chocolate chips
⅓ cup date pieces
½ cup Lighter Bake
1½ cups evaporated cane juice
½ cup enriched vanilla 1% fat soymilk
½ tablespoon pure vanilla extract
freshly ground nutmeg

Preheat oven to 350°. Spray a 9-by-5-inch loaf pan with oil.

Combine the spelt flour, soy flour, wheat germ, flaxseed meal, baking soda, baking powder, cinnamon, salt, allspice, nutmeg, nuts, chips, and dates in a medium bowl. Set aside.

In a large bowl, combine Lighter Bake and evaporated cane juice, blending until smooth. Add soymilk and vanilla; mix until smooth. Fold the dry ingredients into the liquid mixture quickly just until mixed. Pour into prepared pan and sprinkle with freshly ground nutmeg. Bake 40 minutes, or until tester comes out clean.

SPELT SEEMS TO require less liquid than other flours. To use spelt in a recipe designed for wheat flour, start by using less liquid than called for or by increasing the amount of spelt flour.

NUTRITION ANALYSIS: PER 3-OUNCE SERVING

Enlightened Chocolate Chip Walnut Bread
Protein 6 g, carbohydrate 49 g, fiber 6 g, fat 4 g,
cholesterol 0 mg, calcium 45 mg, sodium 242 mg
Calories 238: from protein 9%,
from carbohydrate 76%, from fat 15%

Traditional Chocolate Chip Walnut Bread
Protein 6 g, carbohydrate 45 g, fiber 2 g, fat 17 g,
cholesterol 36 mg, calcium 52 mg, sodium 306 mg
Calories 347: from protein: 7%,
from carbohydrate 50%, from fat 43%

Chocolate Streusel Cake

*A sweet tunnel of spiced chocolate fills the center
of this delicious Bundt cake. Top with a sprinkling
of powdered sugar, if desired.*

*12
Servings*

olive oil cooking spray

Streusel
⅔ cup dairy-free chocolate chips
⅓ cup chopped pecans
¼ cup brown sugar

1 tablespoon unbleached flour
1 teaspoon ground cinnamon
¼ teaspoon ground nutmeg

Cake
3 cups whole wheat pastry flour
½ cup yellow cornmeal
1½ teaspoons baking soda
2 teaspoons nonaluminum baking
 powder
1 teaspoon ground cinnamon

¼ teaspoon sea salt
1 12.3-ounce package lite silken tofu
½ cup unsweetened applesauce
1½ cups evaporated cane juice
2 teaspoons pure vanilla extract
½ cup enriched vanilla 1% fat
 soymilk

Preheat oven to 375°. Spray 10-inch Bundt pan with oil.

For the Streusel: Place chocolate chips in food processor and pulse to chop coarsely. Add remaining streusel ingredients and pulse to mix. Do not process to a fine crumb, but instead create chunky mixture. Set aside.

For the cake: Combine the pastry flour, cornmeal, baking soda, baking powder, cinnamon, and salt in a large bowl and set aside.

Place tofu in food processor and blend until smooth. Add applesauce and blend. Add the remaining ingredients, processing until smooth. Make a well in the flour mixture and fold tofu mixture in quickly. Do not overbeat. Pour ⅓ of the batter into the prepared pan and top with the streusel mix. Pour remaining batter over streusel and bake for 40, minutes or until tester comes out clean.

NUTRITION ANALYSIS: PER 4-OUNCE SERVING

Enlightened Chocolate Streusel Cake
Protein 7 g, carbohydrate 51 g, fiber 4 g, fat 5 g,
cholesterol 0 mg, calcium 92 mg, sodium 312 mg
Calories 270: from protein 10%,
from carbohydrate 74%, from fat 15%

Traditional Chocolate Streusel Cake
Protein 6 g, carbohydrate 54 g, fiber 2 g, fat 28 g,
cholesterol 93 mg, calcium 77 mg, sodium 506 mg
Calories 474: from protein 5%,
from carbohydrate 44%, from fat 51%

Chocolate Rice Pudding

This is rich tasting, sweet,
and really "soysational."

2 cups water
½ teaspoon sea salt
1 cup raw white rice
3 cups enriched vanilla 1% fat
    soymilk
2 tablespoons rice butter spread
1 12.3-ounce package lite silken tofu

1¾ cups evaporated cane juice
⅓ cup liquid Fruitsource
¼ cup cocoa powder
2 tablespoons cornstarch
1 tablespoon pure vanilla extract
⅛ teaspoon ground nutmeg

Preheat oven to 350°.

Bring water and salt to a boil in a medium saucepan. Add rice, stir, and bring to a second boil. Reduce heat to simmer, cover, and cook for 15 to 20 minutes, or until water is absorbed.

In a stovetop- and oven-proof 5-quart casserole, heat soymilk and rice spread over low heat, stirring occasionally. Scrape cooked rice into hot soymilk and bring to a boil over medium heat.

Place tofu in food processor and blend until smooth. Add evaporated cane juice and process to blend.

Place Fruitsource in a small glass measuring cup and microwave 30 seconds, or heat in small saucepan over low heat until hot, but not boiling, about 2 minutes.

Place cocoa and cornstarch in a small bowl and whisk in hot Fruitsource until a smooth chocolate syrup is formed. Add to the tofu mixture along with vanilla; blend. Add tofu mixture to the rice mixture and stir to blend thoroughly. Sprinkle with nutmeg and bake, uncovered, 35 minutes. Serve warm or cover and refrigerate.

NUTRITION ANALYSIS: PER 6-OUNCE SERVING

Enlightened Chocolate Rice Pudding
Protein 5 g, carbohydrate 40 g, fiber 1 g, fat 1 g,
cholesterol 0 mg, calcium 91 mg, sodium 170 mg
Calories 199: from protein 10%,
from carbohydrate 84%, from fat 6%

Traditional Chocolate Rice Pudding
Protein 5 g, carbohydrate 45 g, fiber 1 g, fat 22 g,
cholesterol 87 mg, calcium 87 mg, sodium 221 mg
Calories 384: from protein 5%,
from carbohydrate 45%, from fat 50%

Cinnamon Pecan Muffins

These tasty muffins are made with kamut flour, an ancient wheat that is more nutritious than modern hybridized wheat. These muffins are also fortified with flaxseed meal and soy flour. Serve with luscious Apricot Butter, page 236.

12 Large Muffins

olive oil cooking spray
2 cups plus 2 tablespoons kamut flour
¼ cup soy flour
2 tablespoons flaxseed meal
¾ teaspoon baking soda
1 teaspoon nonaluminum baking powder
1 teaspoon ground cinnamon
¼ teaspoon ground allspice

½ teaspoon sea salt
⅓ cup chopped pecans
½ cup Lighter Bake
1 cup evaporated cane juice
2 tablespoons egg replacer powder
⅓ cup cold water
⅔ cup enriched vanilla 1% fat soymilk
2 teaspoons pure vanilla extract

Flaxseeds are a plant-based source of omega 3 fatty acids, a type of polyunsaturated fatty acid that retards inflammation and is thought to reduce the risk of many diseases.

Preheat oven to 375°. Spray a 12-cup muffin pan with oil.

In a medium bowl, combine the kamut flour, soy flour, flaxseed meal, baking soda, baking powder, cinnamon, allspice, and salt. Stir in the pecans and set aside.

In a large bowl, mix the Lighter Bake with the evaporated cane juice.

In a small measuring cup, whisk together the egg replacer powder with the water until foamy. Add to the Lighter Bake mixture with the soymilk and vanilla. Make a well in the center of the dry ingredients and quickly fold in the liquid mixture. Pour into prepared muffin cups and sprinkle tops with additional cinnamon. Bake 20 minutes, or until tester comes out clean.

NUTRITION ANALYSIS: PER MUFFIN

Enlightened Cinnamon Pecan Muffins
Protein 4 g, carbohydrate 36 g, fiber 3 g, fat 3 g, cholesterol 0 mg, calcium 46 mg, sodium 169 mg
Calories 181: from protein: 9%, from carbohydrate 77%, from fat 15%

Traditional Cinnamon Pecan Muffins
Protein 4 g, carbohydrate 34 g, fiber 1 g, fat 13 g, cholesterol 64 mg, calcium 57 mg, sodium 317 mg
Calories 271: from protein 6%, from carbohydrate 50%, from fat 44%

Cinnamon Spice Pudding

*Lite silken tofu lends its creamy, custardlike texture
to this delightful spiced pudding. Serve with Hip Whip.*

2 12.3-ounce packages lite silken tofu
1 ripe medium banana
1 cup evaporated cane juice
2 tablespoons rice butter spread
2 tablespoons pure vanilla extract

2 tablespoons lemon juice
½ teaspoon ground cinnamon
cinnamon and freshly ground nut-
    meg for garnish

Place tofu in food processor and blend. Break banana into pieces, add, and blend. Add the evaporated cane juice, rice butter, vanilla, lemon juice, and cinnamon. Pulse to mix; then blend until smooth. Pour into a 2-quart bowl; sprinkle with cinnamon and nutmeg. Cover and refrigerate for at least an hour, preferably overnight. Serve chilled.

NUTRITION ANALYSIS: PER 4¾-OUNCE SERVING

Enlightened Cinnamon Spice Pudding
Protein 7 g, carbohydrate 20 g, fiber 0 g, fat 1 g,
cholesterol 0 mg, calcium 60 mg, sodium 114 mg
Calories 124: from protein 23%,
from carbohydrate 66%, from fat 11%

Traditional Cinnamon Spice Pudding
Protein 5 g, carbohydrate 26 g, fiber 0 g, fat 19 g,
cholesterol 164 mg, calcium 114 mg, sodium 182 mg
Calories 286: from protein 5%,
from carbohydrate 36%, from fat 58%

Cranberry Oat Muffins

These delicious muffins are fortified with flaxseed meal and whole oats.
Serve with luscious Apricot Butter, page 236.

12
Muffins

olive oil cooking spray
1 cup whole wheat pastry flour
1 cup rolled oats
½ cup yellow cornmeal
¼ cup soy flour
1½ tablespoons flaxseed meal
½ teaspoon baking soda
1 teaspoon nonaluminum baking
　powder
1 teaspoon ground cinnamon

½ teaspoon sea salt
1 cup dried cranberries
½ cup unsweetened applesauce
¾ cup evaporated cane juice
2 tablespoons egg replacer powder
½ cup cold water
½ cup enriched vanilla 1% fat
　soymilk
¼ cup sliced almonds

ALL WHOLE GRAINS
are carbohydrates and are
rich sources of fiber, which
slows digestion and satis-
fies hunger while reducing
the secretion of insulin
into the pancreas.

Preheat oven to 350°. Spray a 12-cup muffin pan with oil.

In a medium bowl, combine the pastry flour, oats, cornmeal, soy flour, flaxseed meal, baking soda, baking powder, cinnamon, and salt. Stir in the cranberries and set aside.

In a large bowl, mix the applesauce with the evaporated cane juice.

In a small measuring cup, whisk together the egg replacer powder with the water until foamy. Add to the applesauce mixture with the soymilk. Make a well in the center of the dry ingredients and quickly fold in the applesauce mixture. Pour into prepared muffin cups and sprinkle tops with sliced almonds. Bake 20 minutes, or until tester comes out clean.

NUTRITION ANALYSIS: PER MUFFIN

Enlightened Cranberry Oat Muffins
Protein 4 g, carbohydrate 32 g, fiber 3 g, fat 3 g,
cholesterol 0 mg, calcium 56 mg, sodium 147 mg
Calories 163: from protein 10%,
from carbohydrate 76%, from fat 14%

Traditional Cranberry Oat Muffins
Protein 6 g, carbohydrate 37 g, fiber 3 g, fat 15 g,
cholesterol 61 mg, calcium 69 mg, sodium 291 mg
Calories 304: from protein 8%,
from carbohydrate 48%, from fat 44%

Creamy Rice Pudding

Rice pudding is one of my favorite comfort foods. Like all of my recipes, this delicious, rich-tasting rice pudding is completely dairy-free.

2 cups water
½ teaspoon sea salt
1 cup raw white rice
3 cups enriched vanilla 1% fat
  soymilk
2 tablespoons rice butter spread

1 12.3-ounce package lite silken tofu
2 cups evaporated cane juice
2 tablespoons cornstarch
1 tablespoon pure vanilla extract
ground cinnamon for garnish

Preheat oven to 350°.

Bring water and salt to a boil in a medium saucepan. Add rice, stir, and bring to a second boil. Reduce heat to low, cover, and simmer 20 minutes, until water is absorbed. Scrape cooked rice into a stovetop- and oven-proof 5-quart casserole dish. Add soymilk and rice spread and cook mixture over medium heat, stirring occasionally.

Place tofu in food processor and blend until smooth. Add evaporated cane juice, cornstarch, and vanilla; process. Add tofu mixture to rice, stirring to blend. Sprinkle generously with cinnamon. Bake, uncovered, 25 minutes. Serve warm, or cover and refrigerate.

NUTRITION ANALYSIS: PER 6-OUNCE SERVING

Enlightened Creamy Rice Pudding
Protein 4 g, carbohydrate 37 g, fiber 1 g, fat 2 g,
cholesterol 0 mg, calcium 89 mg, sodium 140 mg
Calories 180: from protein 10%,
from carbohydrate 82%, from fat 8%

Traditional Creamy Rice Pudding
Protein 5 g, carbohydrate 29 g, fiber 0.5 g, fat 13 g,
cholesterol 97 mg, calcium 122 mg, sodium 234 mg
Calories 257: from protein 8%,
from carbohydrate 45%, from fat 47%

Gingerbread Spice Bars

This sweet and spicy gingerbread
is easy and delicious.

20 2¼-by-2¼-Inch Cookie Bars

olive oil cooking spray
2½ cups whole wheat pastry flour
¼ cup yellow cornmeal
1 teaspoon baking soda
1 teaspoon nonaluminum baking powder
1 teaspoon ground cinnamon
1 teaspoon ground ginger
¼ teaspoon ground nutmeg
⅛ teaspoon ground cloves

¼ teaspoon sea salt
1 12.3-ounce package lite silken tofu
½ cup prune puree
2 cups evaporated cane juice
½ cup enriched vanilla 1% fat soymilk
1½ tablespoons grated fresh gingerroot
½ tablespoon pure vanilla extract
powdered sugar

GINGER IS AN underground stem or root of a plant that has been prized since ancient times for its ability to stimulate digestion and settle upset stomachs.

Preheat oven to 350°. Spray 9-by-13-inch baking pan with oil.

Combine the pastry flour, cornmeal, baking soda, baking powder, spices, and salt in a large bowl and set aside.

Place tofu in food processor and blend. Add prune puree and blend. Add remaining ingredients (except powdered sugar) and process. Make a well in the center of the dry ingredients and quickly fold in the tofu mixture. Pour into prepared pan; sprinkle with additional cinnamon and nutmeg. Bake 30 minutes, or until tester comes out clean. Cut into bars and serve sprinkled with powdered sugar, if desired.

NUTRITION ANALYSIS: PER 2-OUNCE COOKIE BAR

Enlightened Gingerbread Spice Bars
Protein 4 g, carbohydrate 25 g, fiber 2 g, fat 0.5 g, cholesterol 0 mg, calcium 42 mg, sodium 134 mg
Calories 131: from protein 11%, from carbohydrate 86%, from fat 4%

Traditional Gingerbread Spice Bars
Protein 3 g, carbohydrate 34 g, fiber 1 g, fat 7 g, cholesterol 38 mg, calcium 21 mg, sodium 214 mg
Calories 205: from protein 5%, from carbohydrate 66%, from fat 29%

Glazed Blueberry Surprise with Orange Chocolate Glaze

The "surprise" here is that a gorgeous, rich-tasting cake like this one can be so very low in fat. This luscious dessert is perfumed with orange blossom water, widely used in Mediterranean desserts.

olive oil cooking spray

Cake

2 cups whole wheat pastry flour
⅓ cup soy flour
½ cup yellow cornmeal
1 teaspoon baking soda
1 teaspoon nonaluminum baking powder
1 teaspoon ground cinnamon
¼ teaspoon sea salt
1½ cups evaporated cane juice
⅓ cup dried blueberries ½ cup chopped pecans

1¼ cups firm lite silken tofu
½ cup unsweetened applesauce
⅓ cup liquid Fruitsource
½ cup freshly squeezed orange juice
1 teaspoon orange blossom water
1 teaspoon pure vanilla extract
zest from 1 medium orange
1 tablespoon egg replacer powder
¼ cup water
¼ cup soy grits

Orange Chocolate Glaze

1¼ cups powdered sugar
¼ cup Wonderslim cocoa
¼ cup liquid Fruitsource

½ teaspoon orange blossom water
½ teaspoon pure vanilla extract
¼ cup orange juice (approximately)

Preheat oven to 350°. Spray 10-inch tube pan with oil.

For the cake: Combine pastry flour, soy flour, cornmeal, baking soda, baking powder, cinnamon, salt, evaporated cane juice, blueberries, and pecans in a large bowl and set aside.

Place tofu in food processor and blend. Add applesauce and Fruitsource, pulse to mix, then blend. Add the orange juice, orange blossom water, vanilla, and zest and process.

Glazed Blueberry Surprise with Orange Chocolate Glaze *(continued)*

In a small bowl, whisk egg replacer powder with water and add to the tofu mixture. Make a well in the center of the dry ingredients and quickly fold in the liquid ingredients, adding in the soy grits in the process. Pour into prepared pan; bake 45 minutes, or until tester comes out clean.

For the glaze: Sift sugar and cocoa into a medium bowl. Warm Fruitsource in the microwave 25 seconds, or in a small saucepan for 1 minute, and whisk into the cocoa mixture. Add orange blossom water and vanilla. Add the orange juice by the tablespoonful until you reach the right consistency. The glaze should fall from spoon with a ribbonlike quality and harden at room temperature. Top cake with Orange Chocolate Glaze.

NUTRITION ANALYSIS: PER 3$\frac{1}{2}$-OUNCE SERVING

Enlightened Glazed Blueberry Surprise with Orange Chocolate Glaze
Protein 6 g, carbohydrate 48 g, fiber 3 g, fat 4 g, cholesterol 0 mg, calcium 41 mg, sodium 157 mg
Calories 247: from protein 9%, from carbohydrate 76%, from fat 14%

Traditional Glazed Blueberry Surprise with Orange Chocolate Glaze
Protein 5 g, carbohydrate 50 g, fiber 2 g, fat 18 g, cholesterol 71 mg, calcium 36 mg, sodium 257 mg
Calories 375: from protein 5%, from carbohydrate 53%, from fat 42%

Lemon-Glazed Chocolate Spice Fruitcake

This delectable cake that is low in fat and rich in phytochemicals features brandy-infused fruit and a lemon glaze.

olive oil cooking spray

Cake

¼ chopped dried apricots
¼ cup golden raisins
¼ cup ginger brandy
1¾ cups whole wheat pastry flour
½ Wonderslim cocoa
¼ cup soy flour
2 tablespoons flaxseed meal
1 teaspoon baking soda
1 teaspoon nonaluminum baking powder
1 teaspoon ground cinnamon

¼ teaspoon ground allspice
¼ teaspoon ground nutmeg
⅓ cup chopped walnuts
½ cup prune puree
1½ cups evaporated cane juice
2 tablespoons egg replacer powder
½ cup cold water
1 tablespoon liquid Fruitsource
½ cup enriched vanilla 1% fat soy milk
1 teaspoon pure vanilla extract

Glaze

¾ cup powdered sugar
1½ to 2 tablespoons lemon juice

¼ teaspoon pure vanilla extract

Preheat oven to 350°. Spray 10-inch Bundt pan with oil.

For the cake: Place the apricots and raisins in a small saucepan, add the brandy, and simmer over low heat, stirring occasionally, 5 minutes or until liquid is absorbed.

In a medium bowl, mix together the pastry flour, cocoa, soy flour, flaxseed meal, baking soda, baking powder, and spices. Stir in the walnuts and set aside.

Place the prune puree in a large bowl, add the evaporated cane juice, and blend.

In a small measuring cup, whisk the egg replacer powder with water and add to the prune mixture. Blend in the Fruitsource, soymilk, and the vanilla. Fold

Lemon-Glazed Chocolate Spice Fruitcake *(continued)*

the dry ingredients into the large bowl quickly, until just mixed. Pour into prepared pan and bake 35 minutes, or until tester comes out clean. Set aside to cool.

For the glaze: Sift powdered sugar into a medium bowl. Add 1½ tablespoons lemon juice and the vanilla and stir to blend. If the glaze is too thick, add a little more juice, measured by the teaspoon. Drizzle glaze onto cooled cake.

NUTRITION ANALYSIS: PER 3½-OUNCE SERVING

Enlightened Lemon-Glazed Chocolate
Spice Fruitcake
Protein 6 g, carbohydrate 51 g, fiber 4 g, fat 4 g,
cholesterol 0 mg, calcium 63 mg, sodium 164 mg
Calories 262: from protein 9%,
from carbohydrate 79%, from fat 12%

Traditional Lemon-Glazed Chocolate
Spice Fruitcake
Protein 7 g, carbohydrate 48 g, fiber 2 g, fat 20 g,
cholesterol 81 mg, calcium 53 mg, sodium 320 mg
Calories 391: from protein 6%,
from carbohydrate 48%, from fat 46%

Glazed Date and Nut Bars

*Crunchy walnuts and sweet dates fill these delightful
cookie bars topped with a creamy lemon glaze.*

olive oil cooking spray

Bars

½ cup enriched 1% fat soymilk

1 tablespoon lemon juice

2 cups whole wheat pastry flour

⅓ cup yellow cornmeal

¼ cup soy flour

½ cup rolled multigrain cereal

1 teaspoon baking soda

1 teaspoon nonaluminum baking
    powder

1 teaspoon ground cinnamon

½ teaspoon sea salt

½ cup chopped walnuts

1 cup date pieces

¼ cup prune puree

¼ cup liquid Fruitsource

1⅓ cups evaporated cane juice

1 tablespoon pure vanilla extract

2 tablespoons egg replacer powder

Glaze

¼ cup enriched 1% fat soymilk

½ tablespoon rice butter spread

1 cup evaporated cane juice

1 teaspoon lemon extract

1 tablespoon cornstarch

1 tablespoon cold water

walnut halves (optional)

Preheat oven to 350°. Spray an 11-by-17-inch jelly roll pan with oil.

For the bars: Place soymilk in a liquid measuring cup and add lemon juice.
Set aside.

In a large bowl, combine pastry flour, cornmeal, soy flour, cereal, baking
soda, baking powder, cinnamon, and salt. Stir in the walnuts and date pieces
and set aside.

Combine prune puree and Fruitsource in a medium bowl, and cream with
the evaporated cane juice and vanilla.

In a small bowl, whisk the egg replacer powder with the cold water until
foamy and add to the liquid ingredients. Make a well in the center of the dry
ingredients and quickly fold in the liquid mixture. Do not overbeat. Pour batter into the prepared pan and bake for 30 minutes, or until tester comes out
clean.

Glazed Date and Nut Bars *(continued)*

For the glaze: Heat soymilk and rice butter in a small saucepan over medium-low heat. Stir in evaporated cane juice and lemon extract.

Blend cornstarch and water in a small bowl; then add to the pan. Lower heat and simmer 3 minutes. Remove from heat and place in refrigerator to cool, about 20 minutes. Drizzle glaze over cooled bars in pan and dot with walnut halves, if desired. Place in refrigerator to set for 30 minutes before cutting into bars.

NUTRITION ANALYSIS: PER 2-BY-3-INCH COOKIE BAR

Enlightened Glazed Date and Nut Bars
Protein 2 g, carbohydrate 24 g, fiber 2 g, fat 2 g, cholesterol 0 mg, calcium 27 mg, sodium 101 mg
Calories 117: from protein 8%, from carbohydrate 79%, from fat 13%

Traditional Glazed Date and Nut Bars
Protein 4 g, carbohydrate 26 g, fiber 1 g, fat 12 g, cholesterol 46 mg, calcium 44 mg, sodium 123 mg
Calories 229: from protein 7%, from carbohydrate 47%, from fat 47%

Glazed Mocha Muffins

*Scented with orange blossom water, these sweet muffins are lovely
when made in miniature Bundt-shaped muffin/cupcake pans.*

olive oil cooking spray

Muffins

1¾ cups plus 2 tablespoons whole
    wheat pastry flour
¼ cup yellow cornmeal
2 tablespoons soy flour
1½ tablespoons flaxseed meal
½ teaspoon baking soda
1 teaspoon nonaluminum baking
    powder
¼ teaspoon sea salt
1 teaspoon ground cinnamon

⅓ cup chopped almonds
½ cup prune puree
1½ cups evaporated cane juice
1 tablespoon egg replacer powder
¼ cup cold water
1 tablespoon liquid Fruitsource
1½ teaspoons orange blossom water
¼ teaspoon almond extract
⅓ cup fresh orange juice
⅓ cup strong brewed coffee

Glaze

¾ cup sifted powdered sugar
1½ to 2 tablespoons orange juice

⅛ teaspoon orange blossom water
⅛ teaspoon almond extract

Preheat oven to 350°. Spray muffin cups with oil.

In a medium bowl, combine pastry flour, cornmeal, soy flour, flaxseed meal,
baking soda, baking powder, salt, and cinnamon. Stir in the almonds and set
aside.

Place the prune puree in a large bowl and blend in the evaporated cane juice.

In a small measuring cup, whisk the egg replacer powder with water and add
to the prune mixture. Blend in the Fruitsource, orange blossom water, and
almond extract. Stir in the orange juice and coffee and mix thoroughly. Add the
dry ingredients and fold quickly until just mixed. Spoon into muffin cups and
bake 20 to 25 minutes, or until tester comes out clean. Set aside to cool.

Glazed Mocha Muffins *(continued)*

For the glaze: Sift powdered sugar into a medium bowl. Add 1½ tablespoons orange juice and the flavorings. Stir to blend. If the glaze is too thick, add a little more orange juice, measured by the teaspoonful. If it is too thin, add more powdered sugar. Drizzle glaze onto cooled muffins.

NUTRITION ANALYSIS: PER MUFFIN

Enlightened Glazed Mocha Muffins
Protein 3 g, carbohydrate 32 g, fiber 2 g, fat 2 g,
cholesterol 0 mg, calcium 35 mg, sodium 99 mg
Calories 158: from protein: 8%,
from carbohydrate 80%, from fat 12%

Traditional Glazed Mocha Muffins
Protein 4 g, carbohydrate 33 g, fiber 2 g, fat 13 g,
cholesterol 53 mg, calcium 47 mg, sodium 188 mg
Calories 257: from protein 6%,
from carbohydrate 49%, from fat 45%

Lemon-Glazed Chocolate
Chip Cookie Bars

*Tart cranberries and chocolate chips fill these lovely cookie bars,
drizzled with a sweet lemon glaze and sprinkled with sliced almonds.*

olive oil cooking spray

Bars

1 cup rolled oats
2 cups whole wheat pastry flour
¼ cup soy flour
1 cup wholesome crisped rice cereal
1 teaspoon baking soda
1 teaspoon nonaluminum baking powder
1 teaspoon ground cinnamon
½ teaspoon sea salt
½ cup dairy-free chocolate chips

¾ cup dried cranberries
⅓ cup unsweetened applesauce
¼ cup liquid Fruitsource
1½ cups evaporated cane juice
1 tablespoon pure vanilla extract
½ teaspoon lemon extract
2 tablespoons egg replacer powder
½ cup water
½ cup enriched 1% fat soymilk

Glaze

¼ cup enriched 1% fat soymilk
½ tablespoon rice butter spread
1 cup evaporated cane juice
1 teaspoon lemon extract

1 tablespoon cornstarch
1 tablespoon cold water
¼ cup sliced almonds

Preheat oven to 350°. Spray an 11-by-17-inch jelly roll pan with oil.

Place the oats in food processor and process to flour. Place in a large bowl and combine with pastry flour, soy flour, cereal, baking soda, baking powder, cinnamon, and salt. Stir in the chocolate chips and cranberries and set aside.

Combine applesauce and Fruitsource in a medium bowl, and cream with the evaporated cane juice, vanilla, and lemon extract.

In a small bowl, whisk the egg replacer powder with the water until foamy and add to the liquid ingredients. Fold the liquid ingredients into the dry alter-

Lemon-Glazed Chocolate Chip Cookie Bars *(continued)*

nately with the soymilk. Do not overbeat. Pour batter into the prepared pan and bake for 30 minutes, or until tester comes out clean. Cool.

For the glaze: Heat soymilk in a small saucepan over medium-low flame with the rice butter. Stir in evaporated cane juice and lemon extract.

In a small bowl, blend cornstarch and water; add to the pan, lower heat, and simmer 3 minutes. Remove from heat and place in refrigerator to cool for about 20 minutes. Drizzle glaze over cooled bars in pan and sprinkle with sliced almonds. Place in refrigerator to set for 30 minutes before cutting into bars.

NUTRITION ANALYSIS: PER 2-BY-3-INCH COOKIE BAR

**Enlightened Lemon-Glazed
Chocolate Chip Cookie Bars**
Protein 3 g, carbohydrate 26 g, fiber 2 g, fat 2 g,
cholesterol 0 mg, calcium 30 mg, sodium 115 mg
Calories 129: from protein 8%,
from carbohydrate 80%, from fat 12%

**Traditional Lemon-Glazed
Chocolate Chip Cookie Bars**
Protein 3 g, carbohydrate 28 g, fiber 1 g, fat 13 g,
cholesterol 41 mg, calcium 44 mg, sodium 262 mg
Calories 237: from protein 5%,
from carbohydrate 46%, from fat 48%

Ginger Fruit Ring

*This fragrant cake is moist and delicious, with chunks of luscious fruit
in every bite. Ginger brandy is used in several recipes in this collection, and
in some cases other flavors of brandy can be substituted. In this recipe,
however, ginger brandy adds a special dimension and is much preferred.*

olive oil cooking spray
⅔ cup enriched 1% fat soymilk
1 tablespoon lemon juice
3 cups whole wheat pastry flour
¼ cup soy flour
¼ cup yellow cornmeal
1 teaspoon baking soda
1 teaspoon nonaluminum baking
  powder
½ teaspoon sea salt
1 teaspoon ground cinnamon

1 teaspoon ground ginger
½ teaspoon ground allspice
½ cup chopped dried apricots
½ cup dried cranberries
½ cup chopped walnuts
1 12.3-ounce package lite silken tofu
½ cup Lighter Bake
1¾ cups evaporated cane juice
1 tablespoon pure vanilla extract
1 tablespoon ginger brandy

Preheat oven to 350°. Spray a 10-inch tube pan with oil.

Combine the soymilk and lemon juice in a nonreactive liquid measuring
cup and set aside.

In a large bowl combine the pastry flour, soy flour, cornmeal, baking soda,
baking powder, salt, cinnamon, ginger, allspice, dried fruit, and walnuts. Set
aside.

Place tofu in food processor and blend. Add the Lighter Bake and blend.
Add the remaining ingredients and process while motor is running; pour
soymilk mixture through feed tube. Make a well in the dry ingredients and fold
in the tofu mixture quickly, just until mixed. Pour into prepared pan and bake
50 minutes, or until tester comes out clean.

NUTRITION ANALYSIS: PER 3½-OUNCE SERVING

Enlightened Ginger Fruit Ring
Protein 7 g, carbohydrate 45 g, fiber 4 g, fat 3 g,
cholesterol 0 mg, calcium 62 mg, sodium 199 mg
Calories 232: from protein 11%,
from carbohydrate 76%, from fat 12%

Traditional Ginger Fruit Ring
Protein 6 g, carbohydrate 49 g, fiber 2 g, fat 13 g,
cholesterol 59 mg, calcium 57 mg, sodium 265 mg
Calories 332: from protein 7%,
from carbohydrate 58%, from fat 34%

Lemon Pudding and Pie Filling

*This richly flavored lemon pudding comes together
in a few minutes. Or pour into a prebaked pie shell (page 280)
for a lovely lemon pie. Chill several hours or overnight.*

2 12.3-ounce packages lite silken tofu
1 cup plus 2 tablespoons evaporated
    cane juice
1 tablespoon cornstarch
2 tablespoons rice butter spread

¼ cup fresh lemon juice
¼ teaspoon lemon extract
1 tablespoon pure vanilla extract

Place tofu in food processor and blend. Add evaporated cane juice and corn-starch and blend. Add the remaining ingredients. Process until smooth. Pour into a 2-quart bowl, cover, and refrigerate. Serve well chilled.

NUTRITION ANALYSIS: PER 4-OUNCE SERVING

Enlightened Lemon Pudding and Pie Filling
Protein 7 g, carbohydrate 19 g, fiber 0 g, fat 1 g,
cholesterol 0 mg, calcium 58 mg, sodium 114 mg
Calories 119: from protein 24%,
from carbohydrate 66%, from fat 11%

Traditional Lemon Pudding and Pie Filling
Protein 4 g, carbohydrate 23 g, fiber 0 g, fat 12 g,
cholesterol 150 mg, calcium 94 mg, sodium 238 mg
Calories 205: from protein 7%,
from carbohydrate 44%, from fat 50%

Old-Fashioned Spiced Apple Cake

*This healthful rendition of a popular
classic is chock-full of goodness.*

olive oil cooking spray
2 tablespoons lemon juice
½ cup enriched 1% fat soymilk
3 cups whole wheat pastry flour
⅓ cup yellow cornmeal
1 teaspoon baking soda
1 teaspoon nonaluminum baking
  powder
1 teaspoon ground cinnamon
½ teaspoon ground allspice
½ teaspoon ground ginger
¼ teaspoon ground nutmeg

1 cup date pieces
½ cup dried apples
1 12.3-ounce package lite silken tofu
½ cup unsweetened applesauce
⅓ cup liquid Fruitsource
1 cup evaporated cane juice
1 tablespoon powdered egg replacer
¼ cup cold water
1 tablespoon pure vanilla extract
½ cup walnut pieces
⅓ cup soy grits
cinnamon and nutmeg

Preheat oven to 350°. Spray a 10-inch tube pan with oil.

Add lemon juice to soymilk; set aside. In a large bowl, mix together the next 10 ingredients (pastry flour through dried apples). Set aside.

Place tofu in food processor and blend. Add applesauce, Fruitsource, and evaporated cane juice. Pulse; then blend.

Whisk egg replacer with water in a small bowl until foamy. Add to tofu mixture along with soymilk mixture and vanilla. Blend thoroughly. Fold the tofu mixture into the dry ingredients; do not overbeat. Mix the walnut pieces and soy grits together, and fold into the batter. Sprinkle generously with cinnamon and nutmeg. Bake 45 minutes, or until golden brown.

NUTRITION ANALYSIS: PER 3¾-OUNCE SERVING

Enlightened Old-Fashioned Spiced Apple Cake
Protein 7 g, carbohydrate 44 g, fiber 5 g, fat 4 g,
cholesterol 0 mg, calcium 49 mg, sodium 128 mg
Calories 225: from protein 11%,
from carbohydrate 74%, from fat 14%

Traditional Old-Fashioned Spiced Apple Cake
Protein 8 g, carbohydrate 58 g, fiber 2 g, fat 19 g,
cholesterol 65 mg, calcium 65 mg, sodium 257 mg
Calories 424: from protein 7%,
from carbohydrate 54%, from fat 39%

Orange Apricot Pudding

The rich creaminess and depth of flavor of this delectable baked pudding belie its exceptionally low-fat profile.

12 Servings

1 cup chopped dried apricots
⅓ cup apricot brandy
2 tablespoons cornstarch
2 cups enriched vanilla 1% fat
   soymilk
1 cup lite silken tofu
1 cup orange juice

1 cup evaporated cane juice
2 tablespoons rice butter spread
2 tablespoons pure vanilla extract
2 teaspoons lemon juice
ground cinnamon and nutmeg

Preheat oven to 350°.

In a small saucepan, combine apricots and brandy and simmer over low heat until liquid is absorbed, about 5 minutes. Set aside.

Whisk cornstarch into cold soymilk in a 4-quart stovetop- and oven-safe pan. Bring mixture to a low boil over medium-high heat, and then reduce heat to medium low and cook for 8 minutes, stirring occasionally; set aside.

Place tofu in food processor and blend. Add remaining ingredients (except cinnamon and nutmeg) and blend. Add tofu mixture to thickened soymilk along with apricots and cook over medium-low heat for 10 minutes, stirring frequently. Sprinkle generously with cinnamon and nutmeg. Bake, uncovered, for 20 minutes. Serve warm, or cover and refrigerate.

NUTRITION ANALYSIS: PER 4-OUNCE SERVING

Enlightened Orange Apricot Pudding
Protein 3 g, carbohydrate 30 g, fiber 2 g, fat 1 g,
cholesterol 0 mg, calcium 58 mg, sodium 59 mg
Calories 149: from protein 7%,
from carbohydrate 80%, from fat 4%

Traditional Orange Apricot Pudding
Protein 2 g, carbohydrate 36 g, fiber 2 g, fat 10 g,
cholesterol 34 mg, calcium 63 mg, sodium 125 mg
Calories 240: from protein 4%,
from carbohydrate 59%, from fat 37%

Peachy Almond Spice Ring

This sensational cake is rich in essential nutrients, fiber, and phytochemicals and so much lower in fat, calories, and sodium than its traditional counterpart.

olive oil cooking spray
1 cup chopped dried peaches
½ cup water
2 tablespoons amaretto, or 1
  teaspoon almond extract, divided
¾ cup rolled oats
2¼ cups whole wheat pastry flour
1 teaspoon baking soda
1 teaspoon nonaluminum baking
  powder
¼ teaspoon sea salt

1½ teaspoons ground cinnamon
¼ teaspoon ground nutmeg
⅛ teaspoon ground cloves
½ cup chopped almonds
1 12.3-ounce package lite silken tofu
½ cup prune puree
1½ cups evaporated cane juice
1 tablespoon liquid Fruitsource
½ cup enriched vanilla 1% fat
  soymilk

Preheat oven to 350°. Spray a 10-inch tube pan with oil.

Place peaches in medium saucepan with water and 1 tablespoon amaretto or ½ teaspoon almond extract. Bring to a boil; then reduce heat to low and simmer for 8 to10 minutes, or until liquid is absorbed. Set aside.

Place oats in food processor and pulse lightly to a coarse flour consistency. In a large bowl, combine oat flour, pastry flour, baking soda, baking powder, salt, spices, and almonds.

Peachy Almond Spice Ring *(continued)*

Place tofu in processor bowl and blend until smooth. Add prune puree; blend. Add evaporated cane juice, Fruitsource, soymilk, and 1 tablespoon amaretto or ½ teaspoon almond extract; pulse and process until smooth. Make a well in the dry ingredients and fold tofu mixture in quickly. Do not overbeat. Pour batter into prepared pan and bake 45 minutes.

NUTRITION ANALYSIS: PER 3½-OUNCE SERVING

Enlightened Peachy Almond Spice Ring
Protein 6 g, carbohydrate 43 g, fiber 4 g, fat 3 g,
cholesterol 0 mg, calcium 59 mg, sodium 172 mg
Calories 218: from protein 11%,
from carbohydrate 77%, from fat 11%

Traditional Peachy Almond Spice Ring
Protein 6 g, carbohydrate 49 g, fiber 2 g, fat 17 g,
cholesterol 62 mg, calcium 61 mg, sodium 259 mg
Calories 366: from protein 6%,
from carbohydrate 52%, from fat 41%

Peanut Butter Oat Bars

These healthful cookie bars are bursting with plant-centered goodness and blanketed with a thick fudge frosting. Imagine a rich-tasting peanut butter bar with only 3 grams of fat!

olive oil cooking spray

Bars

1⅓ cups rolled oats
1⅓ cups whole wheat pastry flour
⅓ cup yellow cornmeal
1 teaspoon baking soda
1 teaspoon nonaluminum baking powder
1 teaspoon ground cinnamon
½ teaspoon sea salt

1 12.3-ounce package lite silken tofu
½ cup Lighter Bake
⅓ cup peanut butter, smooth or chunky
1½ cups evaporated cane juice
½ cup enriched vanilla 1% fat soymilk
1 tablespoon pure vanilla extract

Fudge Frosting

1½ cups powdered sugar
¾ cup cocoa powder
⅓ cup enriched vanilla 1% fat soymilk

2 teaspoons pure vanilla extract

Preheat oven to 350°. Spray 9-by-13-inch baking pan with oil.

For the bars: In a large bowl, combine the oats, pastry flour, cornmeal, baking soda, baking powder, cinnamon, and salt; set aside.

Place tofu in food processor and blend until smooth. Add Lighter Bake, peanut butter, and evaporated cane juice. Pulse to mix; then blend. Add soymilk and vanilla and process until smooth. Make a well in the dry ingredients and fold in the tofu mixture without overbeating. Pour into prepared pan and bake 40 minutes, or until tester comes out clean. Set aside to cool.

Peanut Butter Oat Bars *(continued)*

For the frosting: Sift powdered sugar and cocoa into a medium bowl. Stir in soymilk and vanilla. If frosting is too thick, add a tablespoon or so of soymilk. Spread evenly over cooled baked dough; then chill 30 minutes to set frosting before cutting into bars.

NUTRITION ANALYSIS: PER 2-BY-3-INCH COOKIE BAR

Enlightened Peanut Butter Oat Bars
Protein 5 g, carbohydrate 32 g, fiber 3 g, fat 3 g,
cholesterol 0 mg, calcium 44 mg, sodium 171 mg
Calories 169: from protein 11%,
from carbohydrate 74%, from fat 15%

Traditional Peanut Butter Oat Bars
Protein 5 g, carbohydrate 38 g, fiber 2 g, fat 18 g,
cholesterol 61 mg, calcium 38 mg, sodium 241 mg
Calories 324: from protein 6%,
from carbohydrate 45%, from fat 48%

Pineapple Banana Bundt Cake

Sweet pineapple chunks offset crunchy
walnuts in this delightful cake.

olive oil cooking spray
2 cups whole wheat pastry flour
¼ cup yellow cornmeal
¼ cup soy flour
1 teaspoon baking soda
1 teaspoon nonaluminum baking
   powder
2 teaspoons ground cinnamon
½ cup chopped walnuts
1 12.3-ounce package lite silken tofu

¼ cup prune puree
1 cup mashed bananas (2 small)
1¾ cups brown sugar
1 tablespoon egg replacer powder
¼ cup water
1 tablespoon pure vanilla extract
2 tablespoons banana liqueur
1 8-ounce can pineapple chunks,
   drained
ground cinnamon and nutmeg

Preheat oven to 350°. Spray a 10-inch Bundt pan with oil.

In a large bowl, combine the pastry flour, cornmeal, soy flour, baking soda, baking powder, cinnamon, and walnuts. Set aside.

Place tofu in food processor; blend. Add the prune puree and bananas and blend. Add the brown sugar and pulse; then blend.

Whisk egg replacer with water in a small bowl until foamy. Add to tofu mixture along with vanilla and banana liqueur. Blend thoroughly. Make a well in the dry ingredients and fold in the tofu mixture. Fold the pineapple into the batter; do not overmix. Sprinkle with cinnamon and nutmeg. Bake 35 minutes, or until tester comes out clean.

NUTRITION ANALYSIS: PER 3½-OUNCE SERVING

Enlightened Pineapple Banana Bundt Cake
Protein 5 g, carbohydrate 37 g, fiber 3 g, fat 3 g,
cholesterol 0 mg, calcium 60 mg, sodium 139 mg
Calories 195: from protein 11%,
from carbohydrate 75%, from fat 14%

Traditional Pineapple Banana Bundt Cake
Protein 6 g, carbohydrate 35 g, fiber 2 g, fat 17 g,
cholesterol 68 mg, calcium 59 mg, sodium 353 mg
Calories 311: from protein 8%,
from carbohydrate 45%, from fat 48%

Pineapple Carrot Cake

*Dried pineapple and pecans enhance this carrot cake.
Enriched with wheat germ, rolled oats, and soy flour, this
rich-tasting cake is nutritious and low in calories and fat.*

*16
Servings*

olive oil cooking spray
1 cup whole wheat pastry flour
¼ cup soy flour
¼ cup yellow cornmeal
⅓ cup rolled oats
2 tablespoons cornstarch
1 teaspoon baking soda
1 teaspoon nonaluminum baking
   powder
1 teaspoon ground cinnamon
¼ teaspoon ground nutmeg
⅛ teaspoon ground allspice
⅛ teaspoon ground cloves

½ teaspoon sea salt
½ cup chopped pecans
½ cup dried pineapple, snipped into
   bite-size pieces
½ cup prune puree
1 tablespoon egg replacer powder
¼ cup water
1¼ cups evaporated cane juice
1½ cups grated carrots (about 3
   carrots)
½ cup fresh orange juice
1 tablespoon pure vanilla extract
1 tablespoon liquid Fruitsource

CARROTS CONTAIN the highest level of the antioxidant beta-carotene. Beta-carotene is not destroyed by cooking, and it is more easily assimilated by the body from cooked vegetables than from raw.

Preheat oven to 350°. Spray a 9-by-13-inch baking pan with oil.

In a medium bowl, combine the pastry flour, soy flour, cornmeal, oats, cornstarch, baking soda, baking powder, cinnamon, nutmeg, allspice, cloves, and salt. Mix in the pecans and pineapple and set aside.

Place prune puree in a large bowl. In a small liquid measuring cup, combine the egg replacer powder and water with a wire whisk, and then whisk the mixture into the prune puree. Add the evaporated cane juice and the remaining ingredients, mixing thoroughly. Make a well in the dry ingredients and fold in the liquid mixture without overbeating. Pour into prepared pan and bake 35 minutes, or until tester comes out clean. Set aside to cool.

NUTRITION ANALYSIS: PER 2¾-OUNCE SERVING

Enlightened Pineapple Carrot Cake
Protein 3 g, carbohydrate 31 g, fiber 3 g, fat 3 g,
cholesterol 0 mg, calcium 30 mg, sodium 188 mg
Calories 162: from protein 7%,
from carbohydrate 75%, from fat 18%

Traditional Pineapple Carrot Cake
Protein 4 g, carbohydrate 31 g, fiber 1 g, fat 12 g,
cholesterol 56 mg, calcium 31 mg, sodium 260 mg
Calories 241: from protein 6%,
from carbohydrate 50%, from fat 44%

Pineapple Spice Muffins

Diced dried pineapple makes these muffins special. For a unique presentation, bake these in mini-Bundt muffin cups, sprinkle with powdered sugar, and serve with Apricot Butter, page 236.

olive oil cooking spray
1½ cups spelt flour
¼ cup soy flour
2 tablespoons cornmeal
1 teaspoon nonaluminum baking
    powder
1 tablespoon cornstarch
1 teaspoon ground cinnamon
¼ teaspoon allspice

¼ teaspoon nutmeg
½ teaspoon sea salt
½ 12.3-ounce package lite silken tofu
¼ cup prune puree
1 medium banana, mashed
1 cup evaporated cane juice
⅓ cup sparkling mineral water
½ cup dried pineapple chunks, diced

Preheat oven to 375°. Spray a 12-cup muffin pan with oil.

In a large bowl, combine the spelt flour, soy flour, cornmeal, baking powder, cornstarch, cinnamon, allspice, nutmeg, and salt. Set aside.

Place the tofu in food processor and process. Add the prune puree and banana and blend. Add the evaporated cane juice and sparkling water and process. Make a well in the dry ingredients and quickly fold in the liquid mixture, adding the dried fruit at the end. Pour into prepared muffin cups and sprinkle tops with additional cinnamon. Bake 20 minutes, or until tester comes out clean.

NUTRITION ANALYSIS: PER MUFFIN

Enlightened Pineapple Spice Muffins
Protein 4 g, carbohydrate 33 g, fiber 3 g, fat 1 g,
cholesterol 0 mg, calcium 36 mg, sodium 147 mg
Calories 146: from protein 10%,
from carbohydrate 85%, from fat 5%

Traditional Pineapple Spice Muffins
Protein 3 g, carbohydrate 41 g, fiber 1 g, fat 11 g,
cholesterol 65 mg, calcium 41 mg, sodium 237 mg
Calories 269: from protein 5%,
from carbohydrate 60%, from fat 35%

Pumpkin Cranberry Walnut Bars

These delicious cookie bars are moist and
sweet, a really perfect fall treat!

24
Cookie Bars

olive oil cooking spray
1½ cups whole wheat pastry flour
1 cup rolled oats
¼ cup soy flour
1 teaspoon baking soda
1 teaspoon nonaluminum baking
  powder
1½ teaspoons ground cinnamon
¼ teaspoon ground nutmeg
⅛ teaspoon ground cloves
½ teaspoon sea salt

1 cup dried cranberries
⅓ cup chopped walnuts
½ cup prune puree
½ cup canned pumpkin
1 cup evaporated cane juice
2 tablespoons liquid Fruitsource
2 tablespoons egg replacer powder
½ cup water
1 tablespoon pure vanilla extract
½ cup enriched vanilla 1% fat
  soymilk

Preheat oven to 350°. Spray 9-by-13-inch baking pan with oil.

In a medium bowl, combine the pastry flour, oats, soy flour, baking soda, baking powder, cinnamon, nutmeg, cloves, and salt. Stir in the cranberries and walnuts and set aside.

In a large bowl, blend the prune puree with the canned pumpkin, and cream with the evaporated cane juice and Fruitsource.

In a small bowl or liquid measuring cup, whisk the egg replacer powder with the water until foamy. Add to the prune mixture with the vanilla. Make a well in the center of the dry ingredients and quickly fold in the prune mixture alternately with the soymilk. Pour into prepared pan and sprinkle with cinnamon and nutmeg. Bake 30 minutes, or until tester comes out clean.

NUTRITION ANALYSIS: PER 3-BY 1½-INCH COOKIE BAR

Enlightened Pumpkin Cranberry Walnut Bars
Protein 3 g, carbohydrate 23 g, fiber 2 g, fat 2 g,
cholesterol 0 mg, calcium 29 mg, sodium 125 mg
Calories 113: from protein 9%,
from carbohydrate 79%, from fat 12%

Traditional Pumpkin Cranberry Walnut Bars
Protein 3 g, carbohydrate 23 g, fiber 1 g, fat 13 g,
cholesterol 50 mg, calcium 28 mg, sodium 160 mg
Calories 210: from protein 5%,
from carbohydrate 42%, from fat 52%

Spirited Chocolate Chip Squares

*Dried fruits, stewed in brandy, intensify the rich
flavor and texture in this deceptively low-fat dessert.*

olive oil cooking spray
1 cup dried apricots, snipped to bite-size pieces
½ cup dried cranberries
½ cup apricot brandy
2⅓ cups whole wheat pastry flour
⅔ cup yellow cornmeal
1 teaspoon baking soda
1 teaspoon nonaluminum baking powder

1 teaspoon ground cinnamon
½ cup dairy-free chocolate chips
1 12.3-ounce package lite silken tofu
½ cup unsweetened applesauce
2 cups evaporated cane juice
¼ cup fresh-squeezed orange juice
1 tablespoon orange zest
1 teaspoon pure vanilla extract
ground cinnamon and nutmeg

Preheat oven to 350°. Spray a 9-by-13-inch baking pan with oil.

Combine the dried fruit with the brandy in a small saucepan over low heat. Simmer fruit 5 minutes, or until brandy is absorbed. Remove from heat and set aside.

Mix the pastry flour, cornmeal, baking soda, baking powder, cinnamon, and chocolate chips in a large bowl. Set aside.

Place tofu in food processor and blend. Add applesauce and evaporated cane juice; blend. Add orange juice, zest, and vanilla to tofu mixture and process until smooth. Make a well in the center of the dry ingredients. Quickly fold in the liquid ingredients and add the brandied fruit. Pour into prepared pan; sprinkle with cinnamon and nutmeg. Bake 30 minutes, or until tester comes out clean. Top with Hip Whip.

NUTRITION ANALYSIS: PER 2¼-BY-3-INCH SQUARE

Enlightened Spirited Chocolate Chip Squares
Protein 5 g, carbohydrate 49 g, fiber 4 g, fat 2 g,
cholesterol 0 mg, calcium 45 mg, sodium 128 mg
Calories 237: from protein 9%,
from carbohydrate 84%, from fat 8%

Traditional Spirited Chocolate Chip Squares
Protein 4 g, carbohydrate 57 g, fiber 3 g, fat 13 g,
cholesterol 62 mg, calcium 49 mg, sodium 256 mg
Calories 357: from protein 5%,
from carbohydrate 63%, from fat 33%

Strawberry Mango Cobbler

You will love this fruit cobbler, replete with a luscious mix of fruit, and a crunchy walnut topping.

Cobbler

- 1 cup frozen apple juice concentrate
- 1 16-ounce package frozen mango chunks
- 1 16-ounce package frozen whole strawberries
- 2 cups sliced dried peaches
- ¼ cup ginger brandy
- ⅔ cup Sucanat
- 1 tablespoon cornstarch
- 1 tablespoon cold water

Topping

- ½ cup rolled oats
- ⅓ cup walnuts
- ⅓ cup whole wheat pastry flour
- ½ cup Sucanat or brown sugar
- 2 tablespoons olive oil
- 2 tablespoons liquid Fruitsource

Preheat oven to 350°.

For the cobbler: In a stovetop- and oven-safe 5-quart casserole, thaw the juice concentrate over medium heat. Add mango chunks and strawberries and cook until fruit is almost thawed. Add peaches, ginger brandy, and Sucanat. Cook mixture 5 minutes, stirring frequently.

In a small bowl, blend the cornstarch with water and add to the fruit. Cook mixture 5 minutes.

For the topping: Place the oats, walnuts, flour, and Sucanat in the bowl of food processor and process to mix. While motor is running, pour oil and Fruitsource through feed tube. Process until mixture is crumbly but holding together. Sprinkle over top of fruit and bake, uncovered, for 25 minutes.

NUTRITION ANALYSIS: PER 4¾-OUNCE SERVING

Enlightened Strawberry Mango Cobbler
Protein 3 g, carbohydrate 49 g, fiber 4 g, fat 4 g, cholesterol 0 mg, calcium 27 mg, sodium 30 mg
Calories 237: from protein 5%, from carbohydrate 82%, from fat 13%

Traditional Strawberry Mango Cobbler
Protein 4 g, carbohydrate 49 g, fiber 4 g, fat 13 g, cholesterol 26 mg, calcium 25 mg, sodium 139 mg
Calories 314: from protein 5%, from carbohydrate 60%, from fat 35%

Strawberry Shake

*Think you can't have a "milk shake" that is actually bursting with optimal
nutrition? Think again. Light silken tofu has the consistency of soft
custard ice cream when blended and is the base for this healthy shake.*

1 12.3-ounce package lite silken tofu
1 medium banana, peeled and sliced
1 cup frozen sliced strawberries (do
   not thaw)

1 cup enriched vanilla rice milk
½ cup liquid Fruitsource

Place tofu in food processor or blender and blend until smooth. Add banana
and frozen strawberries and blend. Add remaining ingredients and blend until
smooth.

NUTRITION ANALYSIS: PER 8-OUNCE SERVING

Enlightened Strawberry Shake
Protein 7 g, carbohydrate 40 g, fiber 1 g, fat 2 g,
cholesterol 0 mg, calcium 52 mg, sodium 104 mg
Calories 194: from protein 14%,
from carbohydrate 79%, from fat 8%

Traditional Strawberry Shake
Protein 6 g, carbohydrate 55 g, fiber 1 g, fat 16 g,
cholesterol 61 mg, calcium 182 mg, sodium 80 mg
Calories 383: from protein 6%,
from carbohydrate 58%, from fat 37%

Sweet Potato Pie

*A delectable, creamy, spiced filling in a perfect crust is
crowned with an almond crunch topping. This outrageous dessert is
the first recipe that I have offered that exceeds 5 grams of fat per serving.
I think most would agree that 6 grams is still quite low.*

*16
Servings*

olive oil cooking spray

Crust

2 cups whole wheat pastry flour

¼ teaspoon sea salt

¼ cup lite silken tofu (reserve the rest
    of the package for the filling)

2 tablespoons mild olive oil

2 tablespoons liquid Fruitsource

⅓ cup ice water

Filling

Remainder of lite silken tofu

2 cups mashed, cooked yams

¼ cup Lighter Bake

1 cup firmly packed brown sugar

1 teaspoon pure vanilla extract

½ teaspoon ground cinnamon

¼ teaspoon ground nutmeg

⅛ teaspoon ground cloves

¼ teaspoon sea salt

Topping

½ cup chopped almonds

⅓ cup firmly packed brown sugar

2 tablespoons unbleached flour

½ teaspoon ground cinnamon

¼ teaspoon ground nutmeg

1 tablespoon liquid Fruitsource

2 tablespoons mild olive oil

Preheat oven to 375°. Lightly spray a deep dish pie pan with oil.

For the crust: Place the pastry flour, salt, and ¼ cup tofu in food processor
and pulse to mix. Add oil and Fruitsource and blend. While motor is running,
pour in ice water and process until mixture comes together. Turn out on a
lightly floured sheet of wax paper. Sprinkle dough lightly with flour and top
with a second sheet of wax paper. Roll out to a thickness of between ⅛ and

¼ inch. Press dough into pan and trim around edges; using thumb and forefinger, press a decorative edge along the rim. Set aside.

For the filling: Place the remainder of tofu in processor and blend until smooth. Add yams and Lighter Bake and process. Add remaining filling ingredients and blend until smooth. Pour into prepared crust and bake for 20 minutes.

For the topping: In a medium bowl, mix together the almonds, brown sugar, flour, cinnamon, and nutmeg. Add the Fruitsource and oil and mix to a crumbly texture. Remove pie from oven, leaving oven on. Sprinkle topping evenly over top and bake for an additional 25 minutes. Remove, cool, then chill in the refrigerator before serving.

NUTRITION ANALYSIS: PER 10-OUNCE SERVING

Enlightened Sweet Potato Pie
Protein 5 g, carbohydrate 34 g, fiber 2 g, fat 6 g,
cholesterol 0 mg, calcium 42 mg, sodium 113 mg
Calories 205: from protein 9%,
from carbohydrate 65%, from fat 26%

Traditional Sweet Potato Pie
Protein 6 g, carbohydrate 25 g, fiber 0 g, fat 21 g,
cholesterol 82 mg, calcium 113 mg, sodium 197 mg
Calories 316: from protein 9%,
from carbohydrate 31%, from fat 60%

Wholesome Waffles

*These crisp waffles are nutritious and delicious. No eggs, no
dairy, no kidding! This recipe will make at least 8 waffles.*

*4
Servings*

olive oil cooking spray
1 cup plus 2 tablespoons whole
　wheat pastry flour
2 tablespoons soy flour
2 tablespoons yellow cornmeal
2 tablespoons egg replacer powder
1 tablespoon nonaluminum baking
　powder

½ teaspoon sea salt
¼ cup rice butter spread
2 tablespoons liquid Fruitsource
1¾ cups enriched vanilla 1% fat
　soymilk

Preheat waffle griddle and spray lightly with oil.

Combine pastry flour, soy flour, cornmeal, egg replacer powder, baking
powder, and salt in the food processor. Pulse to mix. Add rice butter and pulse;
then add Fruitsource and blend. Pour soymilk through feed tube while processing thoroughly. Place batter in pitcher or large liquid measuring cup and
pour enough batter to cover about ⅔ of the surface of the waffle grid. Close and
cook for 4 to 5 minutes, or until steam stops escaping. If you meet resistance
when opening the iron, the waffle is probably not done. You may need to repeat
oil spray, very lightly, before cooking each waffle.

NUTRITION ANALYSIS: PER 2 WAFFLES

Enlightened Wholesome Waffles
Protein 9 g, carbohydrate 47 g, fiber 5 g, fat 5 g,
cholesterol 0 mg, calcium 437 mg, sodium 674 mg
Calories 267: from protein 13%,
from carbohydrate 70%, from fat 18%

Traditional Wholesome Waffles
Protein 11 g, carbohydrate 50 g, fiber 2 g, fat 28 g, cholesterol 227 mg, calcium 275 mg, sodium 767 mg
Calories 491: from protein 9%,
from carbohydrate 41%, from fat 50%

Blueberry Pancakes

*Spelt is a grain that has been cultivated for more than 9,000 years.
It has an exceptional protein and fiber profile and contains a unique
type of gluten that is easier to digest than common wheats.*

olive oil cooking spray
1¼ cups 1% fat soymilk
1 tablespoon lemon juice
1¼ cups spelt flour
2 tablespoons soy flour
1 tablespoon yellow cornmeal
3 tablespoons evaporated cane juice
1 tablespoon egg replacer powder

1¼ teaspoons nonaluminum baking
   powder
1 teaspoon baking soda
½ teaspoon sea salt
3 tablespoons lite silken tofu
2 tablespoons rice butter spread
⅓ cup dried blueberries

Preheat griddle or electric frying pan and spray lightly with oil.
   Combine the soymilk and lemon juice in a glass liquid measuring cup and set aside.
   Combine the spelt flour, soy flour, cornmeal, evaporated cane juice, egg replacer powder, baking powder, baking soda, and salt in food processor. Pulse to mix. Add tofu and rice butter and blend. Pour clabbered (or sour) soymilk through feed tube while processing thoroughly. Place batter in pitcher or large glass measuring cup and stir in the blueberries. Pour batter onto griddle and flip over when bubbles have appeared and the bottom is golden brown. Stir batter from time to time to keep blueberries evenly distributed. Repeat oil spray as needed.

SCIENTISTS AT TUFTS University have published a study indicating that the antioxidants in blueberries seem to contain an anti-aging boost for the body. Although strawberries and spinach produced some improvement in memory, only blueberries had a significant positive impact on balance and coordination as well.

NUTRITION ANALYSIS: PER 4 PANCAKES

Enlightened Blueberry Pancakes
Protein 9 g, carbohydrate 58 g, fiber 7 g, fat 4 g,
cholesterol 0 mg, calcium 194 mg, sodium 663 mg
Calories 278: from protein 12%,
from carbohydrate 77%, from fat 11%

Traditional Blueberry Pancakes
Protein 13 g, carbohydrate 61 g, fiber 1 g, fat 19 g,
cholesterol 150 mg, calcium 291 mg, sodium 1,039 mg
Calories 470: from protein 11%,
from carbohydrate 53%, from fat 36%

Vegetarian Dog Treats

*Let's not forget treats for those constant mealtime companions,
dogs. More like crunchy crackers than biscuits, these healthy dog
treats are economical and easy to make. They are very low in fat
and calories and made more nutritious by the addition of triticale,
a hybrid grain that is a cross between wheat and rye.*

*Makes about
30 2-Inch-by-
2-Inch Treats*

olive oil cooking spray
1½ cups whole wheat flour
½ cup triticale flour
1½ teaspoons nonaluminum baking
    powder

1 tablespoon flaxseed meal
¼ cup lite silken tofu
1 tablespoon liquid Fruitsource
1 tablespoon olive oil
¼ cup plus 3 tablespoons ice water

Preheat oven to 400°. Spray baking pans with oil.

Place the whole wheat flour, triticale, baking powder, and flaxseed meal in food processor and pulse to blend. Add the tofu, Fruitsource, and olive oil; process. Add the ice water through the feed tube while motor is running; dough should hold together and form a ball. Turn dough onto lightly floured board and knead a few minutes. Cover with a towel and let rest 5 minutes. Divide the dough in half and roll the dough out to a thickness of about ⅛ to ¼ inch. Using a pizza cutter or a sharp knife, cut the dough into 2-inch squares. If you prefer, you can cut the dough into 2-inch-by-4-inch pieces. Place on prepared pans and bake 10 to 12 minutes, or until golden brown and crisp.

NUTRITION ANALYSIS: PER TREAT

Enlightened Vegetarian Dog Treats
Protein 2 g, carbohydrate 7 g, fiber 1 g, fat 1 g,
cholesterol 0 mg, calcium 19 mg, sodium 28 mg
Calories 37: from protein 16%,
from carbohydrate 67%, from fat 17%

Traditional Dog Treats
Protein 1 g, carbohydrate 4 g, fiber 1 g, fat 4 g,
cholesterol 4 mg, calcium 32 mg, sodium 37 mg
Calories 55: from protein 8%,
from carbohydrate 26%, from fat 66%

RESOURCE GUIDE

Advanced Ingredients, Inc.
331 Capitola Avenue, Suite F
Capitola, CA 95010
(831) 464-9891
http://www.advancedingredients.com
FruitSource liquid sweetener

Arrowhead Mills
Box 2059
Hereford, TX 79045
(806) 364-0730
flours, grains, and natural food products

Boca Burger, Inc.
20 N. Wacker Drive, Suite 1360
Chicago, IL 60606
http:www.bocaburger.com
Boca Burger Basics and other products

Bob's Red Mill Natural Foods, Inc.
Milwaukie, OR 97222
http://www.bobsredmill.com
variety of grains and flours

EnerG Foods, Inc.
5960 S. First Ave.
Seattle, WA 98108
(800) 331-5222
http://www.ener-g.com
EnerG egg replacer, tapioca flour, and allergy-free products

Florida Crystals, Inc.
Palm Beach, FL 33480
http://www.floridacrystals.com
Florida Crystals organic and conventional evaporated cane juice

Hain Food Group
16007 Camino de la Cantera
Irwindale, CA 91706-7811
(800) 434-4246
http://www.westbrae.com
a variety of natural and organic foods, including lite soymilk

Imagine Foods
350 Cambridge Ave., Suite 350
Palo Alto, CA 94306
(800) 333-6339
nondairy beverages: Rice Dream Original and Vanilla Rice Milk, Soy Dream; and desserts and soups

Lightlife Foods, Inc.
153 Industrial Blvd.
Turners Falls, MA 01376
(800) SOY-EASY (769-3279)
www.lightlife.com
variety of soy products, tempeh, Lean Links Italian, Gimme Lean, and other products

Live Food Products
Box 7
Santa Barbara, CA 93102
(805) 968-1028
http://www.bragg.com
Bragg Liquid Aminos

Marin Foods Specialties, Inc.
P.O. Box 609
Byron, CA 94514
Wonderslim, Wondercocoa

Miyako Oriental Foods, Inc.
4287 Puente Ave.
Baldwin Park, CA 91706
(626) 962-9633
*Cold Mountain miso: mellow white,
light yellow, red, and others*

Morinaga Nutritional Foods, Inc.
2050 West 190th St., Suite 110
Torrance, CA 90504
(800) 669-8638
http://www.morinu.com
*Mori Nu Silken Tofu and Silken Tofu
Lite, Tofu Hero, Mori Nu Mates*

Nasoya Foods, Inc.
One New England Way
Ayer, MA 01432
(800) 229-TOFU (8638)
http://www.nasoya.com
*soy-based products: Nayonaise, dress-
ings, tofu, VegiDogs, and other products*

Now & Zen, Inc.
665 22nd Street
San Francisco, CA 94107
http://www.nowandzen.net
(800) 335-1959
*A variety of dessert and wheat gluten
products: Hip Whip, Chocolate Mousse,
Unchicken, Unturkey, and others*

Pacific Foods of Oregon, Inc.
Tualatin, OR 97062
(503) 692-9666
http://www.pacificfoods.com
*nondairy beverages: soymilk, rice milk
and almond milk; mushroom broth,
soups, and other products*

Quong Hop & Co
171 Beacon St.
South San Francisco, CA 94080
(650) 553-9900
http://www.quonghop.com
*The Soy Deli reduced-fat organic soy-
foods; baked tofu, firm nigari tofu, and
other products*

San Gennaro Foods, Inc.
9620 ML King Way S.
Seattle, WA 98118-5630
(800) 462-1916
http://www.sangennarofoods.com
*variety of ready-to-use, shelf-stable
polenta*

Simply Delicious, Inc.
8411 Hwy. 86 North
Cedar Grove, NC 27231
(919) 732-5294
http://www.simplydelicious.com
*variety of salad dressings made with soy
and the Wizard's vegetarian worcestershire sauce*

Sokol and Co.
5315 Dansher Rd.
Countryside, IL 60525
(708) 482-8250
http://www.solofoods.com
prune puree (lekvar)

Soyco Foods
2441 Viscount Row
Orlando, FL 32809
http://www.galaxyfoods.com
*dairy-free alternatives, Soymage, Soy
Parmesan Cheese, Soyco Rice Butter
Spread, and other products*

Sunspire
2114 Adams Ave.
San Leandro, CA 94577
(510) 569-9731
http://www.sunspire.com
*a line of confections including organic
dark chocolate chips*

Sunsweet Growers, Inc.
Yuba City, CA 95993-9270
(800) 417-2253
http://www.sunsweet.com
*Lighter Bake and a variety of dried
fruits, such as prunes, apricots, raisins,
and others*

The Mail Order Catalog
Summertown, TN 38483
(800) 695-2241
http://www.healthy-eating.com
*nutritional yeast, wide variety of soy-
foods, dairy and egg substitutes, cook-
books, and other products*

Tree of Life, Inc.
P.O. Box 410
St. Augustine, FL 32085-0410
(904) 825-2009
http://www.treeoflife.com
*variety of soy products and dairy-free
beverages*

Vegi-Deli
(888) 473-3667
P.O. Box 881781
San Francisco, CA 94188-1781
http://www.vegideli.com
email: mark@vegideli.com
*wheat protein–based meat substitutes
and snack foods*

White Wave, Inc.
1990 N. 57th Ct.
Boulder, CO 80301
http://www.whitewave.com
*tofu, baked tofu, seitan packed in
broth, tempeh, Silk soymilk, Silk dairy-
free yogurt, and other products*

Wholesome Sweeteners
P.O. Box 339
Savannah, GA 31401
(800) 241-3785
http://www.wholesomefoods.com
*organic Sucanat and organic evapo-
rated cane juice*

Wildwood Natural Foods
135 Bolinas Rd.
Fairfax, CA 94930
(800) 499-TOFU (8638)
http://www.wildwoodnaturalfoods.
com
*a variety of natural deli and soy prod-
ucts, including baked and smoked tofu*

Yves Veggie Cuisine
1138 E. Georgia Street
Vancouver, BC V6A 2A8
Canada
(604) 251-1345
http://www.yvesveggie.com
*Yves Veggie Canadian Bacon, Deli
Slices, Ground Round, Veggie Burgers,
and other products*

RECOMMENDED READING

Barnard, Neal D. *Food for Life*. Random House, 1994.

———*Eat Right, Live Longer*. Random House, 1995.

——— *The Power of Your Plate*. The Book Publishing Co., 1995.

———*Foods That Fight Pain*. Crown, 1999.

Cohen, Robert, and Jane Heimlich. *Milk: The Deadly Poison*. Argus, 1998.

Fouts, Roger, and Stephen Tukel Mills. *Next of Kin*. William Morrow and Company, 1997.

Klaper, Michael. *Vegan Nutrition*. Gentle World, 1987.

Lyman, Howard, with Glen Merzer. *Mad Cowboy: The Plain Truth from the Cattle Rancher Who Won't Eat Meat*. Scribner, 1998.

Marcus, Erik. *Vegan: The New Ethics of Eating*. McBooks, 1997.

Masson, Jeffrey Moussaieff, and Susan McCarthy. *When Elephants Weep*. Delacorte, 1995.

McDougall, John, and Mary McDougall. *The McDougall Plan*. New Century Publishing, 1983.

——— *The McDougall Program: 12 Days to Dynamic Health*. Penguin Books, 1990.

——— *The McDougall Program for Maximum Weight Loss*. Plume, 1995.

——— *The McDougall Program for a Healthy Heart: A Life-Saving Approach to Preventing and Treating Heart Disease*. Plume, 1998.

——— *The McDougall Quick and Easy Cookbook*. Plume, 1999.

——— *The McDougall Program for Women: What Every Woman Needs to Know to Be Healthy for Life*. Dutton, 2000.

Messina, Mark, and Virginia Messina. *The Simple Soybean and Your Health*. Avery, 1994.

——— *The Vegetarian Way: Total Health for You and Your Family*. Crown, 1996.

Ornish, Dean. *Stress and Your Heart.* Signet Books, 1983.

———*Dr. Dean Ornish's Program for Reversing Heart Disease.* Random House, 1990.

———*Eat More, Weigh Less.* HarperCollins, 1993.

———*Everyday Cooking with Dr. Dean Ornish.* HarperCollins, 1997.

———*Love and Survival.* HarperCollins, 1998.

Pinckney, Neal. *Healthy Heart Handbook.* Health Communications, 1996.

Rhoads, Richard. *Deadly Feasts.* Simon & Schuster, 1997.

Rifkin, Jeremy. *Beyond Beef.* Dutton, 1992.

Robbins, John. *Diet for a New America.* Stillpoint, 1987.

———*May All Be Fed.* William Morrow and Company, 1992.

———*Reclaiming Our Health.* Tiburon, Calif.: H. J. Kramer, 1996.

BIBLIOGRAPHY

Albertazzi, P., et al. "The effect of dietary soy supplementation on hot flushes," *Obstetrics & Gynecology* 91(1):6–11 (January 1998).

Aldercreutz, Herman T., et al. "Soybean phytoestrogens intake and cancer risk," *Journal of Nutrition* 125(3 Suppl):757S–770S (March 1995).

Anderson, James W., M. Bryan Johnstone, and Margaret E. Cook-Newell. "Meta-analysis of soy protein intake on serum lipids," *New England Journal of Medicine* 333(5):276–282 (August 3, 1995).

Anderson, J. W., et al. "Effects of soy protein on renal function and proteinuria in patients with type 2 diabetes," *American Journal of Clinical Nutrition* 68(6 Suppl):1347S–1353S (December 1998).

Anthony, M. S., T. B. Clarkson, and J. K. Williams. "Effects of soy isoflavones on atherosclerosis: potential mechanisms," *American Journal of Clinical Nutrition* 68(6 Suppl):1390S–1393S (December 1998).

Arjmandi, Bahram H., et al. "Dietary soybean protein prevents bone loss in an ovariectomized rat model of osteoporosis," *Journal of Nutrition* 126:176–182 (January 1996).

Arjmandi, B. H., et al. "Bone-sparing effect of soy protein in ovarian hormone-deficient rats is related to its isoflavone content," *American Journal of Clinical Nutrition* 68(6 Suppl):1364S–1368S (December 1998).

Ascherio, A., and W. C. Willett. "Health effects of trans fatty acids," *American Journal of Clinical Nutrition* 66(4 Suppl):1006S–1010S (October 1997).

Barnard, Neal D. *Food for Life.* New York: Random House, 1993.

———. *Eat Right, Live Longer.* New York: Random House, 1995.

Barnard, N. D., et al. "Diet and sex-hormone binding globulin, dysmenorrhea, and premenstrual symptoms," *Obstetrics & Gynecology* 95(2):245 (February 2000).

———. "Effectiveness of a low-fat vegetarian diet in altering serum lipids in healthy premenopausal women," *American Journal of Cardiology* 85(8):969–972 (April 15, 2000).

Beling, Stephanie. *Powerfoods.* New York: HarperCollins; 1997.

Bridge, Fred, and Jean F. Tibbetts. *The Well-Tooled Kitchen.* New York: William Morrow, 1991.

Caldwell, Wayne J. "Land-use planning, the environment, and siting intensive livestock facilities in the 20th century," *Journal of Soil and Water Conservation* 53(2):102-106 (Second Quarter 1998).

Campbell, T. C., B. Parpia, and J. Chen. "Diet, lifestyle, and the etiology of coronary artery disease: the Cornell China study," *American Journal of Cardiology* 82(10B):18T–21T (November 26, 1998).

Carroll, K. K., and E. M. Kurowska. "Soy consumption and cholesterol reduction: review of animal and human studies," *Journal of Nutrition* 125:594S–597S (1995).

Cline, J. M., and C. L. Hughes Jr. "Phytochemicals for the prevention of breast and endometrial cancer," *Cancer Treatment Research* 94:107–134 (1998).

Conil, Jean. *Encyclopedia of Food.* London: Kiln House, 1996.

Craig, W. J. "Phytochemicals: guardians of our health," *Journal of the American Dietetic Association* 97(10 Suppl 2):199S–204S (October 1997).

Crouse, J. R. III, et al. "A randomized trial comparing the effect of casein with that of soy protein containing varying amounts of isoflavones on plasma concentrations of lipids and lipoproteins," *Archives of Internal Medicine* 159(17):2070–2076 (September 27, 1999).

Durning, A. B., and H. B. Brough. *Taking Stock: Animal Farming and the Environment.* WorldWatch Institute, Worldwatch Paper 17(103) (July 1991).

Dwyer, J. "Convergence of plant-rich and plant-only diets," *American Journal of Clinical Nutrition* 70(3 Suppl):620S–622S (September 1999).

Edge, R., D. J. McGarvey, and T. G. Truscott. "The carotenoids as antioxidants—a review," *Photochemistry Photobiology* 41(3):189–200 (December 1997).

Erdman, J. W. Jr., and E. J. Fordyce. "Soy products and the human diet," *American Journal of Clinical Nutrition* 49:725–737 (1989).

Goldberg, A. C. "Perspectives on soy protein as a nonpharmacological approach for lowering cholesterol," *Journal of Nutrition* 125:675S–678S (1995).

Harris, William. *The Scientific Basis of Vegetarianism.* Honolulu: Hawaii Health Publishers, 1995.

Hasler, C. M., and J. B. Blumberg. "Phytochemicals: biochemistry and physiology," *Journal of Nutrition* 129(3):756S–757S (March 1999).

Herbst, Sharon Tyler. *Food Lover's Companion.* New York: Barrons Educational, 1990.

Hu, F. B., et al. "Dietary fat intake and the risk of coronary heart disease in women," *New England Journal of Medicine* 337(21):1491–1499 (November 20, 1997).

Jenkins, D. J., et al. "Health aspects of partially defatted flaxseed, including effects on serum lipids, oxidative measures, and ex vivo androgen and progestin activity: a controlled crossover trial," *American Journal of Clinical Nutrition* 69(3):395–402 (March 1999).

Ji, X. D., N. Melman, and K. A. Jacobson. "Interactions of flavonoids and other phytochemicals with adenosine receptors," *Journal of Medical Chemistry* 39(3):781–788 (February 2, 1996).

Katdare, M., M. P. Osborne, and N. T. Telang. "Inhibition of aberrant proliferation and induction of apoptosis in pre-neoplastic human mammary epithelial cells by natural phytochemicals," *Oncology Reports* 5(2):311–315 (March–April 1998).

Krishnaswamy, K., and N. Raghuramulu. "Bioactive phytochemicals with emphasis on dietary practices," *Journal of Medical Research* 108:167–181 (November 1998).

Kritchevsky, D. "Dietary protein, cholesterol and atherosclerosis: a review of the early history," *Journal of Nutrition* 125:589S–593S (1995).

Mallin, Michael A. "Impacts of industrial animal production on rivers and estuaries," *American Scientist* 88(1) (January–February 2000).

McDougall, John A. *The McDougall Program for a Healthy Heart.* New York: Dutton, 1996.

Messina, Mark J. "Interest in isoflavones continues to increase," *Soy Connection* (The United Soybean Board) 6(2):1–2 (Spring 1998).

Messina, Mark, Virginia Messina, and Kenneth R. Setchell. *The Simple Soybean and Your Health.* Garden City Park, N.Y.: Avery, 1994.

Messina, Mark, and Virginia Messina. *The Vegetarian Way.* New York: Harmony Books, 1996.

Messina M., and J. W. Erdman Jr. eds. "Soybeans and the prevention and treatment of chronic disease." *Journal of Nutrition* 125:567S–569S (1995).

Mindell, Earl. *Earl Mindell's Food as Medicine.* New York: Simon & Schuster, 1994.

———. *Earl Mindell's Soy Miracle.* New York: Simon & Schuster, 1995.

Murakami, A., H. Ohigashi, and K. Koshimizu. "Anti-tumor promotion with food phytochemicals: a strategy for cancer chemoprevention," *Bioscience, Biotechnology, and Biochemistry* 60(1):1–8 (January 1996).

Nelson, G. J. "Dietary fat, trans fatty acids, and risk of coronary heart disease," *Nutrition Review* 56(8):250–252 (August 1998).

Netzer, Corinne. *Encyclopedia of Food Values.* New York: Dell Publishing, 1992.

Newmark, H. L. "Squalene, olive oil, and cancer risk: a review and hypothesis," *Cancer Epidemiology Biomarkers of Prevention* 6(12):1101–1103 (December 1997).

Nicholson, A. S., et al. "Toward improved management of NIDDM: a randomized, controlled, pilot intervention using a low-fat, vegetarian diet," *Preventive Medicine* 29(2):87–91 (August 1999).

Ornish, Dean. *Dr. Dean Ornish's Program for Reversing Heart Disease*. New York: Random House, 1990.

Potter, S. M. "Overview of proposed mechanisms for the hypocholesterolemic effect of soy," *Journal of Nutrition* 125:Suppl:606S–611S (1995).

Potter, S. M., et al. "Depression of plasma cholesterol in men by consumption of baked products containing soy protein," *American Journal of Clinical Nutrition* 58:501–506 (1993).

Shurtleff, William, and Akiko Aoyagi. *The Book of Tofu*. Berkeley: Ten Speed Press, 1983.

Sirtori, C. R., et al. "Soy and cholesterol reduction: clinical experience," *Journal of Nutrition* 125:Suppl:598S–605S (1995).

Telang, N. T., et al. "Inhibition of proliferation and modulation of estradiol metabolism: novel mechanisms for breast cancer prevention by the phytochemical indole-3-carbinol," *Proceedings of the Society of Experimental Biological Medicine* 216(2):246–252 (November 1997).

Tufts University Diet and Nutrition Newsletter. "Scientists spotlight phytoestrogens for better health," 12(2):3–6 (February 1995).

Vastag, B. "Tea therapy? Out of the cup, into the lab," *Journal of the National Cancer Institute* 90(20):1504–1505 (October 1998).

Waladkhani, A. R., and M. R. Clemens. "Effect of dietary phytochemicals on cancer development," *International Journal of Molecular Medicine* 1(4):747–753 (April 1998).

Weil, Andrew. *Eight Weeks to Optimum Health*. New York: Random House, 1997.

Wong, W. W., et al. "Cholesterol-lowering effect of soy protein in normocholesterolemic and hypercholesterolemic men," *American Journal of Clinical Nutrition* 68(6 Suppl):1385S–1389S (December 1998).

Wu, A. H., et al. "Soy intake and risk of breast cancer in Asians and Asian Americans," *American Journal of Clinical Nutrition* 68(6 Suppl): 1437S–1443S (December 1998).

Zhou, J. R., et al. "Soybean phytochemicals inhibit the growth of transplantable human prostate carcinoma and tumor angiogenesis in mice," *Journal of Nutrition* 129(9):1628–1635 (September 1999).

INDEX